Banbury Remembered

Looking Back 1995-2019

Other books by Brian Little

Banbury in Old Picture Postcards (Zaltbommel: Europese Bibliotheek, 1997).

The History of the Horton (Banbury Guardian, 1997).

The Changing Faces of Banbury (Witney: Robert Boyd, 1998).

The Changing Faces of Grimsbury (Witney: Robert Boyd, 1999).

The Changing Faces of Easington (with B Davis, Witney: Robert Boyd, 2000).

Banbury: a photographic history of your town (Salisbury: W H Smith, 2001)

Banbury: a History (Chichester: Phillimore, 2003).

Banbury: a Century of Change (Derby: Breedon, 2005).

From Banbury Cakes to a Bushel of Sweetmeats : A look at trades and trademarks (with B Davis, Witney: Robert Boyd, 2011).

The History of Banbury Spencer Football Club (with D Shadbolt, Witney: Robert Boyd, 2013).

The Banbury Historical Society

Banbury Remembered
Looking back 1995-2019

Brian Little

edited by
Barrie Trinder

Volume 37

2020

Published by
the Banbury Historical Society
c/o Banbury Museum
Spiceball Park Road
Banbury OX16 2PQ

in association with
Robert Boyd Publications
260 Colwell Drive, Witney
Oxfordshire OX28 5LW

ISBN (BHS) 978 0 900129 36 0
ISBN (RBP) 978 1 908738 37 0

This volume has been produced with the aid of a
substantial grant from the Greening Lamborn Trust
which is acknowledged with gratitude.

The objective of the Greening Lamborn Trust is to
promote public interest in the history, architecture,
old photographs and heraldry of Oxford and its
neighbourhood by supporting publications
and other media that create access to them.

Printed by Henry Ling Limited at the Dorset Press, Dorchester DT1 1HD
from computer text generated and prepared by Barrie Trinder

Contents

Abbreviations   8
Acknowledgements for illustrations   8
Acknowledgements   9

Brian Little remembered   11
Editor's Introduction   15

1. Market town business
1.01: Family businesses flourished in town   21
1.02: Banbury Industrial Exhibition 1951   23
1.03: A man of distinction: E Owen Reid   26
1.04: The year of the bulldozer: 1972   28
1.05: P R Alcock, builders   30
1.06: Masters of masonry: George Carter   32
1.07: Town once slated by the Welsh   34
1.08: Characters from inter-war markets   36
1.09: Henry Cooke's Co-op legacy   39
1.10: Dream shopping centre of 1934   42
1.11: Ladies ruled Bridge Street:- the electricity showrooms   45
1.12: Life in Havenfield: - R B Miller's home in Bridge Street   47
1.13: Lamprey & Son, seed merchants   49
1.14: Hoods, the Banbury ironmongers   51
1.15: Bernard Smith, draper   55
1.16: W Ekins, outfitters   57
1.17: Farewell to an old friend: Whitchers's   60
1.18: Mansfields: sellers of leather goods   62
1.19: S R Jones, wine merchants   64
1.20: Mark B Plumb, rope and canvas merchant   67
1.21: Bringing fish and chips to town   70
1.22: Coal in the blood: the Higham dynasty   72
1.23: An iconic store: F W Woolworth   74
1.24: The heydays of Littlewoods   76
1.25: Tommy Dean and the *Sports Argus*   78
1.26: G F Braggins & Co, timber merchants   80
1.27: Excursions for motorists in the 1920s   83

1.28: Some Banbury garages   85
1.29: Sidney Young, garage proprietor   87
1.30: The livestock market: a view from 1950   89
1.31: Samuelson memories   91
1.32: The origins of Northern Aluminium, Banbury   93
1.33: Glory days at Switchgear & Equipment   96
1.34: The Spencer factory   98
1.35: Automotive Products   101
1.36: Paper & Publications, printers   103
1.37: Get on board the double-deckers   105
1.38: Fun on the buses with Sumners   108
1.39: Nesbitts of Banbury, removals   110
1.40: Station's refreshment facilities, 1905   111
1.41: Banbury: Ten years of the M40   113

2. Localities.
2.01: Grime and grind: Calthorpe Street   115
2.02: Castle Street in the 1940s & 50s   117
2.03: Starvation or the workhouse   119
2.04: Behind the bar with Nellie: the *Barley Mow*   121
2.05: St Paul's Church   124
2.06: Neithrop Wesleyan Mission   127
2.07: 1930s estates changed shape of town   130
2.08: Tom Pickston's memories of Grimsbury   132
2.09: 125 years of St Leonard's   135
2.10: Easington formed in the 1920s   137
2.11: Stephen Lake of Springfield Avenue, auctioneers' porter   140
2.12: The Fox fled to Easington   142

3. Schools and colleges
3.01: The last years of the British School, Crouch Street   145
3.02: Harriers' Primary School   147
3.03: Woodgreen secondary technical school   149
3.04: Engineering: North Oxfordshire Technical College   151
3.05: A Block: Banbury Further Education College   153

4. Pastimes and sports
4.01: Menu cards with a history lesson   155
4.02: Michaelmas still a fair old time in town centre   157
4.03: Behind the doors of the Masons   159

4.04: Rotary Club outlasts expectations with 75th anniversary   162
4.05: Banbury's tartan army: the Caledonian Society   164
4.06: Proud history of Banbury Harriers   167
4.07: Easington Sports Football Club   170
4.08: Centenary of Central Bowls Club   172
4.09: Star shone brightly: Banbury Star Cyclists Club   174
4.10: Vintage motor bikes: the Banbury Run   176
4.11: Banbury Auto club's TT thrill   180
4.12: Legacy led to People's Park   182
4.13: Banbury Arts & Crafts Festival 1940s & 50s   184
4.14: Banbury Steam Society   186
4.15: Goodbye to a Grand venue   188
4.16: Methodists took to the stage 1939   191
4.17: Banbury Cross Players   192
4.18: Centenary of the Girl Guides   196
4.19: Banbury Sea Cadets   198
4.20: Banbury Air Training Corps   201
4.21: Winter wonders   203
4.22: Wrestling with the past   205
4.23: Pete Lay and Banbury Jazz Club   207
4.24: Dancing to Brownie's beat   209
4.25: Ken Prewer's big band   212

5. World War 2
5.01: Annie Meadows, billeting officer, 1939   217
5.02: Wartime child's fond memories.   219
5.03: Flying high in Wings Week: raising money 1943   221
5.04: Fires lit to mark end of the war   223
5.05: The election of 1945   225
5.06: Vital roles of those left behind: wartime at NAC   227
5.07: A great war effort: Banbury 1939-45   229
5.08: Alderman W G Mascord: wartime mayor   231

Maps:
1. Banbury's Immediate Hinterland   16
2. Central Banbury   21
3. Social venues in Banbury   163

Abbreviations

AA: Automobile Association
ADCC: Air Defence Cadet Corps
AEI: Associated Electrical Industries
AFC: Association Football Club
Ald: Alderman
ARP: Air Raid Precautions
C&CH: Cake & Cockhorse
CCC: County Cricket Club
Cllr: Councillor
CO: Commanding Officer
GWR: Great Western Railway
LMSR: London, Midland & Scottish Railway
NAC: Northern Aluminium Company
NBC: National Bus Company
RAC: Royal Automobile Club
SWS: Shropshire, Worcestershire & Staffordshire Power Company

Acknowledgements for illustrations

Most of the illustrations in this book are from Brian Little's own collection, and were published with his articles in the *Banbury Guardian*. The editor and publisher apologise to any holders of copyright in these images whose rights have not been acknowledged.

Sources of other images are as follows
Brian Goodey: pp 43, 45, 65, 75.
Stephen & Clare Jakeman: pp 51, 52, 53.
The late John Powell: p 49
Barrie Trinder: pp 31, 40, 42, 118, 125, 131, 133, 137, 138, 143, 144, 158, 166, 178, 183, 190, 193, 214, 232 + back cover.

Acknowledgements

We are grateful to Brian's widow, Margaret Little, without whose co-operation this publication would not have been possible, and to the editor of the *Banbury Guardian* who kindly gave permission for the reproduction of articles originally published in his newspaper. We would also like to thank Alan Sargent for the loan of his collection of copies of Brian Little's articles which made the task of transcription much easier. We must also record our gratitude to Geoff Gwatkin for three excellent maps, to Paul Hayter for ultra-efficient proof-reading, and to Bob Boyd, our joint publisher, for his enthusiastic support.

Helen Forde,
Barrie Trinder,
November 2019.

Brian Little (1936-2019)

Brian Little remembered

Brian Little (1936-2019) lived in Banbury for nearly 60 years, and became a fount of knowledge on many aspects of local history. His weekly columns in the *Banbury Guardian*, maintained over 24 years, stimulated popular interest in the workings of the town past and present, and led to the preservation of countless memories, images and documents for the delectation of future generations of historians.

The following reminiscences of Brian were written by those who knew him best and illustrate his wide-ranging interests, not only local history. His enthusiasm and passion shines through the various accounts together with a love of the quirky sides of life to balance his academic interests and love of teaching. A fuller obituary appears in *Cake and Cockhorse* [vol 21 (2019), 70-71]. In brief he was born in Southampton where he went to school after having been evacuated to Exeter and Brockenhurst during the war. He read geography at Nottingham University, followed by a teacher training course and later a part-time M.Ed. from Reading University. He moved to Banbury in 1961 where he lived with his wife Margaret and their children for the rest of his life, teaching at North Oxfordshire College, from which he retired in 1995 as Head of Art, Design and Further Education.

****

Brian Goodey (professor emeritus, Urban Design Dept., Oxford Brookes University) wrote:

Brian and I not only shared an in-period Christian name but, rather more influentially, an undergraduate training in Geography at the University of Nottingham. Brian was a few years before me, but we had the same team of teachers, especially Professor K.C. Edwards, master of the fieldwork visit. It is their approach and methods I quickly identified on our first meeting. In December 1976, soon after I moved from the University of Birmingham to Banburyshire, Brian invited me to talk to the Banbury Geographical Association, then a thriving and regular gathering of senior school students and their teachers, genially gathered and animated by Brian. We had agreed on an ever-relevant topic, 'Can Planning Save the City?' which is now a reminder of the way in which Nottingham Geography always stressed that planning (at all scales) was a significant element in geographical practice. Over the subsequent forty plus years, Brian and I tended to meet shopping on market day, usually regretting the passing of another local enterprise or building, and the decline of Banbury's market function.

When Brian's reputation as a guide led to visitor overload we sometimes split coach parties and, without any agreed route or script, contrived to offer similar basic stories, except that Brian's progress was likely to be slower, in part at least because he was halted by his very extensive network of informants. Not only was he an expert oral historian, but he also quickly persuaded his contacts and students that they, too, should proclaim the story and current issues in the town. We were present at, and indeed wrote about, the end of Banbury's livestock market, a traumatic event in the rapid disconnection between the human and social meaning of 'Market Day' for the town and especially the surrounding communities. Brian's genial come-on, talk-to-me smile was absent that day; there was no shortage of male tears in those we talked to.

To the end Brian was a traditional geographer trained to observe, describe and understand his chosen patch, then to use this current awareness and synthesis to evaluate future propositions.

At the same time as his newspaper column captured the recent past, he was exploring the latest reincarnation of new communities such as that at Bicester, evaluating the implications of the Oxford-Cambridge corridor (rail matters were always of interest) and quickly spotting events where Banbury's future was to be discussed and possibly determined. In an age where local expertise and identity are too often trumped by career-led mobility and placelessness, and where planning is often seen as obstructing the present rather than visioning the future, Brian's was a rare public voice for a town and its future. His was an important professional and self-motivated role in Banbury and one which few are equipped to continue.

Nick Allen (local historian) wrote:
I first met Brian when I was invited to join the committee of the Banbury Historical Society in the spring of 1996 – we were fellow committee members until I retired in the summer of 2007. A more pleasant fellow to work with I have yet to meet. Brian was very good at sweeping a 'newbie' into the fold as, happily, so were the rest of the committee. Brian was an historian's historian delighting in sharing his knowledge of Banbury's history by taking people on his frequent Banbury walkabouts, imparting his very deep knowledge of the town. I, too, thoroughly enjoyed several of them over the years.

In his world of history he was the consummate historian; his private life was just that, private. It wasn't until I attended his memorial service on a lovely spring afternoon in his charming little church of St Hugh that I discovered that he was passionately fond of soccer and cricket. During that service it was fascinating to learn so much about the man that I, thought, I knew, from his ex-workmates and fellow members of his church – a man of many parts. A pleasure and a privilege to have known him – a week or so before he died we met up in Sainsbury's – I felt someone looming behind me saying 'good morning Mr Adderbury'. I was happy to reply 'and good morning to you Mr Banbury'. I was chuffed – *very* chuffed to be addressed so – but then you always meet the nicest people in Sainsbury's!

Bob Boyd (publisher of several of Brian's books) wrote:
Brian was passionate about his subject; there can be few people who knew as much as he did. He was a kind of hub for local Banbury knowledge. His association with the *Banbury Guardian* made him very well-known and respected and he made a huge contribution over a number of decades.

Don Scott (friend) wrote:

On the basis of a shared sporting interest, I got to know Brian some 25 years ago. On our first meeting, I recognised at once that Brian was no ordinary mortal. His breadth of knowledge covering sporting subjects, as well as issues of the day, was really impressive. I recognised that Brian was a man of many interests with tremendous energy and enthusiasm. Over many years I took Brian to various County cricket matches at Cheltenham, Basingstoke, Northampton, Leicester, Worcester, Trent Bridge and Uxbridge. Charles Woolland [see below] accompanied us on numerous occasions. In fact, in addition to Hampshire, Brian was a life member at Northamptonshire CCC, as well as an annual member at Edgbaston. This venue was easily accessible for him by train and bus, and occasionally I accompanied him there. However, I felt that Brian particularly looked forward to the Cheltenham cricket festival, when Charles and I shared the driving. He enjoyed roaming around every July at this special event, visiting bookstalls, obtaining players' signatures and chatting with like-minded people. He was particularly friendly with cricket correspondents, especially Ivo Tennant.

Brian was an avid collector of cricket memorabilia. Interestingly what mattered to him was the ambience and joy of the days' experiences rather than the scores on the board. We spent many happy hours discussing sporting matters of the day and recent purchases we had both made. As may be appreciated, it was a pleasure to be in his company. Even when there was no play at Worcester, we returned via Alcester so that Brian could visit the local museum.

As far as football was concerned, I know that Brian enjoyed following Nottingham Forest whilst at the local university in the 1950s, whilst his heart was with Southampton FC, his home town team.

He always took the trouble to listen to what people had to say and I regard this as a great virtue. His support to various activities and interests was unswerving; Brian had a great sense of fun and his knowledge of the weather was exceptional.

Charles Woolland (cricket enthusiast) wrote:

I remember Brian at the annual Cheltenham Cricket Festival where the idyllic setting of Cheltenham College provides the perfect backdrop for cricket at the height of summer. Usually the cricket consists of two four day matches and at least one T20 match. Brian always looked forward to attending two matches. I would drive him over to Cheltenham together with our friend Don Scott.

As well as enjoying each match Brian was an avid collector of cricket memorabilia and always spent time in the tent of Wisteria Books trying to find score cards relating to his beloved Hampshire County Cricket Club. He would usually buy books and old score cards from this stall. During the intervals for lunch and tea Brian was outside the pavilion attempting to get autographs from the players and having a word with them and the umpire. A superb lunch at the ground added to the enjoyment of the occasion.

David Shadbolt, Co-Author of *The History of Banbury Spencer Football Club* wrote:
I had the pleasure of working with Brian on *The History of Banbury Spencer Football Club*. At that time I was Banbury United's programme editor and had acquired a good knowledge of the club's earlier history as Banbury Spencer FC from writing articles for that publication. It had even crossed my mind that a book could be produced so that such knowledge would not be lost perhaps for ever but had no idea how to achieve this and so when Brian 'out of the blue' approached the club asking if there was someone who might collaborate on such a project, I was both delighted and excited and was quickly on board.

Brian's contacts and reputation in the local community were invaluable in getting people to come forward and offer information and pieces of memorabilia for the project, particularly photos and old programmes. Much of this was copied and now forms an extended part of the club's historical collection. Brian's previous publication of local books was also key in persuading the publisher that this was a book that would be financially viable.

We worked together on the project for almost two years, meeting every couple of weeks in the early days but less frequently as time passed as we got to know well how we worked best together, Brian letting me get on with my agreed tasks without undue interference and vice versa. At our meetings it soon became evident how much interest Brian had in all sports. Amazingly, when he found out I followed speedway, he would regale me with tales of how in his younger days he would stand on the terraces at Southampton Speedway, watching the racing! It was a pleasure working with Brian throughout the project and thanks to him we have a permanent historical record in print of the local football club's history as "Banbury Spencer".

****

Brian was a highly valued member of the committee of the Banbury Historical Society from 1991 and served as the Society's chair between 1995 and 2004. The Society is privileged to publish this commemorative anthology of some of his best work.

Helen Forde
Chair, Banbury Historical Society,
October 2019.

Editor's Introduction

Shortly before Christmas 1995 the editor of the *Banbury Guardian* invited Brian Little to contribute to his newspaper a series of six articles on historical topics. Brian had been resident in Banbury for 34 years, had recently retired, and at the time was chair of Banbury Historical Society. His first piece appeared on 21 December 1995. An article 'Rail Link gave town its industrial might' published on 8 February 1996 was billed as the 'final part' but the 'short series' extended to more than 1200 'nostalgia columns' which appeared every week until Brian died in March 2019, a remarkable record for any columnist. Whenever Brian went on holiday he wrote several articles in advance.

Brian's weekly column became a hub of local history in Banbury and district. Residents and far-flung Banburians sent him letters, and later emails, with their memories and with sometimes dubious tales of 'what they had always been told'. He was always pleased to re-ignite controversies about the Cross, the rhyme and Banbury Cakes. Some 'Pick of the Post' articles were miscellanies drawn from readers' letters or photographs. In season he looked nostalgically, often beneath punning headlines, at the Michaelmas Fair, Christmas and May Day. Some articles are summaries of published histories, new and old, which have not been included in this collection since the relevant books or pamphlets are easily available.

Brian also talked to many people in the district, and some of his articles are excellent examples of oral history. He extended his range of acquaintances by delivering lecture courses and by leading guided walks. In 1996, for example, he offered town walks in July and two lecture series, 'Discovering more about Banbury' and 'Moments from Memory Lane' from September. Interest was also aroused by his books, the first of which appeared in 1997. [1] He even made his private telephone number available to those who wished to get in touch.

Brian rescued from obscurity a variety of individuals and occupational groups, counter assistants at Woolworths, an auctioneer's porter, an errand boy at Hoods. He provides us with the life story of a member of a family of fairground show people who had a respectable career as a footballer, with the reminiscences of an evacuee billeting officer of 1939, and with recollections of the Warwick Road workhouse in the 1930s.

In many articles Brian picked out the historical significance of printed ephemera, auction and exhibition catalogues, programmes for dramatic productions or fetes, collections of menu cards or bills, in-house journals, timetables and old guide books. Two chapters in this anthology begin with perceptive analyses of ephemera, chapter 1 with an assessment of the range of trades available in Banbury based on bills in the records of the Chestnuts Bowls Club, and chapter 4 with an examination of a collection of menu cards made by a prominent Banburian during his mayoral year, to demonstrate the variety of voluntary organisations in the town. He was able to

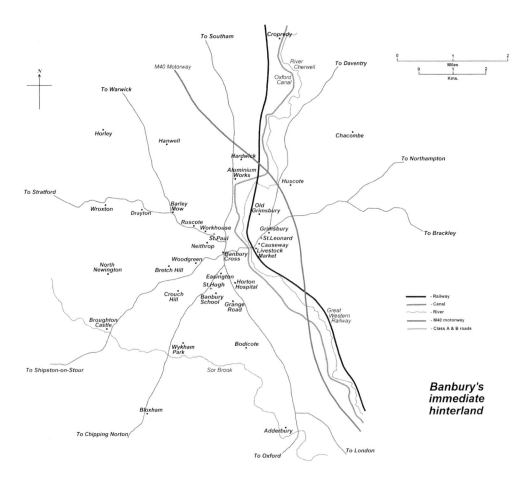

Banbury's immediate hinterland

draw on the files of his employers, the *Banbury Guardian*, but also used those of the *Banbury Advertiser* which ceased publication in 1972.

Many features of life in Banbury that would have seemed immutable when Brian Little arrived in Banbury in 1961 had disappeared by 2019, above all the livestock market, but also the marshalling yard, the aluminium works, Switchgear, Spencers, Automotive Products, Woolworth and Littlewoods. He saw the opening of the M40 and ten years later analysed its impact. As a geographer he was always anxious to gain an understanding of the ways in which the town functioned.

He often quoted the social survey of the town carried out by Margaret Stacey in 1948-51 and replicated in 1966-68 when the late Colin Bell identified Brian as a key figure of influence. His short life story of Alderman W G Mascord (5.08) shows a fascination with the sociograms used in the surveys to demonstrate the links of individuals to various organisations. [2]

Brian Little regularly used his column to promote the interests of traders in Banbury, to attract customers to the town's shops and tourists to historic buildings and the museum. He served for several years on the Borough Council in the 1970s, but his direct involvement with local government ceased after 1974 when Banbury became part of the Cherwell district. Whatever its faults the old town council was capable on occasion of decisive action, as when its members agreed to purchase the panels from the Globe Room within two months of the Banbury Historical Society's discovery that they were available for sale in London. [3] Brian considered that the traditional and much-discussed aspects of Banbury's history would attract tourists, arguing in 2016 that: 'if Banbury is to be a significant destination town for visitors and shoppers more needs to be made of the town's assets: the Cross, the Fine Lady and Banbury Cakes'. [4]

The first section of this anthology, 'Market Town Business', includes articles that chart the disappearance of traditional family shops and businesses, accounts of branches of small regional companies and of the largest national chains of the mid-twentieth century such as Woolworth and Littlewoods. In several cases he does not simply provide a history of a business, but adds details from employees and customers of what it was like to work or buy there. He paid attention to the characters who flourished at the retail market and the livestock market that in 1931 left Banbury's streets for the premises built by Midland Marts off Merton Street. He also looked at the town's principal manufacturing industries from Samuelson's Britannia Works, established in 1849, to Automotive Products and Paper & Publications which both began production in 1962. The articles in this section elide from one into another, showing how businesses operated, planning issues, the effects on retailing and manufacturing of the town's topography, and the roles of individuals, whether entrepreneurs such as Sidney Young (1.29), managers such as Henry Cooke (1.09), or employees. The account of G F Braggins & Co, timber merchants (1.26), shows the difficulty of categorising businesses. The firm's felling teams were well-known across Oxfordshire. They supplied timber in the 1930s to motor car manufacturers and railway companies, exported gates in significant quantities to Argentina, manufactured an ingeniously designed trek cart for Scouts, and at the same time sold timber to local builders and individual customers.

Banbury's only distinctive suburb in 1850 was Neithrop village, a characteristic 'rough suburb', consisting of a variety of generally low quality housing that had grown up around farmhouses of modest architectural distinction. Other hamlets, Wykham, Old Grimsbury, Easington, were no more than accumulations of small numbers of cottages around farmsteads. There were nevertheless areas on the edge of the town centre, Calthorpe Street, the Castle streets, the Cherwell streets and Monument Street, that had distinctive characteristics. The establishment of a Freehold Land Society estate at Grimsbury from 1850 created a distinct suburb, cut off from Banbury by river, canal and railway. The development of Easington and Ruscote dates from the 1920s and 30s. This anthology cannot provide a detailed topographical history of Banbury since 1850, but Brian Little's articles include first-hand accounts of many aspects of living and working in particular parts of the town in the twentieth century.

As a college lecturer Brian Little was naturally interested in education in Banbury. Several articles on schools were drawn on recently-published histories, but his moving account of the last days of the British School in Crouch Street comes directly from an original source, the school log book, and he wrote from varied sources a history of Banbury's short-lived secondary technical school at Woodgreen. Two articles draw on his own experience at another institution whose buildings came and went in his lifetime, the technical college in Bath Road.

In several articles Brian Little quoted Margaret Stacey's identification of 71 voluntary associations in Banbury, in addition to 39 which were connected with religious and political institutions. [5] He used varied sources to demonstrate the variety of sports and pastimes in which Banburians participated. He provides accounts of the local branches of national organisations ranging from the freemasons and Rotary to the Girl Guides and the Sea Cadets. He discusses venues for recreation, the Winter Gardens, cinemas, church halls, the Co-op Assembly Rooms and the People's Park, as well as occasions such as the annual Michaelmas Fair. He was interested in sport, particularly cricket, and articles in this anthology are concerned with football, bowls, cycling and motor sports as well as wrestling, which in Banbury was a sport for spectators rather than participants. His interest in music and drama led him to write about big bands and the local jazz club, a Methodist drama group whose activities were cut short by the Second World War, and the post-war Banbury Cross Players.

The memories of the generation who contributed most, by letter or by interview, to Brian Little's columns were dominated by the Second World War. The account by Annie Meadows of her experiences as an evacuee billeting officer in 1939 is of particular interest, and can be contrasted with the less conscientious exploits of Basil Seal in Evelyn Waugh's *Put out more flags*. [6] This anthology can capture only a few aspects of wartime experiences, but it does show that tanks were parked in Horton View, that many country people were bussed in daily to work at the aluminium factory, and that the mayor in 1945 attended at least 36 street parties around the time of VE-Day.

The 91 articles in this anthology, of which several combine two or three of Brian Little's originals, have been selected because of their originality – they are based on interviews, letters from his readers, or the analysis of printed ephemera or past newspaper items, and include material that is unavailable elsewhere. Brian Little's contribution to the history of Banbury was to rescue from oblivion memories and forgotten documents that, taken as a whole, vividly illustrate the town as it was for the century or so after 1920. Articles have been selected from the whole range of the 24 years of weekly column; the earliest, on the memoirs of Tom Pickston, were published on 7/14 March 1996 and the last, on housing estates under construction in 1939, on 7 March 2019, less than a month before Brian died.

Brian Little's texts have been altered as little as possible - capitals, abbreviations and punctuation have been copied as they appeared in the *Banbury Guardian*. Spellings of some place names have been amended to conform to standard OS usage, obvious typographical errors have been corrected, and the names of newspapers, journals, books, houses, public houses, plays, films and ships have been uniformly italicised. Some continuity passages, usually concerned with past or future articles, have been omitted, and some articles on the same topic have been amalgamated. Brian's articles were produced for a multi-column newspaper layout and are,

High Street and the Cowfair bedecked with flags, probably for Queen Victoria's Diamond Jubilee in 1897.

reasonably, made up of very short paragraphs. For this anthology paragraphs have been amalgamated where that is appropriate. No additional decimal equivalents to Imperial measurements or sums in pounds, shillings and pence have been inserted, nor has any attempt been made to indicate the current usage of buildings discussed in the text. The articles have been re-titled, replacing the original, sometimes lengthy newspaper headlines with concise indications of what they contain. Other amendments to the texts by the editor are few in number and are indicated by square brackets.

References

1. *Banbury in Old Picture Postcards* (Zaltbommel: Europese Bibliotheek, 1997).
2. Stacey, M, *Tradition and Change: a study of Banbury* (Oxford University Press, 1960); Stacey, M, Batstone, E, Bell, C & Murcott, A, *Power, Persistence and Change a second study of Banbury* (London: Routledge & Kegan Paul, 1975).
3. J S W Gibson, 'The Recovery of the Globe Room Panels', *C&CH*, vol 2 (1964), 171-72.
4. *BG* 26 May 2016
5. Stacey, M, *Tradition and Change*, 75;
6. Evelyn Waugh *Put out more flags* (London: Chapman & Hall, 1942).

1. Market town business

1.01: Family businesses flourished in town

In many ways Banbury of the mid to late 1940s was a carbon copy of the town ten years earlier. A walk along the pavements of the central area streets took you past a seemingly endless array of family businesses. At first glance many of these appeared to be competing firms but, as elaborate billheads suggest, the overall impression changes to one of diversity as well as marked individuality. Today's shopper has come to expect little more than a till receipt. Over 50 years ago shop proprietors used the opportunity of account settlement to convince customers that their businesses were well-established and able to create a reputation for quality and reliability of service.

Organisations like the Banbury Green Bowls Club (the Chestnuts) depended almost entirely on local suppliers some of whom were playing or non-playing members. The existence of a licensed bar in the clubhouse meant that several different sources of alcoholic and non-alcoholic drinks were relied on. These included two breweries, Hunt Edmunds of Banbury but also Flowers & Son of Stratford-upon-Avon. However despite the ability of these companies to meet all possible requests, there was always scope for other suppliers to have an involvement. Goodmans at 5 High Street, Thornitts of 28 and 29 Cornhill, Watsons in the High Street, S H Jones of the Old Wine House and A E Kilby at the *Dog and Gun* in North Bar all contributed

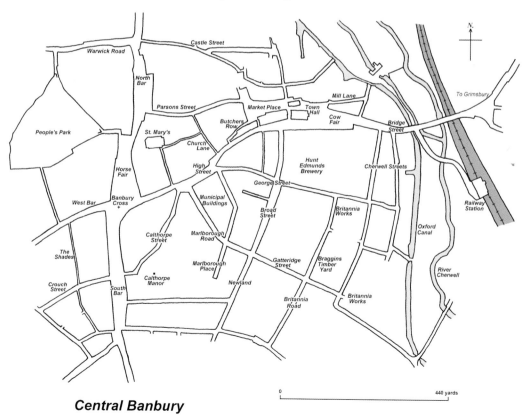

Central Banbury

to a well-stocked bar. On one occasion it was felt necessary to ask the *Red Lion* in George Street to supply one bottle of whisky and one bottle of Booth's Dry Gin for the annual match against the Handsworth Wood club from Birmingham. In the days before health warnings, a club of this calibre had to ensure that smokers as well as drinkers could have their expectations met. Cook's Tobacco Stores, whose proprietor was F J Perkins, could be relied on for all the favourite brands of the day – Players, Gold Flake, Woodbines, Craven A and Capstan.

Applications for renewal of the bar licence stress that the Chestnuts was a social body as well as a bowls club. This carried the implication that apart from drinking a little beer and making conversation, members had the opportunity to play cards and read evening papers. Thomas Dean of Broad Street was contracted to deliver the *Oxford Mail* and the *Evening Standard*. His bills to the club appear to cover great periods of time. Either Dean had great confidence in customers like the Bowls Club or he was not keen on bookwork. A bill issued on October 29, 1947 covered 22 weeks and asked for a payment of £1 5s 8d.

A prominent member, whose business derived some benefit from ongoing needs for repair and replacement, was Joe Bustin. He had an electrical works in Horse Fair but was also well remembered because of his donation of a bowls trophy. Banbury's astonishing number of ironmongers was clearly an asset so far as the Chestnuts was concerned. Bills in equal numbers from Neale & Perkins at 86/87 High Street and Broughton & Wilks in the Market Place demonstrate the importance to Banbury of having firms prepared to meet very differing demands. Neale & Perkins described themselves as manufacturing and furnishing ironmongers whereas Broughton & Wilks laid claim to being agricultural and electrical engineers as well as ironmongers. When the Chestnuts Club needed to repair its scoring board in 1946, the secretary turned to Cox's of Queens Road, successor business to George Eaves who had established originally in Butchers Row. Since a marked feature of the market town was its summer awnings it is no surprise to read on the billhead that the main business of this firm was a concern for shop spring window blinds.

Like Bustin, William Potts was a keen bowler at the Shades green. Unsurprisingly, he too benefitted from the distribution of club contracts. His *Banbury Guardian* printing office at 51 Parsons Street was the source of 200 letter headings, 150 fixture cards and 130 circulars announcing the new season of 1946. With the bill came the reminder, if indeed one was needed, that the *Guardian* of the day was 'the leading advertising medium and business organ in a district of 82,000 people'.

In 1965 the Chestnuts Club offered an honorary life associate membership to Ethel Usher of the Winter Gardens. This gesture set the seal on recognition of local business expertise without which the club would have enjoyed for looser ties with the trades of Banbury.

Banbury Guardian 4 July 2002.

1.02. Banbury Industrial Exhibition 1951

During the week April 21-28, 1951, Festival of Britain Year, Banbury's Horse Fair became the town's own industrial shop window. Exhibitors appeared in Church House and also in a Dutch barn as well as two marquees, one of which was termed agricultural and included space for livestock.

Most of those businesses participating in the Banbury and District Industrial Exhibition must have been looking forward to a surge of orders in the wake of the event. Many had set up in a small way but were already on the road to expansion. A classic example was [Leslie] Hyde of Calthorpe Street. In 1938 one man and an upstairs room had to suffice. However by 1951 cabinets for radio and television manufacturers were being turned out from the premises built within the confines of what had been known as Shilson's Wool Yard.

Several firms used the occasion to profile the history of their development or to show how what they did in the Fifties was in line with town traditions. The Hunt/Usher partnership took exhibition brochure readers back to the mid-nineteenth century when Gazey's *Wine and Spirit Vaults* had retail premises in Calthorpe Street.

The catalogue for the Banbury & District
Industrial Exhibition, 1951.

The Calthorpe Street premises of L G Hyde Ltd, cabinet manufacturers, whose business grew rapidly in the post-war period, and featured in the Banbury & District Industrial Exhibition in 1951. The Tudor-style chimneys in the centre of the picture belong to Calthorpe Manor.

The trading name changed to Watsons in 1860 when George Watson purchased the business. It was also a case of new name, so new location. Under his influence and that of his son Frank a different retailing outlet was established at 39 High Street. By the time of the exhibition this embraced King & Co who had been mineral water manufacturers in Calthorpe Street. Kings had continued a well-established tradition for aerated products in Banbury. Back in 1855 J B Austin was well-known for soda water and lemonade, trading from Parsons Street premises.

Weaving of plush cloth or shag had been a major activity in the 18th and 19th centuries. In 1951 the main manufacturing focus for Ian Steele & Co of Burford Road, Bloxham was the Wilton carpet. Their claim was that this represented a revival of weaving in the Banbury area. At the time of this exhibition, many visitors might well have viewed local industries as synonymous with Northern Aluminium and Hunt Edmunds. Here was an opportunity to get to grips with the scale and diversity of Banbury's industrial scene.

Stand 24 in the marquee was occupied by R A Bone, a metal working company. This firm was born out of wartime conditions when Banbury was regarded as a safe haven in terms of location. They produced First Aid and ARP equipment as well as sub-machine gun parts. By 1951 their manufacturing base had changed dramatically and they were producing all manner of metal equipment for intensive poultry farming enterprises. Another company with wartime origins was the North Bar Tool Company. In 1943, the Ministry of Aircraft Production approved the manufacture of a tool vital to the aero engine industry. This was the Sumner P50 Tension Wrench.

A stand that must have caught the eye was the one belonging to E W Brown. In their brochure notes they draw attention to their restaurant mural which illustrated in colour the history of Banbury from the Bronze to the Aluminium Age. Browns also presented a challenge to the notion that Banbury was known principally because of the Ride a Cockhorse rhyme. To their mind 'Nothing seems to enhance its reputation more than these delectable cakes' (i.e. Brown's Banbury Cakes).

The early 1950s was not a boom time for everyone in the Banbury area. In fact the firm of Braggins, a long established timber company, took the unusual step of emphasising the post war restrictions on felling timber and how this could affect the company's ability to meet some requests. In the years after the war newsprint limitations had affected both the *Banbury Guardian* and the *Banbury Advertiser*. However their entries in the exhibition brochure were both upbeat and reflected an awareness of competition in the newspaper sales business. Whilst the *Advertiser* claimed it had been a public servant for over 97 years, the *Guardian* reminded Banbury people that it had once been the watchdog of a Poor Law Act as well as a non-political paper informing the town and district of happenings local and national.

On April 23, 1951, this outstanding Banbury event was given an added boost by the presence of HRH the Duchess of Gloucester. Her abiding memory of this occasion must have been the astonishing variety of activities in a town where traditions once ensured a much narrower industrial base.

Banbury Guardian 12 September 2002.

1.03: A man of distinction: E Owen Reid

In the early 1930s, keen observers of the local government scene would have noticed a new name in the corporation handbook. Ernest Owen Reid had arrived from Coventry and become Banbury's first full-time town clerk. He succeeded Arthur Stockton who had fulfilled this role but only on a part-time basis. Reid was well versed in council procedures by the time he reached our town in 1932. His previous period of employment in Coventry had lasted since 1912. However, becoming familiar with the structure of Banbury's council could not have been easy. There were no fewer than 19 committees and sub-committees with responsibilities as diverse as health, allotments and the museum, as well as sub-committees to cover school attendance, repairs and the canteen. Familiarisation with local affairs and the development of Banbury must have been greatly assisted by such colleagues as James Friswell (mayor), Ernest Claude Fortescue (clerk to the justices) and Sidney Hilton (borough surveyor and engineer). They had come to know and understand the town. It was said of Sidney Hilton that he was 'the man who built a third of Banbury, which, due to his untiring efforts, was rapidly becoming one of the garden towns of England'.

Interestingly, another significant way in which Owen Reid must have got to grips with his new job would have been through constant reference to which was called *The Directional Printer Guide – Map to Banbury*. This was published by E J Burrow of Cheltenham and London and with the approval of the Banbury Borough Council. His personal copy was annotated to highlight the town centre within the total built-up area. Amongst the miscellaneous information and interesting notes was a statement of the 1931 census population and some observations about the town. A total of 13,953 people lived within the borough which still clung to its established market traditions. Coming to Banbury about a year after the arrival of the Northern Aluminium Company, Owen Reid must have smiled at the remark that 'the uninitiated find it difficult to imagine Banbury as an industrial town. At first glance it appears quite isolated and remote from any fields of industrial activity'.

If Reid's first impression of the town was coloured by these comments then it was not long before he was grappling with Banbury's transformation from pure market town to an industrial centre that retained a continuing interest in livestock. Industrial arrivals generated a need for housing and Reid acquired land such as the Kings Road area in 1936 which allowed Banbury to expand its built-up area. Between 1932 and 1945 he performed other functions with great distinction. In his role as clerk to the local education authority, he was responsible for maternity and child welfare. During the 1939-45 war he was food executive officer, national registration officer and even looked after the billeting of evacuees, which was a very important activity as Banbury was viewed with confidence as a safe haven. After 1945 he contested the trend towards centralisation of powers in the county and enabled Banbury to retain its Commission of the Peace as well as the Borough Quarter Sessions.

Ceremonial occasions brought the best out of Owen Reid. He was the key figure in the successful handling of the visit of HRH the Duchess of Gloucester, the granting of the freedom of the borough to the county's own regiment, the Oxford & Bucks

Light Infantry and not least the fourth centenary celebrations of the incorporation of the borough. This last event took place in 1954. Ernest Owen Reid retired in 1955. Along with Sidney Hilton, he was promptly given the highest honour that it was possible to confer on an individual – the honorary freedom of the Borough. A Municipal Corporations Act of 1885 established that this position of honorary freeman was specifically for persons of distinction. At the ceremony held on December 5 1955, remarks by Fred Boys (the new town clerk) and Councillor Frank Partridge demonstrated that Owen Reid's 23 years of service more than merited the award, the first ever conferred on an individual by Banbury Borough Council.

Banbury Guardian 11 September 2003.

1.04: The year of the bulldozer: 1972

There may be said to have been many different Banburys at different times during the town's history.

Explanations of this can be sought in events such as the Great Fire of 1628 and the sieges of the Castle during the Civil War in 1644 and 1646.The outcomes were considerable havoc at specific locations, which were never going to be the same again. Much more recently change was in the air again but in the 1970s this was prompted by retail demands and new perceptions of service sector needs. This time around local newspapers were able to give substantial coverage to a fresh era of upheaval. In fact 1972 was dubbed the year of the bulldozer, mechanical digger, cement mixer and bricklayer.

In certain cases the construction activity of the seventies included welcome and substantial conservation. This was highlighted in an exhibition at the Oxfordshire Studies Centre of some of the photographs of the late Ken Brooks, who was a solicitor with the West Bar firm of Aplins for several decades. For instance he caught on camera the portico of the old Baptist Chapel in Bridge Street, all that was left of the building when the site was being got ready for a significant expansion of the adjacent Fine Fare supermarket. The company was quick to exploit the words of our nursery rhyme to the effect that:

Ride a Cock Horse to Banbury Cross
To see a fine lady upon a white horse
She's going to Fine Fare
Without more delay
For much better value
At far less to pay.

Further along Bridge Street towards the bridge traffic movements became a major concern following a programme of slum clearance in the Cherwell area, which was preceded by the relocation of the residential population. The entrance to Cherwell Street was widened to 40ft, the first stage in a progression to inner relief road status. In the heyday as a residential neighbourhood the Cherwell area was home to a substantial number of people. It was they who stood to benefit from an offer of recreational land made by Banbury butcher Thomas Hankinson. He made available the flood plain area known as Spiceball Park. Many years later in the early 1970s leisure took on a new meaning with the construction and opening (November 1972) of the General Foods Club as well as substantial building activity, the early stages of the local authority's sports centre.

1972 was also the year in which the original Castle Centre shopping development took shape and, for possibly the first time for nearly 100 years, Banbury folk could see across swathes of land where once Castle Street North, Factory Street and Compton Street were home to communities that could collectively and justifiably be called Old Banbury. In November 1972 it was announced that Sainsburys would secure the anchor store position in the new development. However devotees of this firm had to wait a little longer.

The last *Banbury Guardian* of 1972 contained photographs of the changing face of the town. Central to these was one of the present Cross built in 1859. This symbolised tradition rather than change. The people of Banbury were opposed to the county council's desire to shift or even demolish it to aid traffic flow. The town's response was 'move the traffic instead'. Higher than the Cross and much more modern was the GPO's Castle Street telephone switching centre. This was a 70ft tall fibreglass mosaic. Internally it was expected to take until November 1974 before it could become operational. In the meantime the Church Passage exchange was going to continue serving local subscribers. The Castle Street building with its motifs on a casing of panels largely escaped criticism because the wrath of the town descended on what became known as the Kremlin, the new Crown offices in Southam Road. Perhaps it is a pity that the livestock market did not take shape in the Cope Road/Arran Grove area. This had been the original intention of the borough council in the early 1920s.

Seventies development was not confined to the town centre. Drayton School took shape at the junction of the Stratford and Warwick roads and allowed pupils from Grimsbury Hall to start life in a new environment rather than their early 1900s building. Previously this north-west end of the town had been characterised by the *Barley Mow* and a solitary AA box.

Towns by their very nature cannot stand still but it was to be a whole 20 years or more before the arrival of the M40 started a process whereby Banbury found its market town image considerably distorted, even if a national newspaper writer in the '90s could claim that 'the Cockhorse town gallops on'.

Banbury Guardian 14 December 2006.

1.05: P R Alcock, builders

On April 16, P R Alcock, the Castle Street firm of builders, celebrated 78 years in business. The company was established in 1927 by Percy Reginald Alcock, a man with a most interesting background. Born in 1886, Percy was the son of a carrier at Epwell who brought his cart to Banbury. Percy did not follow in his father's footsteps but instead he became apprenticed as a carpenter with a firm called Booths who were [the] principal builders in the town during the early years of the 20th century. On leaving this company Percy sought to widen and extend his training by joining Franklins of Deddington who were specialists in church building and restoration work. After five years with them Percy joined the work force at Samuelsons in the Cherwell area of Banbury. Here he was involved with the making of timber moulds and various parts for agricultural implements.

At the outset of the First World War and wishing to help the war effort, Percy cycled from Banbury to Coventry where he found work with an aircraft manufacturer whose specialised interests included timber-framed aircrafts and wooden propellers. In the aftermath of war Percy reverted to being a carpenter, this time with Henry Boot, a Sheffield firm in origin. It was at this point in his career that job progression resulted in promotion first to foreman and then a site agent for schemes of council house construction at Horley, Wroxton and North Newington. When these contracts were completed Percy faced redundancy but instead turned himself into a sub-contractor in order to be redeployed by Boots on new private house work in the Bloxham Road in Banbury.

Henry Boot left this area in 1922 and Percy seized the opportunity to take over the firm's yard in the Warwick Road. He formed a partnership with a stone mason with whom he had already worked and the outcome was a firm known as Alcock and Cronk. Sadly within a few years a motorbike accident forced Mr Cronk to take early retirement and it was at this point, in the year 1927, that the firm was renamed P R Alcock & Sons. The business remained under Percy's control until his death in 1958 when his son Harold, who in turn directed the affairs of the company for the next 22 years, succeeded him. Since 1980 a third generation, John and Mike Alcock, have been in charge of this family concern.

P R Alcock's first yard in Banbury was rented from a Mrs Sharman and was located in North Bar Place. ... In 1936 the opportunity to move the business to the present site came with the auctioning of a property that had previously been occupied by Mr Wall, a prominent rope maker in Banbury.

In common with one or two other local family construction businesses in Banbury, Alcocks established a name for diversity of activity and involvement with buildings of great significance in the history of the town and surrounding area. The firm had their share of both the council and private housing construction market in villages like Bloxham and Chacombe as well as in Banbury. Certain other contracts won by the firm can rightly be deemed as prestigious. Quite apart from restoration work at places such as Broughton Castle, Canons Ashby and Farnborough Hall, the company was responsible for the Great Hall and entrance gateway at All Saints School, Bloxham, Tudor Hall School's dining room, dormitory and some classrooms,

The Castle Street premises of the builders, P R Alcock, formerly the rope-making workshops of the Wall family.

Easington Girls' School (later Broughton Hall of Banbury School) and St Hugh's Church in Ruskin Road. This last building, which gave Easington its own Anglican church in 1933, was built brick by brick by Harold Alcock.

Bearing in mind recent concerns about listed property in Banbury, it is interesting to record the involvement of the company with the Market Place building occupied by the Nationwide Building Society. Before Alcocks' restoration work led to a short-listing for a European award, the property was going to be demolished. This would have been a scandal to rival that of the destruction of the Parsons Street cake shop.

One consequence of the firm's growing involvement in the Banbury area construction scene was a significant increase in the size of the labour force needed; this reached a total of 130 in 1960. Now, 45 years on, the company has found a moment to enjoy a dinner to mark past achievements and long service contributions. In the photograph with the line of happy smiling faces are those whose total period of employment with P R Alcock amounts to 185 years. This celebration of loyalty and allegiance comes at an appropriate time in the history of the firm because of its recent involvement in the foundation for the Lady on the White Horse statue. This sub-contract is just one more milestone in the life of a company that has contributed so much to preserving the Banburyness of our town while remaining a family concern throughout its existence.

Banbury Guardian 12 May 2005.

1.06: Master of masonry: George Carter

Four brothers by the name of Cakebread came to the Banbury area in the early 19th century. Their move from Loughton in Essex was motivated by a desire to secure construction work. One of these was George. He is listed under stone and marble masons in Rusher's directory published in 1832. At that time George is said to have been in Bloxham and the only Banbury- mason is John Nelson of Scalding Lane (now George Street). Seven years later George Cakebread appears to have established his business at 69 Bridge Street. By then other masons were Robert Mander at 70 Bridge Street (was he linked to the same yard?) and John Nelson, who was in the Horse Fair. Directories between 1832 and 1856 reveal that Nelson moved about a lot and had periodic addresses in Bridge Street and Cherwell Street, as well as his original location of Fish Street (the re-named Scalding Lane).

The period from the mid-19th century to 1888 was dominated in the stone mason business by Alfred Claridge and Robert Mander and it was not until 1889 that the name of a George Cakebread is recorded again. This time the location was in North Bar. A man who became a great rival was William Sturley who started in Broad Street but later moved to Southam Road. In 1904 the name Cakebread appeared on a board fitted to the front wall of 3 Castle Street West. This was home to George (father) and Thomas (son). Their work appears to have been carried out in a shed in the Southam Road which was surrounded by allotment gardens. In 1916 Thomas Cakebread was in a position to expand his stone mason activities because of the financial support that came from his wife's side of the family. Her resources made it possible to buy the business of William Sturley who had acquired 18 Southam Road from a pots and pans man by the name of Badger. Despite this much larger base for his operations, Thomas retained his shed opposite as it was well-adapted for sawing large blocks of stone into more manageable slabs.

Seven years later Thomas accepted George Carter into apprenticeship. George had spent his early years in East Street and was educated at Grimsbury Council School. Five years stretched ahead of George before he was qualified to work in marble. In 1930 at the age of 21 George Carter went into partnership with Thomas Cakebread. This lasted until 1938 when George became sole owner of the business. It was not long before he discovered the extent of the competition. Clutterbucks and Humphris & Sons were prominent rivals. However George developed a good relationship with undertakers over a 30-mile radius and exploited markets abroad including Canada, India and Yugoslavia.

During his working life George evolved an interest in the renovation of coats of arms. These were as bizarre as the iceberg and rib of beef of Lord Vestey at Stowell Park near Burford and as difficult to fit together as the weathered stones at Broughton Castle. The latter assignment during the 1950s exercised George's mason skills because the pieces had not been numbered, as was the custom, by the original creator of the arms of Lord Saye and Sele. Different and other notable tasks included the successful repair of the apex of Banbury Cross in 1977. He might well have had a much greater involvement with the monument ten years earlier but Banbury Borough Council decided against accepting his tender of £5,000 to move Banbury Cross to a site outside the *Whately Hall Hotel*. Another unsuccessful tender was for Bath Stone renovation of the old post office in Banbury High Street.

George's pricing policy was usually a key to his success especially over and against the other firms of masons. Another factor was the very name of Carter which became linked to high standards and quality service as had the name of Cakebread in the past. Banbury is indeed fortunate in having some fine examples of the work of George and his apprentices. The coat of arms at the entrance to the Castle Quay Shopping Centre was carved by Dennis Morrison who subsequently went to Cheltenham. Current restoration work at St Mary's Church is in the capable hands of Brent Hayward, managing director of Hornton Quarries Ltd. Brent was also an apprentice with George Carter.

Christopher Carter, George's father was a gardener whose skills were highly regarded, especially by the well-heeled occupants of properties in South Parade, Middleton Road, Grimsbury. His son chose a very different route to success but one which perpetuated the earlier skills of George and Thomas Cakebread.

Banbury Guardian 24 January 2002.

1.07: **Town once slated by the Welsh**:

Circular P/2 dated July 1, 1910, was an attempt by Davies Brothers of Portmadoc [Porthmadog] in North Wales to encourage Dalby interest in Precelly green and rustic slates. Not content with listing the contents of their stock, the owners of Gilfach Quarry were out to demonstrate the universality of their roofing materials across the country. Apparently, 600 tons of green slates had been used for schools and cottage homes in Brentwood, Essex, while the rustic variant covered buildings such as Oban Pier and Stores in Scotland and a new asylum for Leicestershire. The latter absorbed 1,300 tons.

As much as anything the strength of the Banbury area market for these Cambrian slates was dependent on favourable rail freight rates and the willingness of house and other property builders to think slate, rather than thatch, as an answer to the perennial problem of local marlstones not cleaving. An early letterhead of Dalby & Co reveals that slates were one item in an astonishing range of materials. An extant notebook of 1846 contains several pages of customers, what they bought and at what cost, who collected the items and where the purchasers came from – Banbury or a village within the town's catchment.

Some people who bought from the Bridge Wharf company were regulars and by careful cross referencing with Rusher's Lists and Directories it is possible to understand why they needed to place regular orders. One of these was Edward Hollowell of South Bar Street who was a carpenter. Typically, on Monday, April 1, 1839, he purchased two lots of pine board for 2/6d and 5/3d. Both were collected for him by Mr Wyatt who was one in a veritable army of local carriers. Another regular was Robert Cockerill of Parsons Street. He was in Rusher's list of cabinet makers and upholsterers. On April 16 of the same year, his timber purchases amounted to values of 8/- and £1 8s 0d.

In the case of customers who were village-based, the need to use the services of a local carrier were probably even greater. Mr Grant of Fenny Compton relied on W S Edwards who was from that village. Edwards came to Banbury every Monday and Thursday and based himself at the *Reindeer Inn*, Parsons Street. Not all the carriers mentioned in the Dalby book can be traced in the local directories. A man called Hunt collected planks for Mr Simpson of Eydon and George Coles was the man in charge when Samuel Franklin of Weedon wanted to shift £1 16s 0d worth of timber back into Northamptonshire.

Certain people who relied on Dalby & Co were regarded as safe in terms of making payments. They were permitted accounts. Mr Dumbleton of Middleton Cheney and Mr Dods of Banbury were good examples. Dods was a cabinet maker in Church Lane. The social status of customers is interesting. A few can be traced to a Rusher list of nobility, gentry and clergy. There was George Warriner of Bloxham Grove and the Rev Charles Dayman of Duns Tew. Today's researchers can only guess at why Dayman wanted a 42ft pole which cost him or his church committee 24 shillings. A few other names shine out of the book, notably John Drinkwater who was landlord of the *White Lion* in Banbury's High Street. A quantity of pine board cost him one shilling and eight pence.

A thick address book of Dalby & Co is also a fascinating item. There are qualitative statements about some people and their ability or otherwise to pay promptly. On that front, H A Dalby had set out his stall early. In a public notice about the start of his business in 1834, he remarked: 'The above establishment is commenced upon the principle of supplying the trade with the best articles in the market at the lowest possible price and FOR READY MONEY'. A Deddington slater was described as honest and straightforward, whereas an Alkerton carpenter was bluntly termed 'not good'…

Banbury Guardian 28 October 1999.

1.08: Characters from the inter-war markets:

In 2001 I tutored a local history course entitled 'Banbury: the Changing Faces of its Communities'. Two of the topics were 'A Market Place fit for a town of traders' and 'Bridge Street – haven of the little shop'. Both were based on my earliest experiences of this town which coincided with the start of the sixties. In this article I have decided to go back further in time to the 1920s and 1930s when the Market Place was a sea of stalls manned by a wide range of personalities. A significant number of these were local but there was also a good representation of traders who brought wares from as far away as the East Midlands.

Amongst the best-remembered and ever present people was Rocky Leach. He was renowned for his Banbury rock that was available in a wide range of flavours and colours. However on hot summer days cut up sticks of rock tended to attract a host of insects as well as close attention from children. Confectioners in the 1920s also included Salmon & Catch. A proportion of their sweets were made in North Bar and owed much to the skills of Violet Beale and Dolly Rutter. The latter was best known for her hand-made chocolates. Carriers with their carts ensured that consignments of sweets found their way to village shops. On Saturday their stall stayed open until 9.30pm in order to catch people going into the *Palace* cinema.

Market traders with an East Midlands background included Jack Spencer who was a popular figure and from the 1920s travelled from Leicester to find buyers for stockings, socks and underwear. In 1945 he moved to Banbury and lived locally until his death at the age of 93. Competitors in the underwear business were Peacocks, also from the East Midlands. They had a large square stall where work was offered to several local girls.

Cornhill and the western end of Market Place circa 1910. The premises of the confectioners Salmon & Catch are on the extreme right.

The Market Place in the early 1920s.

Many market traders had shops in the town as well as their stalls. Wyncolls came from Birmingham to Banbury in the early 1920s. They had a pitch outside the Picture House and this was exclusively for selling bananas. Success in this business prompted the opening of a shop towards the top of Parsons Street. Continuously good trade led to the family taking over the old *Windmill* pub in North Bar.

At the beginning of the 21st century the development of Castle Quay Shopping Centre led to Bridge Street becoming a partially blighted area. However the history of this street suggested a more important past when family businesses flourished and people lived above their shops. It is impossible to mention everyone but a family trader from just before the Second World War was F J Mason, the butcher at No 60. In 1938 he took over the building from Andrews transport business. Mason enjoyed a 50-year association with the Banbury Stockyard in Grimsbury. Right up until 1988 he bought livestock to generate his supply of well-hung meat. Within a short distance and on the same side of the road was the bakery and café of Arthur Wincott. The bakehouse was in Mill Lane but the café faced Bridge Street and was visited by many of those whose journeys began and ended nearby. Like many other bakers they claimed their version of the Banbury Cake was the genuine one. Beyond Wincotts were Butlers the fruiterers who were agents for the Oddfellows Friendly Society. Until the 1960s another distinctive retailer was Jimmy Cluff whose footwear business had been handed down by his father. The firm made its own shoes using hides tanned in a workshop close to the *Strugglers* public house in Mill Lane.

Hoods the Banbury ironmongers was where you could buy almost anything from a nail to a roll of chicken wire, including fork handles. Unsurprisingly the shop merited the title 'emporium'. Customers included undertakers and owners of fairground rides. In fulfilling more regular demands, Hoods delivery van enabled the firm to reach customers as far away as Chipping Norton and Eydon.

Banbury Guardian 1 February 2018.

1.09: Henry Cooke's Co-op legacy

The *Wheatsheaf* was a Co-operative Society magazine designed to appeal to home readers. Issue No 423 and dated to September 1931 has come to light but within the context of local news concerning Banbury Co-operative Industrial Society Ltd. A major feature of the issue was an appreciation of the life of Henry James Cooke, JP, by Bill Lickorish who was the author of a 1936 booklet about the CWS in our area. Cooke had been general manager of the Banbury Society from 1891 to 1931 but also local editor of *Wheatsheaf* for some years. Lickorish is almost lyrical in the way he appraised Cooke: 'In our struggle for the people's economic betterment, in our work for better business structures, in our work to educate the public mind, in our work for social advance, we shall feel his influence yet while … we may catch the echoes of his fine tenor voice pleasing for the continued harmony in life and peace in industry by the co-operative principles he held'.

The Cookes lived at 21 Newland Road and it was from here that his widow wrote an open letter of gratitude for the many tributes received from employees of the Banbury Co-operative Society Ltd. At the funeral wreaths came from all walks of local life and the origins of these was a reflection of Henry's involvement in the town and area. Sport seems to have been high on the list. Apparently he was a founder of the Banbury Cricket and Sports Club and also had an involvement in the Banbury Early Closers Athletic Club. Bill Lickorish hinted that Henry Cooke had a good voice when he said 'While from the eternal hills we may catch the echoes of his fine tenor voice'.

The principal grocery shop of the Banbury Co-operative Society on the west side of Broad Street before 1908. The placard to the right of the entrance advertises brawn and pressed beef. Pelaw polishes took their name from the Co-operative Wholesale Society factory at Pelaw, Co Durham.

The Banbury Co-operative Society's shops at the corner of Broad Street and George Street, designed by the architect A E Allen of 35a Bridge Street, and opened on 29 August 1908.

It is obvious that he devoted a lot of time to Marlborough Road Wesleyan Choir as well as to the Banbury Co-operative Choir. His retail connections within the town were understandably strong. Floral tributes appeared from Mr and Mrs Salmon, the Chidzeys and Ernest Butler.

Cooke in particular and the Banbury Society generally had a big impact on life locally. The society was one of the organisations in the town with both cottages and allotments to let. Its members contributed significantly to the Horton Infirmary by supporting the Workpeople's Hospital Fund. Between April 1910 and August 1931 employees raised a grand total of £641 16s 11½d for this fund.

The quarterly meeting of the Banbury Industrial Co-operative Society Ltd was also reported extensively in this issue of the *Wheatsheaf*. It was held on Wednesday, July 22, 1931, in the Society's Assembly Room at 47 Broad Street. At the time Henry Cooke was still alive but obviously very ill. A major cause of concern was the quality of bread being produced. A Mr Bird claimed that, in the case of bread in tins, there was a too high incidence of burnt crusts. Bill Lickorish, the secretary, explained that there had been a decline in bread sales as a result of which their mill was not working economically and efficiently. The mill had to be placed on short time working.

The same meeting was also an opportunity to refer to an announcement in the local press that the Banbury Society had acquired land behind the clothing and other shops in Broad Street. It seems that there was a delay in conveyancing and only on completion could the Co-operative Society think about up-to-date equipment in the premises for their drapery, clothing, boots and other dry goods departments.

One very interesting issue raised at this quarterly meeting concerned the age of members of the committee. Mr R H Gardner of Centre Street in Grimsbury suggested that there should be an age limit of 70. He coupled this with an appeal for younger men to come forward. A Mr Hartrop spoke on the same motion and was quick to acknowledge the part played by older people in the Society's past progress. Maybe he had a point especially as the report about the meeting was followed by an advert in praise of the CWS fish section. 'All the fish is delightfully clean and sweet'. If indeed 50,000 Co-operative families ordered fish every week, some at least must have included elderly members who had done their bit sustained by these nourishing morsels from the sea.

Banbury Guardian 24 May 2001.

1.10: Dream shopping centre of 1934

During March 1934 a new chapter was written in the history of Banbury's shopping developments. This was the outcome of an initiative by the Banbury & District Industrial Co-operative Society. At 3pm on the 10th of that month Mr W H Lickorish, local managing director, accompanied by Sir William Dudley (chairman of the Co-operative Wholesale Society Ltd) officially opened one of the most imposing buildings of its kind in the town. This was Banbury's first ever shopping arcade. Together with the 1909 Society building on the corner of Broad Street and George Street the total effect was 'a wonderful improvement in this increasingly important thoroughfare'.

Public interest in the latest addition to Broad Street was huge, as witness the massive turnout of people at the opening ceremony. They would not have been disappointed as the sales floors were open plan 'just like big city stores', and could be reached by a lift – later an escalator was installed (the first in Banbury). In addition the first floor level had mirrored pillars whilst the central cash system was operated

The Banbury Co-operative Society's shopping arcade in Broad Street which opened in 1934.

The store opened by Montague Burton in March 1934, which stood *'like the Crystal Palace, glistening in the sunshine and adding dignity to the High Street'*.

by what was known as Dart Control. Central to the arcade was the dome that offered a pleasing effect under artificial lighting conditions.

Departments at this level included outfitting, footwear and hair dressing for men, while female interests were served by drapery, ladies' footwear and hairdressing. Customers in need of refreshment found the ideal answer on the first floor in the shape of Cosy Café where 'dainty' teas were served. The final stage at the top of the building was also remarkable – a world of polished brass devoted to office and administration purposes. This was where steel revolving pass book safes had been installed. Unsurprisingly at the time of the official opening Mr Lickorish remarked that 'a long-cherished dream has at last been realised'.

In a letter to the *Banbury Guardian* published on April 9 1998, Pauline Grain (his granddaughter) of Poole, Dorset, recalled how proud her grandfather had been to be accorded the honour of opening the premises. Other people who shared his excitement were members of the General and Educational Committees of the local co-operative movement who attended the official tea and afterwards a grand concert given by the Banbury Co-operative Choir and string orchestra.

Someone with vivid memories of life and work in the building is Nigel Ashley. He started as a hairdressing apprentice there in the mid-1960s following a period during which he gained experience through a Saturday job, working a 9am to noon and 2pm-4pm day. The day was divided by a lunch break during which the proximity of fish, chips and peas was an obvious attraction at 1/9d (9p) as his Saturday wage was 7/9d (30p). For Nigel the cash margin was tight even when the apprenticeship started. However this did not deter him from venturing into Cuban heeled shoes at 19/- (95p) the pair. Social life at the Winter Gardens demanded some attention to fashion. Nigel's five-year apprenticeship included time spent at the Art College, then on the Green. Tuesday morning and Wednesday evening were spent in this way.

As for Tuesday afternoon, the Co-op followed the town pattern of half-day closing. At the time the arcade was opened the Society went so far as to enter a soccer side in the local Tuesday Junior League. A typical fixture was the one played on March 6 1934 when Sports Villa (forerunner of Banbury United) met the Co-operatives.

Many names of people who worked for the company in Nigel's time have coming flooding back to him. Aubrey Griffin (shoes), Neil Barton (haberdashery) and Elsie Milne, his boss in hairdressing, are amongst these. Now in February 2012 the shopping dream centre of 1934 looks sad and forlorn marked by FOR SALE boards.

Banbury Guardian 2012.

- In an article of 20 January 2011 Brian Little briefly describes the opening of the Co-op arcade and also that of the Montague Burton store at 68/69 High Street on 24 March 1934. The firm's publicity proclaimed, '*The busy crowd that swing daily into the heart of Banbury have watched with interest the growth of the mammoth building until it stands like the Crystal Palace, glistening in the sunshine and adding dignity to the High Street, a notable contribution to the architectural beauty of Banbury*'.

1.11: Ladies ruled Bridge Street:- the electricity showrooms

Ownership and occupation may be equally important in determining the character of any part of our town. Bridge Street provides a good example. In 1890 an Inland Revenue form to do with duty liability outlined the estate of the Trew family. A significant element of the estate was in Bridge Stret itself. The core members of the Trew's were the Misses Ellen, Alice and Priscilla. They were resident here but there was also a Henry Fredrick Trew whose address was not known. Among their properties was one of Banbury's many public houses. This was the *White Hart*, complete with yard, stables and outbuildings. The name of Franklin was associated with the inn which was a tied house of Hunt Edmunds. Annual rent for these premises was £70.

Elsewhere in the street, the ladies had three houses, one of which was close to two cottages. All are described as freehold and were let to married persons. In one, William Burton paid a rent of £34-8-0d

28 Bridge Street consisted of a house, garden and premises occupied by Ellen and Alice Trew. Their Bridge Street properties were said to be in a bad state of repair at the end of the 19th century. Elsewhere in Banbury, the Trews had cottages in Fish Street (now George Street) and in Calthorpe Lane.

The Art Deco building at Nos 15-17 Bridge Street, built by Humphris & Sons and occupied from 1929 by the Shropshire, Worcestershire & Staffordshire Power Co.

With their portfolio of properties ranging as widely as this, it should be no surprise that back in 1849, Samuel Lovell of King's Sutton and Thomas Hunt, founder of Hunt Edmunds Brewery, were appointed executors to manage affairs for the ladies. Income for the Trews was also available from a 29-acre farm at Pin Hill. In 1890 this was let to William Woodhull at an annual rent of £80. By 1912 Elias Bonham had become the sitting tenant and was deriving benefits, especially from the grass cutting opportunities. An associated and not uncommon feature of 19th century ownerships was the possession of a pew in St Mary's Church. This south aisle pew was occupied by Miss Tysoe Smith for which she paid £5 a year to the Trews.

In 1929 Messr Humphris and Sons added substantially to the architecture of Bridge Street. In place of cottages with premises at number 15 and a house and shops at numbers 16-17 there appeared a single Art Deco style building. For some while it did not attract a tenant, it was even seen by local people as a white elephant. This phase finally ended when the Shropshire, Worcestershire and Staffordshire Power Company decided it was ready made for them. The showroom – 16th in the country – was opened by the mayor, Coun[cillor] Mascord in 1929. Until recently it housed the business of Baron Motorists' Centre. He commented that, although it was not possible to commit the council, nevertheless he would like to see electricity in the streets of Banbury.

On behalf of the company Mr Wheelwright presented the mayor with a momento – an engraved silver cigarette box. From the outset Banbury was part of a 3,000 square mile SWS catchment and this was soon to grow and embrace Adderbury, Bodicote, Twyford and Hook Norton. It was anticipated that the main supply of electricity would come from Stourport but that Banbury would be the main distribution centre. As the showroom took early shape so it became an integral part of a street which by the 1930s had turned into a haven of family business with domestic life well established above the shops.

Banbury Guardian 21 May 1998.

1.12: Life in *Havenfield*, R B Miller's home in Bridge Street

In the 1930s and 40s Bridge Street had a life all of its own. This was especially true of the south side between Hunt's Yard and the offices of the Shropshire, Worcestershire and Staffordshire Power Company. A prominent building in this section was called *Havenfield*, which was home to the family of Raymond Bernard Miller who was company secretary to Hunt Edmunds Brewery for some 25 years and also an alderman of Banbury Borough Council. The location of this house, together with the size of the garden, meant that the brewery was a major factor in the daily cycle of events. Recollection of these make most interesting reading. It seems that the garden belonging to *Havenfield* backed on to Hunt Edmunds' building yard. In general terms this was a wilderness just made for inquisitive youngsters. An added bonus was a sand pit.

Access to this adjacent property was greatly increased when the brewery staff were on holiday. Then workmen were less restrictive about visits to the carpenter's shop or the cooperage. Were the health and safety regulations of today in place the, circumstances would have been very different. The presence of the brewery was equally apparent on the Cherwell and railway side of the garden. Here was the company's despatch area which was known as Lundie's Yard. It was so called because the manager responsible for operations was Mr Lundie. His house was at the entrance to the yard but during working hours an office annexe enabled him to be aware of movements. In time-honoured manner Lundie inscribed his ledgers, these were so large that they had to spread across huge continuous desks. High stools allowed their surfaces to be reached with ease.

Apart from the comings and goings other memories of this yard related to the nearby malt house tht towered over it. Play areas for the Miller children extended to this enormous building which always appeared deserted of Hunt Edmunds staff. Piles of barley appeared as if by magic and fluctuations in the amount gave the only evidence of an occasional human presence. Another nearby feature was the motor transport garage, which may well have had steam lorries. A real treat for youngsters of the 1930s era was being allowed to travel on the lorries that were destined for country pubs. Entry to the licensed premises was not permitted and so the best someone under age could expect was a bottle of fizzy lemonade, which was not always well received. Journeys themselves were sometimes not without interest. On one occasion all but the driver had to get out of the cab so that the lorry could negotiate a hill near Banbury.

Shovelling grain in the malthouse at
Hunt Edmunds brewery.

During the Second World War, *Havenfield*'s garden was extended so as to enable the Miller family to 'dig for victory'. As flour was in short supply and largely imported, the replacement commodity was the potato, which people were invited to consume in a variety of guises. The garden extension was on to brewery yard land and it was not an uncommon sight to see employees lending a hand. Even before the war the end of the garden was especially fascinating because a raised path marked the line of a tunnel along which full beer barrels were rolled from the production part of the brewery to the dispatch area.

Other aspects of life at *Havenfield* related to the Bridge Street frontage. On Thursdays this implied the cattle market. A slightly raised footpath in front of the house was the sole means of keeping livestock at a distance. Come the end of the day and there was the sight of men cleaning up the mess. Their tactics were less vigorous than those of the stockmen.

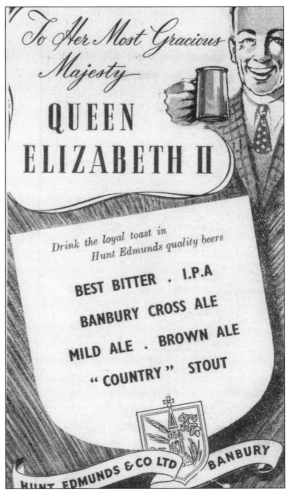

Hunt Edmunds products in Coronation year, 1953.

In October the Michaelmas Fair moved in and this meant a good deal of noise. Directly in front of the house was a coconut shy but night-time disturbance came from elsewhere and was so intensive that the youngest members of the family had to be put to bed in the bedroom of their parents. More regular occurrences and part of everyday life sometimes meant a greater awarenesss of the town. Mr Viggers of Drayton not only delivered milk but also permitted rides on his float. The village of Drayton was a world away from those whose lives were geared to the comings and goings of Bridge Street.

Banbury Guardian 23 October 2003.

- For the brewery see Anon (R B Miller), *Hunt Edmunds & Co 1896-1946* (Banbury: Hunt Edmunds, 1946); C L Harman, *Cheers, Sir! From the Vicarage to the Brewery* (Cheddar: Challis, 1987), also J Portergill, 'RB – a Tribute', *C&CH* vol 2 (1963), 61.

1.13: Lamprey & Son, seedsmen

Benjamin Lamprey was one of the early clock-makers in this country. His life spanned parts of the 17th and 18th centuries during which time he is best known for a lantern clock. Married three times, Benjamin and his wives looked after 13 children. The name Lamprey, however, is better known for a major corn merchanting business. A significant date is 1834 which is when John Barrett Lamprey acquired the business of Edmunds and Son. The shop catered for the feedstock and horticultural needs of the farming community as well as the townsfolk.

It was housed within a property which was to become a landmark building on the fringe of both the 12th century Market Place and the Cow Fair with its regular livestock movements and sales. John lived over the shop and was joined by his son William Linnell Lamprey. Between them they launched the company into an expansionist era by exploring new channels of trade. One of these was the evolution of a brick, tile and pottery works near to Duke Street in Grimsbury. This side of the business attracted the attention of the *Gentleman's Journal*. In their edition of June 27 1908, much is made of Lamprey's ability to exploit a huge outcrop of Oxford Blue Clay. … What is certain is that in the years following the early 20th century closure of Lamprey's works, local children, especially from Merton Street and the Causeway, were deriving endless amusement from the abandoned site. It was fun to shoot down the sides of a large pit on a sheet of corrugated iron and when your journey ended beside a deep pool where there were newts to be found.

The building once occupied by Lamprey & Son at No 34 Bridge Street.

Another big element of the Lamprey business related to their Wharf Mill on Lower Cherwell Street and Bridge Wharf where there were huge lime kilns using materials worked at Shipton-on-Cherwell and brought to Banbury by way of the Oxford Canal.

In 1901, a new name became associated with Lampreys. This was Bradshaw. William Lamprey married Mary June Bradshaw. Her father was miller and baker at Wykham Mill, half way between Banbury and Bloxham. This was a water mill fed by a watercourse derived from the Sor Brook. Between 1919 and 1939 the key figure within the company was Nelson Bradshaw. He steered the business through the depression years of the 1920s but inevitably had to close a wharf and mill in Banbury in order to ensure Wykham's viability. Nelson was not merely wedded to his business activities – many a tennis player found him a very competitive opponent and his love of the game extended to being a founder member of the West End Lawn Tennis Club. With the drive to get the most from the land during the Second World War came the opportunity to diversify into chemical sprays. The 1950s and 1960s saw Wykham Mill business grow and the company took over the Cherwell-side mill of Edmunds and Kench. These were the decades of Roger Bradshaw's influence. By 1980 computerisation has taken Lampreys into a new world remote from 17th century clocks.

Banbury Guardian 11 March 1999.

1.14: Hoods, the Banbury ironmongers

This year is exactly 80 years on from when Stephen Hood and Edward Henry Hood – ironmongers and co-partners – entered into an agreement with William Stephens Orchard and Ernest Walter Orchard. The outcome was that the two Orchards secured the business and the goods which went with it. In effect this means 35 and 36 Bridge Street – of which the latter was occupied by Walter Richard Sansbury. Their deposit was £200 and the rest of the money was due to be made in instalments by July 1, 1920.

Banbury people have not only cause to celebrate an anniversary but every reason to treasure a unique part of the town's trading fabric. Few customers can ever have emerged from Hoods empty-handed even if what they carried away was but a single nail. In some delightful jottings about the shop, an unnamed employee has recorded memories of the old Hoods, a place of numerous rooms of varying sizes split up by passageways that turned shop heating into a nightmare occupation.

The Banburyshire that this business was structured to serve was largely rural lacking in many amenities we now take for granted and lived in by a dwindling number of blacksmiths, wheelwrights and saddlers. There was paraffin in abundance and no shortage of Duplex lamps with spares. Grates and ranges catered for the numerous coal fires while tin kettles for repair nearly equalled tin kettles for sale. Shoeing iron went to blacksmiths over an area that ranged from Ettington to Waddesdon. Little did it matter that the wheelwrights were left only with repair work by the 1940s – Hoods held the materials for the job.

A trade display by S & E H Hood, probably at a local agricultural show.

Staff at S & E H Hood, ranged around the firm's lorry, probably decorated for participation in a hospital carnival.

A significant part of the Hoods reputation tag has been attributable to the long service combined with civility. Someone who typified this was Percy Miller who gave over 50 years and saw the workings of most aspects of the firm's activities. Like several other members of the shop and office staff down the years, Percy entered fully into the wider life of the town. He kept goal for Stones and played in the Black Diamond Dance Band that gave pleasure to many in the 20s and 30s. Length of association was also true of the management level. A good example was the Stanleys, Fred and his sister. When the *Banbury Guardian* photographer caught them lifting glasses charged with something good, they were able to lay claim to 108 years between them – 1953 was his 60th year in the shop. Much later, in 1993, the paper recorded the passing of Cyril John Baylis. Full- and part-time Cyril gave 60 years to the Hoods brand of ironmongery and this included a spell as manager. He finally departed the shop aged 80. So great had been his involvement that the shop closed on the day of his funeral.

Richard Edmunds's [ironmongery business] in Bridge Street was acquired by S and E H Hood in 1872. Sixty-five years later an advertisement appeared in a 1937 Coronation supplement that included the proud statement, 'Through 5 Reigns we have served the Public well'. This claim is no less true today than it was when George VI came to the throne. … In an early 1930s directory … the firm emphasised that its stock could not be 'excelled anywhere in the district' nor could service be anything less than 'second to none'. The advertising style of the time permitted them to add 'our prices, too, give us a right to solicit your orders'. An impressive list of potential customers showed that they confidently expected to hear from country houses, estates, farmers, motorists, builders, wheelwrights, plumbers, painters, engineers and shopkeepers. They were even visited by Banbury Fair showmen.

Since 1948 the business has come under the able direction of the Jakemans, first Kenneth and now Stephen. Remarkably both had the same background of education and work experience in metallurgy before turning to the retail trade. Stephen first became involved in 1972 ... Hoods then became even more a family business when Stephen's wife Clare joined him in the running of the firm and later their daughter Elizabeth helped out in her school and university holidays. During the Jakeman era several members of their staff have continued the good old tradition of long service. With closure looming many people are reflecting on the old shop. In this context some notes written by former manager Cyril Baylis make fascinating reading. He stressed the large number of rooms of varying sizes with nearby passages

William Orchard who purchased the Hoods business in 1917.

and the need to moisten wooden floors before dust could be removed. A wander through this emporium would reveal the paraffin lamps associated with country establishments, grates and ranges, horseshoes for blacksmiths, spokes for wheelwrights, as well as cast-iron pumps. His recollections covered the now famous drawers for the likes of nails and screws and confirmed that whether you wanted fork handles or four candles you always got them on a shopping trip to Hoods.

In 1983 a new version of Hoods rose from the ashes of the old store. A change of style and presentation with the coming of the Castle Centre made this necessary. Fortunately many of the old trading practices remained. Stock size and variety were undiminished. There was still a willingness to sell items in small quantities, and on hand was the ever present Jimmy to cut keys and repair locks, even though from the late 1980s his workshop had moved upstairs.

The closing of Hoods, as many letters to the *Banbury Guardian* have revealed, is the end of an era. Certain items will be more difficult to acquire and there is the inevitable concern that the disappearance of this fine old family business is one more step along the road to town centre cloning. Over many years the confident title 'Hoods the Banbury Ironmongers' generated a sense of place, purpose and pride. In a recent Operatic Society programme for *Oklahoma*, Hoods' advertisement included the shrewd observation that this shop is 'where every visit is filled with a sense of discovery'. You can't get nearer the truth than that....

The recent closure of Hoods the ironmongers on March 10 [2007] has been an occasion for sharing nostalgic memories of this wonderful old family business. Among those people with a tale to tell is Brian Hilton of Banbury. He first worked for Hoods at the outset of the 1950s when he was still at school. Two hours in the evening combined with being a Saturday boy earned him 25/- (£1.25) a week. This early experience probably explains why Brian opted to work for the Bridge Street ironmongers when his school days were over. Hoods needed an errand boy and Brian soon became familiar figure on his trade bicycle. ...In 1952 Brian was upgraded to the trade department of Hoods, a move that was worth a mere 5/- (25p) a week extra, but did make him more aware of who was who at Hoods. In particular he made the acquaintance of the firm's commercial traveller, a Mr Gill, who travelled everywhere in his familiar Morris Minor.

During four years spent on Hoods's pay roll Brian got to know the regular customers, many of whom were famers and plumbers. Much requested items included rolls of netting that were stored in a warehouse in Factory Street. One hundred yards of wire mesh could be rolled out along the roadway and a mark on the wall of a building ensured that this measure was accurate. Factory Street and the way it was orientated in relation to the shop meant that the canal was but a short distance away. Here, Tooleys at their boatyard sharpened tools and overhauled lawnmowers. Mr Plester, the associated blacksmith at the boatyard, burnt out handles of forks and replaced them. When wheelwright customers arrived on Hoods doorstep this same combination of forge and yard provided the expertise for coping with spokes and rims.

A feature of Hoods day-to-day trade in the 1950s that has remained long in the collective memory was the incessant queues despite the availability of up to four or five shop assistants. Maybe the fact that all the money had to go through one till was responsible for this.

Banbury Guardian 2 July 1998; 8 March 2007; 12 April 2007.

- On 6 February 2014 Brian Little devoted a whole article to 'The life of Percy Miller', principally to his sporting achievements.

1.15: Bernard Smith, draper

In December 1988, Arthur W Jones of East Close in Grimsbury, who was a regular contributor to the *Banbury Guardian* letters page, wrote about his memories of Parsons Street. He recalled that this part of the town was 'interesting and varied with owners living above their premises'. In his estimation they were 'good tradespeople who knew what they were selling'. High on a well-remembered list of early businesses was the drapery of Mark Bernard Smith.

At the time of the census of 1901 Mark and his brother John were living in Crouch Street. Both were born at Weedon in Northamptonshire and had the same trade description, that of general draper. They were members of a family of nine born to Mary Smith and at least three of her sons achieved business success. Mark traded as Bernard Smith and opened a shop at 4 Parsons Street in 1902. Nearby were rivals Harlocks who had two premises selling drapery and household goods. Not to be outdone Mark acquired 59 Parsons Street in 1911 (today this is Barnado's Charity Shop) and subsequently made the necessary alterations.

Throughout his working life Mark demonstrated a commitment to serving people. This was reflected in the way No 4 Parsons Street was organised. Outwardly it had two display windows. Once inside customers would first have been aware of an old stove that on cold winter days emitted a certain warmth. Shoppers were then faced with a wide counter designed to display a range of materials, everything from tweeds to muslin. Lengths required were determined by using a metal tape measure. Further into the ground floor of the shop was a haberdashery area while at the bottom of a flight of stairs there was space for linens. Those who explored further discovered a range of coats, dresses and hats on the first floor. Here it was possible to try on clothes before buying and there was also that usual addition of a button machine. As with most town businesses, Christmas was a time for seasonal adjustments, in particular the locating of a large table for display of goods likely to attract customers hunting for presents or the means of making them. By contrast, No 59 only had a ground floor where the emphasis was on lingerie, corsets and baby clothes. Arthur Jones notes that near neighbours to these premises were Brummitt's toyshop, Baker's store for menswear, Chard tobacco dealer and Dunn's shoe business.

Among those who worked in the original shop was Irene Amos. Her memories take us back to the 1930s when she was first apprenticed to Bernard Smith and employed as an assistant. Early experiences embraced such activities as cleaning the premises and putting buttons on to inspection cards. These were forerunners to a more responsible sales position in the likes of haberdashery, hosiery and dress materials. Once a year in the spring there was a clearance sale, which attracted bargain hunters if not the long queues that were a feature of McIlroy sales in the late 1940s.

The working day at Bernard Smith's lasted until 6pm Monday to Friday with an extension to 8pm on Saturday. Irene was near enough to her home to get a midday break for lunch. As for holidays she was given 14 days in addition to the bonus of Tuesday afternoons, the early closing day. One of her most vivid memories is the way in which her boss greeted customers. They would have been impressed by his height but also by the way he came across as a true gentleman.

However, unlike many of his business contemporaries, outside of business hours he did not seek political office or move within time honoured social organisations such as Rotary or the Masons. As a result he got very little newspaper coverage. Despite this, no-one locally could have doubted the sincerity of the firm's claim to offer 'dependable quality at a reasonable price'.

Banbury Guardian 3 June 2010.

1.16: W Ekins, outfitters

Traditionally Banbury's importance as a place of retail activity has revolved around a miscellany of family-run businesses. However, in recent years most shopping streets have altered in character as one by one the familiar names have disappeared. On Wednesday, December 31 2003, Ekins of Church Lane closed and another chapter in the story of our market town was brought to a conclusion.

In origin the Ekins family were bespoke shoemakers in Northampton. From their shop in Bridge Street, Northampton, Harry Ekins used to ride out to village customers on his motor cycle and side car. The appearance of an Ekins in Banbury in 1938 can be traced to Harry's brother Bill who rented No 13 Church Lane from Messrs Humphris for the sum of £52 per year. With the bespoke shoemaking no longer viable the new focus became footwear repair work. In the early 1950s came the move to No 11 where a shop for the sale of shoes was established. This marked the start of successive expansions that diversified sales into clothing, fabrics, household linens and knitting wools.

David Hitchcox, whose retirement has been the reason for the recent closure of Ekins, joined the business in the mid-1950s. He started as an assistant and was expected to do all the odd jobs; these included tea making. The liquid refreshment had to be brought down two flights of stairs, an activity that often inspired ribald comments from the boss. The shop's stock at that time was very much dominated by the needs of the working man. Farmers were especially important customers and often departed clutching their Derby tweeds or Bedford cords. One person in particular left an indelible impression on David's memory. He was a well-known farmer from the Wigginton area for whom a typical day started at Midland Marts cattle market. Business there was followed by attention to the inner man at the *Catherine Wheel* pub in Bridge Street. Suitably oiled, and enlivened by a spell of gambling, he would set out for Ekins shop where he tried to persuade the manager to accept a double or quits solution to transactions. This was agreed upon on one occasion only. However his gambler's luck deserted him and cash payment became the only option.

By the late 1950s workwear fashion influences had become significant. The jeans era had arrived and so too had trendy items such as skiffle ties, Davy Crockett hats and Beatles boots. This was also a time when many people were keen on camping. Ownership of tents became popular and Ekins wanted to be part of this. The business regularly participated in displays of camping equipment in the town hall. Another aspect of the great outdoors was the boom in scouting. Ekins became official stockists for related clothing which came from Scout headquarters in London. A similar area of demand was school uniforms and sportswear.

Apart from individual customers, lucrative contracts with large companies and organisations were established. Ekins supplied workwear to the employees of R O White, structural engineers, the Northern Aluminium Company and Export Packing. The Horton Hospital had an agreement and so did Upton House and the farming Jacks of Swalcliffe. An especially interesting contract was negotiated by Ekins during the early sixties construction of Alfred Bird's factory. Matthew Hall was working on

An Ekins advertisement of 1958 offering a remarkable range of clothing as well as uniforms and camping equipment for the Scout movement.

the site and had 'an insatiable hunger for wellies'. Because boots had to be worn only by the person to whom they were issued, David Hitchcox soon discovered that his arrival at the works in Ruscote coincided with the incineration of discarded rubber. Halls employed a sizeable itinerant labour force, so the wellie wastage factor was firmly embedded in their health and safety practices.

When, in 1979, the *Banbury Guardian* devoted an advertising feature to the Church Lane firm they were able to headline the accompanying article 'Expanding Ekins are now operating on four fronts'. Bulk purchasing for the Brackley and Northampton shops as well as Banbury meant competitive prices and a wide range of men's clothing, curtain fabrics and household linens. This commercial buying may well have been the key factor in David Hitchcox's decision in 1988 to buy the lease of the Banbury shop from Geoff Ekins, son of Harry.

With the advent of Castle Quay Shopping Centre, the footfall factor in Church Lane became less potent. The shoe shop had already closed in 1987. There were still regular customers for wools and fabrics but farmers' heavy macs and Dr Martens boots belonged to the past. Down the years many of those who have kept faith with Ekins have turned into friends of David and Ann Hitchcox, a relationship they will miss greatly. In its heyday the business was synonymous with the market town culture. An extremely loyal support staff ensured that this happened. Its closure in 2003 is part of a relentless trend towards the probable extinction of the family firm from the central part of the town. Something of the town's Banburyness is slipping away.

Banbury Guardian 15 January 2004.

1.17: Farewell to an old friend: Whitchers's

Somehow Parsons Street will not be quite the same without the name of Arthur Whitcher on the shop front. Trading finished at closing time on Saturday, June 13 [2015], when those immortal words 'are you being served?' were heard for the last time. This left the business card of shop manager Peter Buggins as but a memory of a ready-made clothes world that was a vital part of Banbury's market town image. It promised quality menswear which was not merely stocked but also presented.

The earliest home of Whitcher stores was the Isle of Wight. Newport and Ryde were favoured locations which were established around the turn of the 19th/20th century. The former had the merit of being the Island's capital and the latter was where most visitors from the mainland arrived by steamer. Ambition for growth favoured market towns: Stroud in Gloucestershire, Hinckley in Leicestershire and Chesterfield in Derbyshire were typical choices. Wednesbury, a Black Country hub, opened in 1927, whereas Coventry and Banbury had to wait until 1954.

Kelly's Directory for 1950 reveals an earlier business with an emphasis on menswear at the same address which went under the unusual name of Wildgoose. It occupied only half the site acquired by Arthur Whitcher. Through chance rather than planning the property 61 Parsons Street was at the Market Place end. A onetime circulation manager of the *Banbury Guardian*, which itself was for many years only a few doors distant, always maintained that it made economic sense to be nearer the produce market than North Bar.

The Banbury of 1954 had about 19,000 people but the shopping catchment was greatly influenced by a long-standing tradition of the town acting as focal point within its area. A thriving livestock market ensured that farming families were prominent amongst those people who made the Thursday pilgrimage and enjoyed market ordinary lunches in the leading pubs and hotels. A 1950s guide book confirms this by means of a photograph of the whole Market Place ocean of stalls and the convergence of roads and railways from all directions. Farmers and their friends played an important part in the pattern of sales, which were dominated by suits and jackets as well as a volume business in shirts, especially those with the extra collar. The average buyer was around 40 years old. However a surprising infusion of younger shoppers were looking for the ever-popular tweed jackets.

If there were decades when it could be argued that the good times were rolling these were the 1970s and 1980s. From time to time there were so many customers you could not get into the shop. In spite of this popularity it is interesting to record that Whitchers joined the ranks of the early closers on a Tuesday.

During my second meeting with Arthur Whitcher he was in a reflective mood about changes in the sourcing of clothing items. He clearly recalled the days dominated by the 'Made in Britain' label. His run-in to retirement had largely seen this replaced by the likes of 'Made in China'. Interestingly since knitwear has increasingly been composed of synthetic fibres the local element at Leicester is beginning to take over. In his time as an owner of several branches he had seen a few instances of changes of practice. The firm was one of the first to put clothes on hangers and company shops were serviced by a Bedford van that toured the various locations.

The Banbury shop never succumbed to the age of the till receipt. Each item sold was accompanied by a traditional invoice finished off with a polite 'Thank You'. Ultimate closure was a matter of progression of years. The Wednesbury branch is the last survivor of a proud empire.

Menswear at Banbury as exemplified by independent family shops is fast vanishing. Henrys in the High Street is the sole survivor. Moss Bros and Burtons have been other losses to this kind of business. Banbury's old town will be the poorer for the loss of the Whitcher name and personal service approach.

Banbury Guardian 2 July 2016.

- An advertisement printed with this article shows that the Whitcher company was established in 1901.

1.18: Mansfields: sellers of leather goods

Frederick Roland Mansfield was born at Long Itchington, Warwickshire on December 22, 1916. In reflecting on his career it is possible to detect the strong family influences associated with parents who believed in the merits of work hard, play hard culture. Frederick's father Harry was a successful businessman and more particularly a talented saddler who ran leather factories and shops. Ultimately he hoped that Frederick would enter the same world. Before that stage was reached the right education was paramount. Leamington College provided an appropriate learning environment and Frederick took full advantage both academically and on the playing field. Arithmetic was a strong subject but he also excelled at sports. The latter included a place in a Rugby XV as well as an ability to swim part of the Avon. In a more carefree moment it was he who put a football through the headmaster's window while enjoying a lunchtime kick about. His sense of humour extended to drawing on the pristine white collar of a contemporary lad in his class.

Whereas Harry was the brains behind a high quality High Street leather and glassware business which started in 1952 where Malcolm Douglas of Henry's menswear trades today, Frederick will always be remembered for the way Mansfields became a cherished source of gifts and how he got into the sportswear business by supplying members of the armed services based both in Germany and the United Kingdom. He believed in the personal touch and would spend several days visiting bases beyond the Rhine. It helped that Frederick was naturally a charismatic person but at the same time had recognised the importance of a strong work ethic, determination and confidence, self-discipline and self-respect. No wonder the goods he sold had to be of the highest quality.

Not content with the retail shops selling such diverse items as prams, sports trips and tops (remember the Toy Fair in the Market Place), Frederick also had factories located in Britannia Road, Banbury, and in Charlbury. At the height of his activity there were six shops including a pram shop with sports goods upstairs in Parsons Street. It was at the Toy Fair that he experimented with special promotions such as inviting children of service families and ensuring that their visit concluded with a presentation of labelled packs. This side of his business was in marked contrast to his own childhood with very few toys. On the sportswear side his greatest moment came when he kitted out FA Cup Final officials, especially referees. Whenever he sold sports kit it helped that he was 'one of the lads'.

Outside of working hours Frederick was something of a socialite and as with the goods he sold quality mattered. Roses for his wife were always carefully chosen. As for his sons, motoring had to be in the best cars and horses from top stock. He himself was very much a racing man. Sunday mornings were for riding but he also hunted with the Warwickshire pack. On the race course he had a National Hunt permit to train horses. Personal experience enabled him to recognise quality runners of the likes of 'Have a Care' and 'No Trouble'. If racing left him with spare leisure time it was often spent shooting pheasants at Gaydon. After such enjoyable pursuits the logical locations were typically the *Whately* in Banbury and the *Wykham Arms* at Sibford

Gower. Frederick's death not only occasioned great sadness locally but also revived many happy memories of the businesses he built up. Mansfields will always remain a retail gem in Banburyshire's commercial history.

Banbury Guardian 4 July 2013.

1.19: S H Jones, wine merchants

Memorabilia come in all shapes and sizes but few more curious and fascinating than a sequence of early tally marks on a ceiling beam of those purveyors of fine wines in Banbury, S H Jones. Today, these marks have been varnished to record them for posterity. At the time they had a material significance, each tally equalled a gallon of whisky drawn off at some time during the years before the Second World War. Elsewhere inside No 27 High Street there is a massive chimney breast, sole reminder of the day when the building was a bakery. Between this function and the arrival of the wine business, the property had the evocative title borrowed from the world of antiques – Ye Odds and Ends.

The parent company of today's wine merchant was set up in 1848 but the earliest Banbury presence was in 1886 when a building was purchased on the site of what in 1996 is the forlorn hulk of Church House. Fifteen years later came the move to 62 High Street. The present property was secured in 1913.

A letter to a customer and date-stamped Banbury 6.15, of April 20th 1897, tells us a lot about the company and its approach to business. The full title was S H Jones and Co: wine, spirit, hop and cigar merchants and it was not at all unusual for a visit to be made to customers based away from Banbury. This particular piece of correspondence was sent to Miss A Baker of the *Old Stag's Head* at Wellesbourne. It reads:-

Dear Madam

Our Mr S H Jones hopes to have the pleasure of waiting upon you on or about Friday 23rd instant when the favour of your commands will be esteemed.

We are,

Yours faithfully,

S H Jones & Co.

On the reverse side of the letter there is a note about the hiring of plates, dishes, glasses and cruets and a hint that these might be for the occasion of a harvest home. …

Among the company treasures are two little booklets with price lists. The earlier one dates to shortly after the turn of the century and informs us about the prices of the day. Sherries ranged from 18/- to 50/- per dozen bottles while 51/- would secure 12 bottles of an excellent champagne. Old Tom gin could be had for 2/- a bottle. An equivalent list of the early 1930s reflects an increase in prices but with a fascinating tailpiece on wine management and some useful recipes. Who could resist Manhattan Cocktail, Barney Barnato cocktail or indeed Spion Kop cocktail….

… By the time this article appears [25 June 1998] the directors of S H Jones and Company will have held their 150th anniversary tasting at Heythrop Park. I wonder how many people who sipped their tipples spared a thought for Sidney Herbert Jones. It has been my opportunity and privilege to examine a very fine ledger containing copies of his letters written between 1909 and 1919. Most are to do with Sidney's huge concern about an anticipated increase in the duty on wines and spirits.

No 27 High Street when it was still occupied by S H Jones & Co, wine merchants.

He wrote about what he perceived as an iniquitous tax to members of Parliament, Government Ministers and the Wines and Spirits Association – in fact anyone able to take up the cause. For his own part S H felt there was every prospect that his business, so painstakingly put together, would be eliminated. Personal endeavour and integrity in the trade were linked by him to long hours of work. On another and slightly more amusing front he referred to health implications for those people forced by price increases to resort to lower grade spirits.

The grandfather of the present Michael Jones who brought his business acumen from Bristol started in Horse Fair, Banbury in 1886. Sidney Herbert became tenant of a property which was on the same site as the later Church House (consecrated 1905). His shop front faced St Mary's Church but custom of the day demanded that he was seen to operate from an office. Most of his business was associated with publicans tied to breweries such as Bass, Flowers (Stratford) and Morrells (Oxford). Goods were conveyed to carriers' carts or through the services provided by the Great Western Railway. Sidney Herbert used a pony and trap. By contrast and in the early 1920s Harold Henry Jones (Michael's father) made use of a motorbike and sidecar. Ten years later the market for wines and spirits was diversifying into the working men's clubs and miners' welfares.

However it is time to return to Sidney Herbert and another side to his letter writing. There is a series penned from 62 High Street about SH's desire to rent the premises on the corner of Marlborough Road. He was against outright purchase and bargained quite considerably on the rent level as well as the length of the lease period, preferring seven or 14 years but settling reluctantly for three or five as well as other options. With no cellars, Sidney wanted to adapt the building to allow wines to be stored at controlled temperatures. The need for modification was partly related to the building's previous use – it was Miss Halliday's antiques business called Odds and Ends. Jones the wine came to this building in 1912. Ceramic jars, bottles of sherry, pipes of port and hogsheads of wine have all come and gone but not so the tradition for loyalty and long service. Michael Jones tells me that ten people can account for over 200 years. Celebrations of such a notable anniversary have extended beyond tasting fine wine out of Riedel Glass. Members of staff and some customers have been to the champagne region of France where two days of visits to companies have provided insights into the special characteristics of the chalk region.

Banbury Guardian 5 September 1996/25 June 1998.

- Riedel. One of Europe's most celebrated glass manufacturers, founded in Bohemia in 1756 and now based at Kufstein, Austria.

1.20: Mark B Plumb, rope and canvas merchant

In 1932, Mark Bunting Plumb took over the business of G Eaves and Son. Established back in 1810, Eaves had a shop at 10 Butchers Row but also a works in the hamlet of Williamscot. An extant wholesale price list reveals an astonishing range of items including plough reins, grocers' tea twines, nose bags, tennis and cricket nets, billiard pockets and hammocks. Plumb established his business at 6 Market Place. He did so by entering into a lease agreement with Matthew Balfour who was a draper. The lease was for seven years and involved annual rents starting at £52 but rising to £55. Unlike many retailers of the time, Mark did not live above his shop but at 3 Alma Terrace in Grimsbury where his wife adapted a front room so that she could serve teas to farmers attending the livestock market.

Here he and his wife were not affected by a variety of clauses which had been inserted into the document concerning 6 Market Place. These clauses reveal several interesting points about the property. Internal timber work had to be treated carefully and not cut in any way. Certain uses of the premises were distinctly frowned upon, included in these was 'the trade or business of an innkeeper or retailer of wines, spirits or beer'. Equally unwelcome was the sale and repair of cycles, motor cycles and motor appliances or accessories. Drapers and furniture dealers were also not favoured within the terms of the lease. Renewal of Plumb's agreement made in June of 1939 was an opportunity for the landlord, still Matthew Balfour, to increase the rent. By 1946 and the end of the war, Plumb was expected to find £65 – ten pounds more than in 1939.

A lease of 1967 reveals that both landlord and tenant have changed. The former is Douglas Stewart of College Farm at Aston Clinton in Buckinghamshire. Joan Mary

Telephone : Banbury 2031

MARK B. PLUMB
(M. E. PLUMB)

6, MARKET PLACE, BANBURY

MARQUEES and TENTS for HIRE

Camp Equipment, Canvas Goods, Rick Sheets, Lorry Covers

MATS and MATTING MADE UP TO CUSTOMER'S SIZES, DURSLEY REVERSIBLE RUGS, STAIRCARPET, ROPES and TWINES, SCAFFOLD CORDS, COAL BAGS, PLOUGH REINS, HALTERS, HAYNETS, BROOMS and BRUSHES, WRAPPING PAPER, PAPER BAGS, INSIDE and OUTSIDE BLINDS.

Repairs and Renovations Promptly Attended to.

Mark Plumb's advertisement from the catalogue for the
Banbury & District Industrial Exhibition, 1951.

Tom Parkin and Bill Wyatt at Plumb's on its final day of trading.

Parkin is the new tenant. She is described as a married lady, living at Barton House in Alma Terrace. Both had changed their addresses by the time of the lease of 1972. Balfour had moved to Somerset while Joan was said to be resident at Satch'll Edge in Shotteswell. Interestingly the late 1960s to early 1970s leases omit the reference to restricted uses.

Marquees and tents could be bought and hired. Many a marquee was made by Bill Wyatt who also worked for Joan Parkin. In an age when a walk along any of the main streets was a stroll past a succession of awning-shaded windows, there was space for sun blinds. With Banbury as the centre of an agricultural district, it is not surprising to learn that stock extended to rick sheets, corn sacks, plough reins, halters, nose bags and wagon covers. Several types of bag could be found by the discerning customer but most notably containers for coal and paper bags. Mats and matting, wool rugs, brooms and brushes completed the picture of an emporium enterprise. Their storage in the basement of the shop demanded a position above the level to which this space occasionally flooded.

Mark Plumb had been apprenticed to Eaves and, living as he did at Cropredy, he may well have been aware of the Williamscot works. His involvement within and knowledge of the Banbury area was very much influenced by Mary Eliza Thornton, whom he courted and later married. Her time as a commercial traveller for Brummitts, the Parsons Street toys and fancy goods store, enabled her to develop an eye for business. Mark soon appreciated that location matters. Nearby Hoods and Broughton & Wilks could well have been seen purely as rivals. Instead Plumb came to view then in a complementary relationship, willing to help out with the supply of items demanded but not always in stock. ..

Many of Plumb's contemporaries as shop owners rooted themselves in the administration of Banbury's affairs, by becoming town councillors, but Mark Plumb was distinctly different. Although his wife was active within the Chamber of Trade, he devoted his efforts and money to the cause of Methodism. This may explain why he and Mary moved from a house in Grimsbury's West Street to 3 Alma Terrace, which had been in the ownership of a leading Methodist solicitor, William Smith. Otherwise known as Barton House, this property developed into a kind of outpost for Plumbs. The explanation has to be sought in the location near the Midland Marts Livestock Market, which is where Mary set up a wooden hut for the sale of brushes, brooms, halters and marking sticks....

This house became a farmers' haunt on business days. They went there to enjoy cooked meals and talk about their buying and selling while enjoying a plate of something hot and filling. The doorstep availability of a Market Ordinary (farmers' lunch) may well have strengthened the belief of town centre traders that relocation to Grimsbury of livestock marketing was going to lose them the knock-on benefit of farmers' spending power. Provision of meals was quite an enterprise. It involved several ladies in tasks such as rolling up carpets and relocating chairs to a greenhouse. Steak and kidney puddings (a popular meal) were cooked in a huge copper that had to be checked for the presence of a family of mice amongst the kindling located beneath the copper. It was always the task of a Mrs Whitlock to poke these with a stick while uttering her favourite expression: 'I will see if them mice is there, my duck'.

Catering courtesy of the Plumbs and their helpers was not the only enterprise of this kind. Next door was the Talbot café run by a Mrs Kerridge who focussed here attention on the likes of drovers and lorry drivers, where it was exclusively farmers who dined at Barton House. Cooking on such a scale inevitably resulted in a mass of dripping which was subsequently wrapped in pieces of greaseproof paper and taken to the poor of Grimsbury. Clearly the Plumbs had a social conscience as well as a spirit of commercial enterprise.

Banbury Guardian 3 August 2000, 27 September 2007.

- Joan Parkin was M B Plumb's daughter.

1.21: Bringing fish and chips to town

The history of fish and chip businesses supports the widely held belief that it appeals to working class appetites and is an essential feature of seaside resorts, especially close to promenades and piers.

In the case of Banbury, however, a heart of the town location near the town market place and a past predominance of street trading have encouraged a different tradition best recalled in the name of Needles and Truss.

Forty years ago Jim and Mary Christoforou completed a move from Coventry to Banbury and established what he termed a fish saloon with a parade of shops on the new Park Farm estate just off the Queensway/Mewburn Road junction. Location was the key to both the timing and perceived ability to apply Tile Hill experience to Banbury. By the year 1978 Jim had learnt the trade in Coventry courtesy of his uncle where business had been brisk in a working class district and readied him for the move.

As much as anything the Banbury enterprise was about taking advantage of the increasing significance of the suburbanisation of certain forms of retailing. The context was the Park Farm estate, which came to extend from Beargarden Road across the ridge and valley terrain to the outer fringes of Crouch Hill. As with the later Cherwell Heights estate there was a well-defined need for a parade of shops. That this was set up close to Queensway, destined at the time to become an inner relief route, was a real bonus as was the continuation beyond this boundary. A good flow of custom to the other shops which included a Lo Cost discount grocery store, a newspaper business, motoring accessories and tool hire also helped.

Not everyone in the local area was enthusiastic about the site of the shops and in particular there were concerns about the inclusion of a fish saloon due to worries about potential pollution, smells and litter. Fortunately over time many more people have treated the white plumes as evidence that the shop is open and the smells generated by the Preston & Thomas frying unit only serves to hasten footsteps of customers including whole families both local and from further afield, off-duty paramedics, dustmen and tradesmen working locally. The Queensway Fish Saloon is the first place where you catch up on local news while waiting for your fish to come out or for the next batch of chips to emerge all hot and glowing.

With the continuing problems of parking and accessing town centre outlets, locations such as Queensway with adjacent parking and easy access will reflect the growing trend towards the suburbanisation of shop businesses. Offshoots of the fish saloon may well appear on the larger new developments.

The week commencing Monday, April 23 will mark the start of trading 40 years ago when Jim and Mary welcomed their first customers. From the beginning although cod and haddock were popular choices diversity opened up a range of opportunities. 'Two chicken wings please Jim' was a frequent call from the back of the queue. Chicken nuggets and fillets are now popular choices. Another change is fish coming in a recyclable box which preserves its shape rather than out of paper.

The inspiration and experience that Jim and Mary brought to the trade in the 1970s is still evident today. Occasionally Jim's' white-coated presence is a welcome sight

Staff at the Cherwell Heights fish and chip shop owned by Jim and Mary Christoforou.

behind the counter. With a second shop in the Cherwell Heights district, Queensway has become the hub of a larger enterprise. Jim's sons, Andrew and Peter, have shouldered more and more of the workload and continue to feed in new ideas, some of which originate in Cyprus and are popular there. Walk into the shop today and you can't miss the invitation to try squid and chips. A visit to the shop during the week April 23 to 28 to join in the 40th anniversary celebrations should be an occasion to remember.

Banbury Guardian 19 April 2018.

- In an article *Beloved British institution of fish and chips is in safe hands in Banbury*, published on 6 January 2011, Brian Little discusses customers at the Queensway Fish saloon, including college students, farmers returning home from the market, Tony Baldry MP, Terry Biddlecombe the jockey, and 92-year-old Ted Roberts, a native of the Forest of Dean, who preferred traditional haddock to ling or red snapper.

1.22: Coal in the blood: the Higham dynasty:

Today is a red letter day for a lady who was once described as 'Banbury blonde with coal in her blood'. By the time most of my readers discover the subject of today's column, Rosemary Higham will have donned the robes of town mayor. Although her great-grandfather was a coal merchant in Northamptonshire, the story really begins in 1899 when her grandfather Robert Kitely Higham found his way to Banbury with just a fiver and possession of a horse and cart. He came in from Chipping Warden encouraged by the vision of making his fortune. Robert's first action was to rent a house in Calthorpe Street. This provided him with a base from which he sold and carted sand, bricks, cement, and, of course, coal.

When Robert married Ellen Goode of North Newington, little did he know the extent to which she would get involved in the business. The 1920 purchase of 15 as well as 14 Calthorpe Gardens for the sum of £364 became possible because she had money from savings. Then there were the occasions when their horse could not negotiate some steep hills and Ellen carried as much as 10 cwt of coal so as not to disappoint customers. It was very much within the same spirit that Rosemarie helped to fill sacks and weigh coal at the tender age of seven.

Robert Higham led a full and active life. Apart from the coal business, he found time to help ring the bells of St Mary's Church and his name is recorded in the belfry. When he died in 1936 at the relatively early age of 62, responsibility for the firm passed to Ellen who persuaded her son Harold to help her run the business. Harold, who had married Mary Humphris of Aynho in 1936, took sole charge on her death in 1952. Harold and Mary had four children, the second of whom was Rosemarie.

Harold's background had been entirely different from that of his father. Educated at Dashwood Road School, he left school at the age of 14 to become an apprentice mechanic at the County Garages which was located at the corner of Horse Fair and West Bar. The work there was made more interesting by the fact that he taught people to drive. One of his pupils was Mrs Needle, best known in Banbury for her fish and chip shop in Mill Lane. It was there that Harold met his future wife Mary because she was housekeeper to Mrs Needle. Once married the couple made their home at 16 Manor Road in Grimsbury, a house that cost them £380. Later they moved to Old Grimsbury Road to a superb property with a large garden and garages backing on to Gibbs Road.

These garages provided spaces for the repair of company lorries once the switch from horses had been made in the teeth of strong resistance from Robert. Harold kept the coal business going throughout the war years when he was exempt from military service because of his occupation, working long hours. However he did get involved in civil defence activities in the evening.

Old Grimsbury Road meant to Harold what the Calthorpe Street area had been to Robert and Ellen. Rosemarie was brought up in the former but loved her childhood visits to the latter. The coal business was a booming one and it continued to expand despite Ellen's death. By then the Highams had some big customers in town. One was Hunt Edmunds, the brewery firm. Coal had to be delivered there on most days. Apart from the early experiences with shovelling and bagging coal, Rosemarie

A horse-drawn vehicle, advertising solid fuels and conveying Santa Claus with presents for patients in the children's ward at the Horton Hospital, pauses by Rosemarie Higham's 'By the Fire' shop.

became seriously involved in the business when she went to work in her father's office. At the age of 26 she was made a partner and subsequently took the Coal Board Diploma. Notably she was the first woman to achieve this distinction. Rosemarie was now knowledgeable in all aspects of the trade. Sadly arthritis put a bar on her father's mobility and increasingly she was running the business but with the same sense of customer loyalty as had been true of her parents and grandparents.

This was demonstrated in the miners' strike of 1984-85 when the BBC Panorama programme got wind of this determination to ensure that the public did not go without their solid fuel. Four years previously there was a significant growth in Rosemarie's entrepreneurial activities when she opened 'By the Fire' in White Lion Walk. This development was in part recognition of the way gas was superseding coal. By the time her father died in 1988 King Coal was no longer in the ascendancy

The era of distinctive coals from a range of collieries, a dedicated coal yard close to the railway and customer satisfaction expressed in poetry may be recorded history now but the name Higham lives on in the town's residual coal business. Rosemarie herself has diversified her life and become a dynamic personality in the affairs of the town, trade organisations and charity work, raising money for local hospitals, victim support and other local causes. It was altogether appropriate that Colin Sully's interview with her for *Solid Fuel Magazine* for November 1997 should be entitled 'To Banbury Cross to see a fine lady'.

Banbury Guardian 8 May 2003.

- In a *Guardian* article of 25 October 2007 Brian Little recorded the retirement of Rosemarie Higham, who was born in 1942, and the closure of the premises in Calthorpe Street to which 'By the Fire' had moved.

1.23: An iconic store: F W Woolworth

In a recent editorial the *Times* newspaper made the interesting comment 'the fate of commercial enterprises is ultimately decided not by nostalgia but by competition'. The advantage of a column such as this one is that articles can be made nostalgia-focussed. Today's … is about what was once 'the wonder of Woolies'. In it I am turning back the pages of store history with the help of Nancy Mullis whose career and experience embraced many different aspects of running the High Street store. Nancy left St Mary's School in Southam Road on March 17, 1942 and joined the staff of Woolworths as a trainee sales assistant on the following day.

It was not long before she got into the rhythm of life at Woolies. In common with most other shops in the town, doors were firmly shut every Tuesday afternoon - the tradition of half-day closing. At that time by way of compensation Saturday trading was extended to 9pm at which time assistants could rush to the tea bar to collect their wages. Nancy's first take home pay was 19s 6d (97½p) before hurrying down to the Market Place where a few stalls were still open. Counter experience was, where possible, with someone known to her but occasionally an especially busy section might have to claim her attention.

When the first Christmas arrived Nancy looked after the sale of cards and calendars. The typical counter style was almost like a lucky dip – cards loose and spread haphazardly across the allotted space. Customer selection required assistants to match their purchases with envelopes of appropriate size and shape. During the war years a special attraction was the low price. Many cards were no more than 1d, others were 1½d and the dearest 3d (under ½p to 1½p).

Down the years Woolworths was always happy to make provision for certain groups of shoppers. It seems they were the first retail enterprise in Banbury to introduce late-night shopping for the elderly. Increasingly there was an immediate reaction from Littlewoods management who commented that if they had known of the intention to make such a provision they would have been willing to participate. Woolworths was also willing to meet the Christmastide needs of Horton Hospital nurses when they visited the High Street store armed with a list of patients, each of whom would receive a gift on Christmas morning. The nurses were covering all the wards so needed a wide variety of presents. Similarly nuns from St John's Church bought gifts for children. In those days, the forties and fifties, a little discount on items might be available but it was not widely or freely given.

Difficulties caused by the Second World War and by the weather have remained as memories down the years. One day in snowy 1947 (a very severe winter) only four assistants reported for work when the store opened for business. Even with so few able to reach Banbury's High Street the expectation was that the whole store would be accessible to customers. One other reason for so few assistants checking on was that a high proportion of them lived outside the town and were marooned in their villages. That day there were very few early customers and so it was an opportunity to play the Good Samaritan and provide cups of tea for corporation workmen clearing snow from the centre of the town.

During the course of our conversation I was keen to discover Nancy's views on

The neo-Georgian building which replaced the *Red Lion* hotel at No 7 High Street in which Banbury's Woolworth store was located from 1931.

what made Woolworths such a successful business. Top of the list was the comprehensive nature of the stock, a very wide range of everyday necessities that served the whole spectrum of the local area shopping public. Another important aspect of the way the store was organised was the tight control over sales staff by those on the supervisory and management side. At all costs those behind the counters were expected to maintain politeness and to be good timekeepers. A 9am opening necessitated a counter presence by 8.50am.

During the Second World War there were also extra chores. At the end of each day during the war big black shutters had to be put in place and getting them positioned was no mean task. Voluntary activities included fire watching, which earned participants 3/- (15p) for a night. The effect on normal store work was that the day's firewatchers left the store at 4pm, returned to cover 7pm to 7am and then were required to be back at work by 10am the following day. In Nancy's time computer-linked cash machines were unknown. All calculations involved mental arithmetic so the most help each assistant received was a scribbling pad and a pencil. During her earliest years in Woolworths Nancy was aware of how the store deployed space and expanded the square footage available [into the former *Red Lion* stables, and premises previously occupied by Colebrooks and the National Provincial Bank]. Internal refits were also important and, during one of these, Blinkhorns were commissioned to record the new-style layouts…. One of these pictures shows a notice exhorting customers not to block doorways with perambulators and push chairs. Doubtless this had more effect than the store could exercise over the odd loose cow in High Street which on occasions was an unwelcome guest in the wonderful world of Woolies.

Banbury Guardian 1 January 2009.

- The F W Woolworth store at No 7 High Street opened in 1931.

1.24: The heydays of Littlewoods:

The story of Littlewoods is the story of John Moores. Back in 1919 few people would have guessed that a junior telegraphist working in a Manchester office would one day be hailed by biographer Barbara Clegg as 'the supreme entrepreneur, the billionaire who was also "Uncle John" the family patriarch'. Moores's achievements were built around a succession of business notions. The first manifested itself in 1924 with the issue of Littlewoods football pools coupons. Eight years later came the incorporation of Mail Order Stores. These too proved successful and by 1936 were organised from headquarters set up in a redundant textile mill in the Lancashire town of Crosby. During the remainder of the decade John added a third strand to his business empire. This time it was the American retail concept of chain stores. Despite stiff competition from the already established Woolworths and Marks & Spencer chains, 25 Littlewoods stores were up and running by 1939.

The first store was in Blackpool where trading commenced on July 6, 1937. Banbury, the 62nd, did not appear on the company map until March 1956. At 11am on opening day a substantial crowd gathered outside 2 High Street, formerly the home of Chapmans. With more than 20,000 sq ft in which to spread its wares, especially textiles and food, Littlewoods was set to live up to the initiation advertising image - 'where you spend in shillings and save in pounds' and 'where you shop in the brightest and best planned and most streamlined store in Banbury'.

Such was the lure of the High Street's latest recruit that two ladies though it was worth waiting some three hours for the opportunity to sample the Littlewood experience. The *Banbury Advertiser* identified these ladies as Mrs Tyler of Milcombe and Mrs Ascoli of the Marshes, Southam Road, Banbury. Their immediate rewards were bouquets and baskets of groceries presented by the store assistant Gwen Lees. Caught on camera at the same time was seven-year-old Maureen Cherryman of Brackley who was delighted to receive a doll as well as a cutlery set. When asked what she thought of the store, Mrs Ascoli asserted with confidence 'it will be a boon to the working classes'.

The *Advertiser* reporter was drawn to the tinned fruit, all the textiles, glassware and a 12-piece tea service at 8s 6 d (43p). If this was not enough for you, then a venture into the cafeteria could end with a three course meal for 2s 9d (just under 14p). There were also considerable staff benefits, notably a rest room and a canteen where employees paid only 11s 6d (58p) for a whole week's worth of meals. On the day prior to the opening a civic party was hosted by Messrs Chowins (company sales manager), Burgon (stores superintendent) and Dutton (store manager).

Littlewoods remained a key part of the High Street scene until 1978 when pressures were mounting to find a larger site that would allow the company to meet the challenge of encouraging more and more people to shop in Banbury and halt the drift away to larger towns. On Thursday, November 9, 1978, came an announcement that caught the eye of *Banbury Guardian* readers. 'Littlewoods new superstore opens 16th November, Bridge Street, Cherwell Centre'. Encouraged by a Keynote voucher worth £10, those who spotted the advertisement were exhorted to 'look around our new superstore, you'll find a fantastic selection of high quality goods'. Ironically this

The opening day of the Littlewoods store in Banbury in March 1956.

was a time when there were rumours of the prospective closures of International Stores but also a resounding challenge from Woolworths who reopened on their existing High Street site and on exactly the same day.

Banbury's version of the John Moores retail road show paraded Miss Littlewood, Gail Turnbull, on the occasion of her first official engagement. Significantly she received a charm bracelet from Janatha Stubbs, daughter of John Moores who had been born just two days before the opening of the very first store at Blackpool.

So far as staff were concerned the company continued on its caring way, with a rich tapestry of day trips, regional dances, arts and crafts festivals and fashion shows that featured employees in the role of models. Special dinners and presentations rewarded long service to the company. Staff members in need of occasional recuperations from illness were permitted to stay at a Scottish fishing lodge owned by Littlewoods and used by the Moores family. Locally Lynne Garrett was able to convalesce in these idyllic surroundings.

The many shoppers who have valued the Littlewoods style and quality at a reasonable price will greatly regret its departure from the local scene. Company employees, some of whom have made long, loyal commitments, will shed a tear when the lights go out for the last time.

Banbury Guardian 12 January 2006

1.25: Tommy Dean and the *Sports Argus*

On May 13, 2006 the Birmingham *Sports Argus* newspaper made its final appearance as a stand-alone Saturday issue. It had been in existence since 1895 and in the words of former Walsall and Republic of Ireland goalkeeper Mick Kearns, the Pink 'Un 'was part of footballing folklore'. The last edition contained a fascinating souvenir that included this and other observations by Mick. His contribution was especially interesting because of a boyhood spent in Banbury. He recalled the regular Saturday night trips to a newsagent where he encountered a long queue of mainly men all waiting for the *Argus* to arrive. Mick was conscious of the fact that failure to secure a copy coupled with not hearing the soccer results on the radio or evening tuning in to Charles Buchan's football round-up, meant waiting until the Sunday papers became available.

One such news agency was that run by Tommy Dean in Broad Street. The ground floor of No 6 was home to a flourishing business and no more so than on Saturday evening when customers could be found in a line back along Broad Street and then quite a distance into Bridge Street. When finally these eager customers reached the shop they were confronted with three separate sports papers, the *Oxford Mail* green 'un, the *Birmingham Mail* blue, and of course the *Argus*, pink. Grimsbury residents were given an opportunity of buying their sports papers at the railway station when Tommy Dean collected the bundles …

… It is interesting to speculate about why sales of papers like these were sufficient to keep them alive. Between season 1934-1935 and the mid-sixties the flag for soccer in Banbury was well and truly carried by Spencer FC. It was at the earlier date that the club was invited to take over the fixtures of Rugby Town and play in the Birmingham Combination. This meant that there were fixtures against 'A' sides of Aston Villa, West Bromwich Albion, Coventry City and Wolverhampton Wanderers. By Easter of 1948 they also had to confront the likes of Birmingham City Trams and Stafford Rangers. Both in the 1930s and after the war gates at Spencer Stadium reflected a soccer euphoria, which after the game extended to a desire to read about the action and to check on the other results. In this respect the *Argus* especially was highly regarded for its coverage of the local leagues.

Less easy to assess is the extent to which *Argus* sales locally were boosted in the mid-1960s by Birmingham folk who moved to the area with Birds, the custard people. Many of the 600 or so employees at Deritend who sought new homes in Banbury would certainly have been looking for ways of keeping in touch with their home town. For some the wrench was too great and they missed big city features such as frequent buses. However being able to continue to read news of their favourite West Midlands sides may well have helped the transition from second city to market town.

Another reason for the former popularity of dedicated sports newspapers must surely have been the demand for them within such organisations as the Trades and Labour Club in West Bar. Here copies of the newspaper would be dropped off by the driver of the *Birmingham Mail* van or introduced into the bar area by keen followers of the soccer scene on whom friends and mates depended for a look at 'the pink'.

The recent demise of the *Sports Argus* has much to do with changing habits and life styles. Fewer people 'do the pools' now, electronic information systems, the ending of Saturday dominance within the programme of football matches, new directions on how we view the game (on the 'box' rather than on the 'terraces') have been responsible for declining circulation figures...

Comments made to me by people whose love of sport has not diminished down the years suggest that the custom of going out for a Saturday evening special has long since become a thing of the past. The Banbury area in common with other parts of the country will be the poorer for the departure of the great sports newspapers. Its reporters had an uncanny knack of getting inside clubs and being the first with the news about players and performances. Perhaps the writing was really on the wall back in the autumn of 2005 when the Newcastle area, renowned hot bed of soccer, lost its own 'pink'. Now long term *Argus* readers, and there are still some locally, can only join the ranks of those for whom Saturday night will never quite be the same again.

Banbury Guardian 1 June 2006.

1.26: G F Braggins & Co, timber merchants

In 1850 Banbury was at the dawn of a new era of industrialisation. A major participant in this process was Bernhard Samuelson but other people played their part as well, and one of these was a man by the name of James Braggins. This 32-year-old son of a Northamptonshire timber merchant and sawyer, based in Silverstone, was attracted to Banbury by the opportunity offered by a contract for sawing timber for Samuelson. James managed to locate suitable premises at the rear of the *Catherine Wheel*, a Bridge Street coaching inn, and secured an access to the land by way of Fish Street (now George Street). Here he founded the firm that was later known as G F Braggins & Company and lived conveniently nearby in Windsor Street. In 1859 James Braggins was sufficiently well-established … to explore new product avenues. It was in that same year he patented an adjustable hinge for gates.

This achievement enabled him to manufacture oak entrance gates to such a standard that his company had a competitive edge in the business. Each set of gates was the outcome of real workmanship and not mass production. The gate side of the business flourished exceedingly well. Markets were opened up in many parts of the world but especially in Argentina where there was an insatiable demand on large agricultural estates within the hinterland of Buenos Aires.

Pride in the gate side of the company's affairs was accompanied by success at numerous shows and exhibitions. Awards, often in the form of medals, were accumulated. Typical of these was success at the Worcestershire Agricultural Society Show of 1868 when James Braggins gained recognition for improved gate hanging.

By 1879 the Fish Street premises could not cope with the volume of work. James himself had died in 1873 and it was left to his sons George Frederick and James Henry who had inherited the business to start the hunt for a larger site. The outcome of their search was a move to Gatteridge Street. Here they built a sawmill with accompanying chimney and set up machinery driven by a beam engine, comprising a single blade reciprocating saw, a circular saw and a hand saw. A few years later, in 1881, carpenters' shops, painters' shops and a smithy were erected on the new site. The stage was set for the transfer of the gate and hinge business. This was not the end of the development as in 1897 the timber yard at the Gatteridge Street site was extended and a year later a larger smithy put up. The specialised area of gate production continued until about 1930 when changing methods within the building trade meant that here was less scope for quality work such as a remarkable contract for copies of Sulgrave Manor screens and doors. These were fashioned out of 16th century wood from Warwick Priory and sent to an American customer, Alexander Weddle.

The decline of the gate business coincided roughly with the period when electricity replaced steam and tractors took the place of horse-drawn timber wagons. The last horses were seen about the yard in 1926 and petrol and diesel powered tractors appeared from 1934 onwards. Donald Braggins, son of George, grew up in the age of horses and his playground was the timber yard. He entered the firm in 1936 and after the Second World War guided the timber business through the difficulties due to shortages. In this period of austerity the company was pleased to provide the public with off-cuts for their fires at a modest price of a few pence. Every Saturday morning people – many of them children – queued with handcarts of all shapes and sizes.

The occasion of the firm's centenary dinner in 1950 was a time to reminisce about how the company had been handed down within the family. Tom Haskins, who was mayor from 1950-51, remarked that the name of Braggins was built on good workmanship. It was in recognition of this that Jack Young, the oldest member of the workforce, presented Donald with a silver-backed dressing set.

Unsurprisingly, a firm with the fine traditions of a family business had evolved some labour friendly practices. One of them was recalled by Henry Herbert who had been yard foreman from 1908-1928. He remarked on how birthdays were celebrated by the buying of one shilling buckets of beer. No wonder Donald said of his father that he was 'big in stature and big in personality'.

…, in 1910, the firm of G F Braggins and Co patented a Kit Cart which was designed especially to be of most use to uniformed organisations, notably Boy Scouts, the Cadet Corps and Boys' Brigades. The company issued a well-illustrated pamphlet which demonstrated the versatility of their product. Not merely were the wheels of the cart interchangeable, but the timber materials were selected with performance in mind. English hardwood was used for the framework of the body while the sides relied on selected English oak. Native ash scout staves were available for the handles, either of which could be replaced by a Scout's staff in the event of an accident...In its totally finished shape the cart weighed 143 lbs …The space needed when dismantled and stacked in a pile was a length of 5 ft 3 in, a width of 3 ft 6 in and a height of not more than 11 in.

…The Braggins Company found it necessary to stress to all users that the cart was not to be regarded as a toy. In patriotic language, they proclaimed the cart 'is made from all British materials by British workmen'. Khaki was the chosen colour and each cart came with three towlines. The price back in 1910 was £6 10s 0d and more distant purchasers did not have to worry about rail charges. The name Braggins is well remembered in Banbury, especially for community involvement. Twelve years from the patenting of the Kit Cart, maypoles used in Bridge Street for elementary school childrens' celebrations at a shopping festival were constructed at the renowned yard in Gatteridge Street. If a beer house such as the *Strugglers* wanted to cover its bar floor with sawdust, Braggins was again the man, this time with his bags of sawdust priced at 3d.

Early in 1959 the news broke that Banbury was about to lose a business and so change the lives of the Gatteridge Street area. Braggins yard had been synonymous with the timber trade since the mid-19th century…. In a press interview G D M (Don) Braggins recalled the age of the horse and securing access to Oxfordshire timber. Strong draught animals were the key to success. He accompanied the teams from the age of nine or ten who set out for the likes of Tackley round about 5am. At 7am they could be found in the vicinity of Deddington where it was time to seek breakfast at one of the village's public houses. Three hours later they reached Hopcroft's Holt and shortly after Tackley where the timber was located. Unsurprisingly it was often midnight or later before the welcoming lights of Banbury were spotted on the return journey…

The Braggins firm became renowned for their handmade gates. Craftsmanship ensured that they did not sag nor were they adversely affected by the weather. With obvious pride the late 1950s owner of the business was able to point to some 30 or 40 gates at intervals between Banbury and Woodstock. Those fashioned out of oak were viewed as 'works of art'….The cost of producing gates has varied over time. In 1936 buyers could get one for £15 10s 0d (£15.50). By the late 1950s the same item cost ten times as much. It was then that alarm bells began to ring for the firm. The explanation offered by the company was that metal had become the material of choice leading to a decline in the wood trade.

Mr Braggins reckoned that there was a time when motor cars were 90 per cent timber. His comment was that the amount of wood required for a vehicle in the 1950s 'could be carried under one arm'. In the railway industry carriages and wagons were steel framed and not made from English oak, which also played a less significant role in house building. As for the furniture trade, imported timbers had assumed increasing importance.

There was much more to George Donald McLeod Braggins than the boss of a timber company. He was a long serving Borough Councillor, later promoted to the rank of Alderman, and County Councillor. 1946 was an especially busy time for him, when he took on the office of Mayor and President of Rotary in the same year. On the wider front he belonged to the Banbury Voluntary Fire Brigade, an interest he shared with Frederick Anker.

Closure of Braggins yard was seen as 'the breaking of another link with Old Banbury'. The impact on those employed by the firm was substantial especially as the likes of Jack Cartwright and Harold Tubb had seen 26 years of service. Their predecessors had been viewed as 'hard drinking, hard living timber fellers who were known throughout Oxfordshire'.

Banbury Guardian 22 March 2001, 2 December 2004, 2 August 2012.

- For the trek cart see T Parry, *Scouting for Banbury's Boys* (2009), 19-20.

1.27: Excursions for motorists in the 1920s

A lone signpost, amiable clouds and just one open touring car in an otherwise empty country road – hardly a vision of the late 1990s. Indeed this very scene can be found on the front cover of Sidney Ewins' poplar guide to motor runs around Banbury. It was published in the 1920s. The language of its foreword is reminiscent of tourist pamphlets. One line alone says it all about what awaits the exploring motorist: 'Charming little villages away from the high road … delightful scenes of water, wood and meadow, roadside curiosities enshrining the quaint conceits of past generations … all become accessible to the possessor of the car'.

In brief the book is a passport to what you can see in a day. Ewins Garage was close to the Cross. In a photograph its distinguishing features were the word 'Garage' etched boldly into an extended roof line from which sprouted a pole bearing a flag with the name of the firm. Among the advertisements which doubtless helped to offset the cost of publication is an invitation to expend up to 67/6d on a Sirran Tea Case – the complete picnic set. Source of this attractive and well-presented item was that emporium of hardware, Hoods.

Ewins gave details of ten routes radiating from Banbury and ranging in distance from 24 and a half to 52 miles. They are arranged as a clockwise fan of journeys designed to combine the best of town and country. Any possible fears are allayed, notably and amusingly that the 'Marsh' in Moreton-in-the-Marsh does not imply boggy land. By contrast Stow-on-the-Wold is regarded as 'breezy and bracing'.

Publications like this slim pocket-size volume did much to encourage away days. These were popular with groups as well as individuals. The history of churches like St Leonard's in Grimsbury includes numerous references to choir outings. Past members of that body will have memories of a trip to Swindon Railways Works –

Excursions by charabanc were popular in the 1920s and brought visitors to Banbury as well as taking Banburians into the countryside. These City of Oxford vehicles were photographed at the junction of Marlborough Road and High Street.

A motor coach of a later generation circumnavigates Banbury Cross, the town's principal tourist attraction.

ideal for boys keen to top up their lists of loco numbers, less appealing to choristers with silver hair….

While Cheney employees were waygoosing in the Cotswolds, supporters of Banbury United Homing Society had pigeons in mind … The BUHS charabanc took them to Leys Farm at Great Tew, home of the Society chairman, Mr Tustain. After a stop here for tea they went on to Rousham Parish Church where the Rev Ward-Jackson, a member himself, took as his appropriate sermon theme: 'Let them have dominion over the fish of the sea and over the fowl of the air'.

Banbury Guardian 16 March 1999.

1.28: Some Banbury garages

...A small pocket guide issued with the compliments of County Garages ... (published by) ... Motor Guides (Great Britain) Limited of Chesterfield...The County Garages needed this publicity to help keep ahead of their competition by stressing the location of their showroom and services in such a prime position. It was on what was then the key local crossroads as well as opposite the most famous monument n Banbury, known the world over. The booklet, possibly produced in the 1950s, contains a lot of useful information for drivers. There are eight pages of motor index marks, together with a guide to routes from Banbury. The latter section even comments on gradients. In anticipation that many purchasers of cars from their showroom would not be paying outright, the balance of the pages were fill with a hire purchase calculator.

This was not the first occasion when a local firm had been enterprising in this way. Back in 1920 Ewins Garage, also located near the 1859 Cross, produced a larger booklet about the joys of motoring from Banbury. As this was closer in time to ownership of early car models, there were advertisements by retailers anxious to parade the very latest garb and gear for those behind the wheel.

Sidney Ewins was an enterprising man and a good example of how Banbury entrepreneurs played a leading role in local government. After years as a councillor he became mayor for the year 1934-35 and enjoyed all the excitement of involvement in George V's silver jubilee celebrations. The business enterprise established by Sidney included roadside pumps in the Horse Fair and a service building at the top of Marlborough Place which referred to its location as Marlborough Mews – as befitted a business that started as a horse and carriage dealership in 1897, the year of

A trade card issued by Sidney Ewins, when his family firm were concerned with horses and carriages and before they became involved in the motor trade.

Queen Victoria's Diamond Jubilee. More than 40 years later the firm was official repairer to both the AA and the RAC.

By the 1930s competition amongst garages in Banbury was becoming intense. The Warwick Road attracted developments by Young's Garage, Shires Motor Company Ltd and the Banbury General Motor Company. Each enterprise was agent for a different range of vehicles, yet such was the determination to succeed that the last of these firms made much of the slogan in relation to his Riley 'cars being for the man who would reach the heights of performance without plunging into the depths of his pocket'. Mr Young was equally determined about sales and in 1938 organised a visit to Fords at Dagenham for prospective buyers.

Another part of Banbury which attracted garage owners was the east side of Middleton Road in Grimsbury. Here the Lido Service Station, Grimsbury Motors, City Motors and Bridge Motors have all at some stage contributed to the street scene, but perhaps the most remarkable initiative was by George Mumford. His lifetime in the garage world started by selling cans of petrol out of a corrugated iron hut. This was located in the yard of the *Bell* and financially was underpinned by Strouds the butchers. In his heyday George had four pumps and offered a repair service. If he knew the customer well but was otherwise too busy, he would offer the use of tools to save loss of time. Described by his contemporaries as squat, George had a physical strength that belied his brown-smocked appearance. If a wheel needed changing, George had the strength. When George gave up the business, Tommy Gascoigne took over and so the spirit of Mumford's garage lived on....

Banbury Guardian 13 March 2003.

1.29: Sidney Young, garage proprietor

A half-page advertisement in an early 1930s *Banbury Advertiser Directory* contains a fine testimony to the entrepreneurial activities of Sidney Branson Young. He established a small service garage fronted by a short forecourt and directly facing the *Warwick Arms* public house in the Warwick Road. Initially he sold cycles but quickly diversified into agricultural vehicles, a form of business that was complemented soon after by a Ford (Fordson) Dealership. It quickly became Sid's proud boast that he and his staff could carry out 'repairs and complete overhauls to any make of motor vehicle'. In those days – the start of the 1930s – he could also say with some justification that all work would be 'personally supervised'.

Certainly substantial early experience in the motor trade at a garage (either Wrench's or Station Garage) in Bridge Street and his friendship with Sidney Ewins primed him for Banbury's boom in garage ownership. By the second half of the 1930s Sidney had really established himself as a Ford dealer. His advertisement in the *Banbury Guardian* for May 13, 1937 was the chance to release breaking news about the new Ford Ten, which is described as 'unusually modern' and 'the last word in mechanical efficiency'. Three variants were on display: a saloon at £143, a double entrance saloon with a £150 price tag and a touring car also at £150. All these quotes were works prices.

Despite the thrill of selling the new models, Sidney was also interested in stewardship of the land. This meant the two aspects, farming and hunting. Sid's concern for agriculture may well have been a factor in his decision to take on Bill Webb as an improver (apprentice) in December 1939.

Bill was one of three people who started their working lives with the firm in this way. In his case learning the trade meant acquiring the skills needed to effect repairs to tractors. With the war now a reality, this was part of getting a vital message across to farmers. 'Buy now before tractors get scarce'. 'Be ready to respond to the Government's challenge to plough a substantial proportion of what it termed idle acres'. For his part Bill Webb was heading for the navy. However it was Sid's hand that pulled him back, the reason being that agricultural work was of paramount importance and those involved stood a chance of war service exemptions. Bill remained at Young's Garage and had a workload of some 85 hours a week. During this time he focussed strongly on overhauling the sort of used tractors that Sid had included in an immediate pre-war front page newspaper box. They were priced at £50 and £75 respectively.

These tractors were not the only used ones to come the way of Sid Young. The decision to locate military camps within short distances of Banbury meant that old redundant vehicles were readily available. By 1949 Bill Webb had joined the marriage stakes and advanced his status to that of a foreman. He discovered to his amazement that his weekly earnings made him better endowed than the nearest equivalents at Alcan. Four years later Bill found himself part of a new business structure. In 1953 Sid Young sold out to Hartwell Properties Ltd and this was a signal for larger showrooms. Sid himself was made managing director of the new set-up and the name Young was retained probably because everyone knew it and what it stood for. Within what later became Hartwell Motors Bill Webb retained his control of the repairs to the agricultural and commercial vehicles. By 1963 he had become manager of a department responsible for this work, though within seven years the agricultural aspect had passed to P A Turney. Bill retired in 1980 and left work to reflect on those happy early years when Sid Young's name was the first that sprung to mind as far as repairs were concerned.

Life in the Warwick Road was not all daily grind. There was a strong social side including darts and especially football. Young's employees played teams from other garages and also from insurance firms. Matches happened on Sundays and may well have been the start of Sunday leagues locally.

Both the *Banbury Guardian* and the *Banbury Advertiser* for mid-June 1964 carried short obituaries of Sidney Young. By then he was living out of town at Fenny Compton. In his address the vicar of the Anglican church recorded a life devoted to the motor trade but diversified through his strong attachment to the Warwickshire Hunt and his position as president of the North Oxfordshire Car Club. Bill Webb was a pall bearer at Sid Young's funeral. As he and his colleagues bore the coffin it must have been a poignant moment to recall how Sid had launched him on a lifetime connection with the agricultural side of the business. Just before Christmas last, Bill's colleagues joined him in celebration of his 80th birthday. It was my privilege to be there and to share something of the remarkable world of Bill and Sid.

Banbury Guardian 18 January 2007.

1.30: The livestock market: a view from 1950

Banbury Livestock Market was established by Midland Marts on its Grimsbury location in 1925. The site was adjacent to the lines of the Great Western and London & North Western [in 1925 LMSR] railway companies. Interestingly this development was very much a farmers' movement. In part it was a response to the situation whereby in the Banbury of 1919 buyers and beasts had become mixed up with motor buses, cars, carriers' carts and passing traffic of all descriptions.

Ten years later the prospectus of Midland Marts Ltd revealed that out of nine members of the Board of Directors, five were farmers, one was a stock broker and the remaining two were auctioneers. Not one of these appears to have been connected with Grimsbury though company shares were offered to people living in Merton Street. The driving force behind the enterprise was Alexander Patrick McDougall of Prescote Manor near Banbury. This Scotsman had the vision to appreciate that the location was likely to make the market a mecca for buyers and sellers. The decision about the Grimsbury site became a government one. On April 2, 1925, Edward Wood, Minister of Agriculture, declared the new enterprise open. This action inspired a letter written to the *Banbury Guardian*, which appealed for purer language in the new market than had been the norm with street gatherings.

In 1950 Midland Marts Ltd celebrated their Silver Anniversary. By then they were one of the largest livestock auctioneering concerns in the country and had headquarters in Banbury. Patrick McDougall chose the occasion of the AGM which was held in the Corn Exchange … to make several significant statements. He began by commenting on the sharp decline in revenue from the Ministry of Food in respect of duties carried out, notably the handling of fat cattle, sheep and pigs. This revenue was below the level reached when stock was sold by open auction as in pre-war years. The question on everyone's mind was 'can competitive distribution be achieved via auction rings or wholesale meat traders who still have the craftsmanship in slaughtering and making use of all parts?'. McDougall noted especially that there were people of ability still in Banbury. Overall he observed that the world of 1950 was not the same as that of 1920. Despite this he was quite clear that 'a really great market means so much to the citizens of Banbury'.

The chairman then turned to future ventures amongst which was entry into the pedigree sphere. By the autumn of 1950 he planned to have opening shows and sales of Jersey, Shorthorn and Friesian cattle. Location in the heart of England meant that Midland Marts was well-placed for this activity. McDougall's second move was to extend the existing Corn Exchange so that local Corn Merchants could be accommodated and sales of furniture promoted. The latter would benefit the housewives of Banbury Borough and Rural District areas. His third and last enterprise was the grading of stock which would be carried out on days other than Market Day (Thursday). The proposal was Fridays and close co-operation with the Borough authority would be required. One outcome of this additional activity was the necessity to wash out transport vehicles. To date haulage authorities had been very critical of delays in this process. With many journeys in morning time it was clear that stock carrying capacity would depend on effective cleaning.

During the AGM several leading Midland Marts people, but especially Mr A F Nicholson, viewed Banbury as a convenient transport centre (road and rail). To that end it was decided to invite British Rail[ways] to erect an arrival and departure indicator board at the market. Anniversary celebrations were inevitably tinged with sadness at the death of well-known local farmer Arthur Lawrence Tew of Blackpits Farm, Barford. A specialist in beef production he had clocked up no less than 40 years at Banbury Livestock market and witnessed the move from scattered street locations to Grimsbury's consolidated site.

Banbury Guardian 12 November 2015.

- Edward Wood, first Earl of Halifax (1881-1959), Minister of Agriculture 1924-25, Viceroy of India 1925-31, who came close to being Prime Minister in May 1940.

1.31: Samuelson memories:

In September 1954 the *Banbury Advertiser* published a fascinating conversation between a man called Joe Herbert and a reporter. This took the form of a series of reminiscences about the Britannia Works owned by Sir Bernhard Samuelson, which were situated on two separate sites linked by a tramway with a depot adjacent to the GWR station. Joe went into the works from school during the early years of the 20th century. He was employed in the blower fitting department where the foreman was his father Harry Herbert.

Letter headings about that time identify a diversity of products made by this company of engineers and machinists. These included Roots 'Acme' blowers and exhausts, flour milling machinery, Samuelson's patent power hammers, Foundry moulding machinery, and harvesting machinery. Until about 1912 there was a big emphasis on agricultural items such as reaper binders but this situation changed when on a night before Banbury Fair the carpenters' shop was burnt down. The result was that a consignment of flour milling machinery was lost in the flames.

Britannia Works' products were shown at numerous leading events at home and abroad. Probably their first involvement was with the Great Exhibition of 1851 at the Crystal Palace. Their display reflected the early emphasis on items such as turnip cutters, chaff cutters, ploughs and horse hoes. In Class 9 the firm secured a prize medal for a turnip cutter. By Joe's time blowers were its world famous speciality.

The Britannia Works was not only famous for numerous products but renowned

A list of the products of the Britannia Works which includes the blowers mentioned by Joe Herbert.

The workforce at the Britannia Works, probably photographed before 1914.

for the stable of horses kept in immaculate condition. Their function was for haulage of trucks on the light railway that linked the upper and lower works and conveyed timber to extensive wood yards on the opposite side of the Oxford Canal.

Joe's remarks about his working day and some of his colleagues are especially revealing. Ernest Samuelson, the managing director, walked to the factory from his home at Bodicote Grange and always arrived just before 9am. Frequently he was accompanied by his dog which he let loose at the Upper Works so that the animal could find its way to its kennel in the Lower Works. A personality at the firm was Dick Stanley who got out of his bed every working day at 5.15am so that he could rouse his workmates in case they did not hear the 5.30am hooter. Work started at 6am and ended at 5.30pm (noon on Saturdays). Apparently the hooter was so loud that it could be heard as far away as Middleton Cheney. Many employees lived in villages and of necessity became good walkers …Nicknames were common at the works. These included 'Knacker' Bedlow, 'Foxy' Fairfax and 'Stodger' Jones.

Many of the workers were involved in the considerable number of sports activities on offer. The firm's Recreation Society catered for football, cricket, tennis, shooting, quoits and skittles. There was a large sports field by the railway where the pavilion sported a full licence and the grandstand was thatched. The works also had a good brass [band] under the direction of Harry Webb, a foreman blacksmith. Joe concluded the interview by stressing how much Banbury as a town owed to this company. Sir Bernhard Samuelson was a remarkable benefactor and his money helped underpin the Municipal Buildings and Library as well as Britannia Road School.

Banbury Guardian 17 March 2016.

- In a *Guardian* article on 22 March 2018, 'Britannia – more than just a place of industry' Brian Little again quoted the memories of Joe Herbert, and also drew on G C J Hartland, 'The Britannia works from Living Memory', *C&CH*, vol 4 (1971).
- Ernest Samuelson (1865-1927) was succeeded by his brother Sir Francis Samuelson (1861-1946). A Potts, 'Ernest Samuelson and the Britannia Works', *C&CH* vol 4 (1971).

1.32: The origins of Northern Aluminium, Banbury

On February 15 1930 the Northern Aluminium Company and Mr W I R Lidsey signed the contract which committed the firm to Banbury and a site on Hardwick Farm. This was the most significant industrial event in the town since the middle of the 19th century when Bernhard Samuelson transferred his business interests from France. Prior to the signing, several notable dignitaries were involved in the discussions. They were Alderman Collingridge who was mayor, his town clerk, Arthur Stockton and Mr G H Oakes the borough accountant.

The NAC's advertisement in the catalogue for the Banbury & District Industrial Exhibition, 1951.

The Northern Aluminium Company factory nearing completion in 1931, with queues, probably of applicants for jobs. The works began production in November 1931.

The story is told in the *Banbury Guardian* for February 20 that a chance element was involved. A Mr Myers, of Northern Aluminium engineers, happened to meet Mr Oakes' brother-in-law on board an Atlantic liner and heard about Banbury's keenness for industrial development. At a time of economic depression the prospect of several hundred jobs had great appeal. However the first few months were not easy for the company or the workforce and it was not long before the threat of strike action loomed. During the ensuing troubles people like Frank Partridge and Tom Haskins were prominent.

In the early stages of growth several company employees transferred from Northern Aluminium's West Bromwich site and among these was William Whittle who became production manager. At the time of the 50th anniversary of the company he was still living in the Banbury area. Volunteers for the move from West Bromwich were also sought from the staff of shorthand typists. One of those who agreed to leave the Black Country was Olive Simmons (née Watton). She was then 18. Here new boss was Commander Merrett under whom she received £1 5s a week. Compared with West Bromwich, Banbury seemed relatively rural. Olive and her companions were young girls away from home for the first time in most cases and so forced to seek lodgings. Unfortunately Olive's first base in Grimsbury turned out to be less than satisfactory. In 1933 wedding bells sounded for her and she married John Simmons who joined Northern Aluminium as a draughtsman from the London area. He was responsible for designing the floor layouts for new machinery.

Despite poor working conditions in the early days of the company's operations, there were happy social occasions recorded in the in-house publication *Safety First*. Children's Christmas parties were always a feature. With tea out of the way and crackers pulled, it was time for Mickey Mouse and natural history films. Works sport ranged widely. 1938 was a vintage year for soccer. The Banbury Charity, Banbury [Brackley?] Myer's and Tysoe Challenge Cups all came home to roost. Later the same year company anglers competed for the Cherwell Fishing Association Challenge Shield. It was reported that NAC teams finished fifth and sixth.

Banbury Guardian 19 February 1998.

- G H Oakes was convicted during 1931 of embezzling £7369 of the borough council's money. B Trinder, 'Fifty years on', C&CH vol 8 (1981), 120. The article reproduces several *Banbury Guardian* reports on the progress of the aluminium works during 1931. The best account of the factory is R Hartree, 'The Banbury Aluminium Works 1929-2009', *C&CH* vol 20 (2015), 3-30.

:

1.33: Glory days at Switchgear & Equipment

In 1942 William Potts, who was *Banbury Guardian* editor, published an informative booklet about the development of the town over 100 years. It was designed to coincide with the centenary of the newspaper which had been celebrated four years earlier. Chapter three is about the growth of industry and one of the companies featured, Switchgear & Equipment Ltd, whose presence in the town no longer illuminates the Banbury scene. The origins of the firm can be traced back to the early thirties when rural electrification was introducing a new dimension in village life. Messrs Dean, Laverick and Oxley, as founders of Switchgear, were men of perception who were also aware of a market for small electrical items such as isolators, circuit breakers and clamps, as used on the London Underground system.

So why Banbury for their enterprise? As so often the town's centrality within the country was undoubtedly a factor but so too was the existence of a pool of labour. The Britannia Works had closed and, along with the Northern Aluminium Company, Switchgear & Equipment met an urgent need for jobs. The company was born into premises close to the Great Western Railway line. It was not an 'easy birth', as evidenced by the fact that Arthur Oxley had to work round the clock to get ready. He even slept on the premises! In the words of Potts, 'the firm met with success and a steady progress'. The inevitable consequence was that by 1937, the company had outgrown its capacity and had to utilise part of the former Britannia Lower Works.

At that time, some 30 to 40 people were involved, one of whom was Rowland Humphrey who lived at Woodford Halse. His memories include the experience of cycling with parts between different buildings, but also the occasion when Albert Boote, his foreman, asked him to go to a shop on the bridge. The purpose was to collect two lardy cakes and a bottle of Tizer! Rowland's 7/6d a week no way allowed for coping with such informal requests.

A serious roof fire was probably one of the reasons that Switchgear moved to the Southam Road in 1938, still under the controlling interests of Arthur Oxley. In a strange way, the intervention of war actually promoted company fortunes. Admiralty contracts fell their way and Banbury's contribution to the age of hostilities took the form of mines and depth charges. The main building itself was also geared to war. There was a lookout at the top of the factory and, alongside, a firing range between this building and an electricity sub-station. Switchgear's payroll was dominated by female names. Women worked on one or two 12-hour shifts.

Between 1945 and the early 1970s, when the name Switchgear & Equipment could no longer be found in the local telephone directory, many people made their mark within the company. Eric Woodbridge was works director, Jack Turner had responsibility for technical matters and Bill Betts guided sales. Many apprentices who also turned up at the North Oxfordshire College will have cause to remember Bill Beake.

Like so many Banbury businesses, Switchgear & Equipment was more than the sum total of what it made. There was a social and sports life, as well as a shop floor existence. Indeed for members of the 25-year club, meals out and trips to the theatre were occasions to remember. A link with Grimsbury took the form of darts at the

Blacklocks. Into this pattern of work and play, Rowland Humphrey used the post war years to fashion his contribution to the tool room before transferring to the maintenance department. Between the 1930s and the end for the road for S&E, Rowland experienced the evolution of a business that had a presence at Brackley, sent finished products all over the world, and tested equipment for that wartime arrival in Grimsbury, the Cold Store.

At the top of the employment tree, Arthur Oxley was able to live in the splendid surroundings of the Green at Adderbury. *Woodlands* was not only home, it symbolised a successful career with a company that rightfully takes its place in Banbury's hall of industrial memories.

Banbury Guardian 16 September 1999.

1.34: The Spencer factory

In my article about Ernest Owen Reid [1.03], who became town clerk in 1932, I referred to a *Directional Pointer Guide Map to Banbury*, which had been published by E J Burrow & Co Ltd. This copy had Reid's signature at the top. Someone, maybe Reid himself, had colour shaded the central area. Advertising was a strong component and would have given him a good idea of the mix of commercial businesses in the town. Firms such as E W Brown (the Original Cake Shop), Hoods (Ironmongers) and Cluffs (shoes) must have impressed themselves upon him very early on. Burrows' useful guide also had a section entitled 'Some Interesting Notes'. This told the visitor about such important historical features as Banbury Castle and Banbury Cross. In addition it gave an insight into the manufacturing base and highlights the products of weaving, stationery goods and office equipment, printed matter, linen goods and aluminium sheets. Curiously no mention is made of a company which is currently in the news because of the building it occupied in Britannia Road. Spencer House was designed by Wallis Gilbert & Partners in the art deco style of the period. As readers will have gathered from last week's *Banbury Guardian*, developers by the name of Bovis Homes (South Western) hope to be allowed to demolish the structure and erect apartments suitable especially for key workers and first-time buyers.

Spencer House first became associated with the manufacture of underwear in 1927 when Dorothea Allen set up business following the purchase of an American franchise. Ten years later significant expansion ensured that the premises were

The entrance to Spencer House, designed in the 1920s by Wallis, Gilbert & Partners.

A production room at the Spencer factory in the 1930s.

planned to meet company needs. This industrial initiative was located on the western fringe of the Cherwell area, which experienced a much earlier and contrasting manufacturing boom due especially to the success in Victorian times of Bernhard Samuelson's Britannia works and of Barrow's business. The 1920s Spencer enterprise was a new departure for Banbury and diversified the working environment of Britannia Road, which was also home to Stone's box factory and Kimberley's builders' yard. The last two have gone though the company names have been used for new development and as a nostalgic way of reminding us of their long associations with this part of town.

By the end of the 1930s the Spencer factory was capable of sustaining a large workforce. Along with the Northern Aluminium Company in Southam Road, Spencers was a vital part of Banbury's industrial renaissance. The building this underwear firm occupied became a substantial symbol of town recovery after the closure of the Britannia Works at the end of the 1920s had plunged Banbury into a run of depression years.

It is perhaps not surprising that back numbers of the *Banbury Guardian* newspaper contain several articles which feature the company, which finally closed in 1989. One of the most interesting of these was by Keith Wood who was the senior reporter for many years. In July, 1989, he wrote about the firm's proposal for change of use of its site and relocation of the manufacturing activity. Appropriately, the banner headline was 'Corset Company bursting at the seams'. It appears that continued economic success was dependent on the company making a move to an industrial estate on the fringe of Banbury. Accordingly, Spencers applied to Cherwell District Council for

One of Spencers' neighbours in Britannia Road, the premises of J S Kimberley, builder.

permission to develop their Britannia Road site as flats. The scheme was for 38 two-bedroomed flats and 15 one-bedroomed ones in a complex that would be a three to four-storey block. The sale of this site was going to pay for a move to a new location where it would be possible to continue the company's growth in turnover. This scheme was approved in outline only and was made subject to a considerable number of conditions. Subsequent resubmission of the proposals by Spencers' successors were rejected.

The present day revival of this idea of replacing a long established landmark building with apartment blocks has to be seen in the context of the town's built heritage much of which is beyond the conservation zone and has little or no individual protection.

Banbury Guardian 18 December 2003.

1.35: Automotive Products

Back in the 1960s Banbury had a land windfall of more than 80 acres free of the need to obtain an industrial development certificate. This made the town a very attractive location for industry. A company keen to seize the opportunity was Automotive Products. Their Banbury factory was built 'to house the largest spare parts and replacement organisation in Europe' according to the caption that greeted readers of the book published to celebrate the firm's Golden Jubilee.

The story of AP goes back to 1920 when Edward Bishop Broughton, Willie Emmott and Denis Taber Brock (the so-called Three Musketeers) agreed to the manufacture of Lockheed Hydraulic brakes in the Clemens Street factory in Leamington Spa. By the time the Banbury works opened in 1962 the market was a potential 13 million vehicles on British roads. The way to realise this was perceived as having 'the right part in the right place, at the right time'. In today's article I shall ... reveal how a 1960s' workforce of 2,000 was drawn into a variety of social and leisure activities, which extended to sponsorship of major local events. A valuable ... resource for achieving this is the in-house magazine called *AP News*, Parts and Service edition. Towards the end of the 1970s the firm decided to create a sports ground at Milcombe and landscape it with more than 100 trees, including oak, beech, poplar and sycamore. 'Put your name on an AP tree' was a front page invitation to take advantage of a low-cost opportunity to have your own commemorative plaque.

The diversity and excitement of the official opening of the ground merited a double page spread of pictures. ... No less attention grabbing was a display of steam engines. Pictures of them were accompanied by a caption which summed up the occasion - 'The rural setting provided an ideal back drop for these splendid survivors from the age of steam. The only feature of the day to cause disappointment was the weather – 'rather chilly for July'. However by way of compensation the Suzanne Taylor dancers gave a warming performance and not a little heat was generated when Accounts Department took the strain against Computer Giants in the tug-of-war.

Whoever edited *AP News* was good at whipping up enthusiasm for company-backed events. Typical was a February 1979 reminder to the female workforce that the New Year brought a fresh opportunity to become Miss AP Parts and Services. When the competition first began in 1977 Banbury's Susan Boss 'stormed to victory'. No in-house newspaper would be complete without a photographic reminder of that seasonal event, the AP children's Christmas Party. The background to this occasion is recorded in *50 years of Progress*, the Jubilee booklet. Way back in 1930, Mrs E B Broughton, wife of one of the three musketeers, demonstrated her love of children by persuading families to hold parties at each of the company's factories. The idea took root and literally hundreds of four-eight year old enjoyed 'the feast and fun'. Another good source of AP memories has been John C Webb's recollections published in *Four Shires* in March 2003. In this piece he recalled the distinction between 'staff girls' and 'works girls' in terms of what they were permitted to wear. Until Asian women joined the workforce and introduced their traditional costume, the former were limited to skirts and dresses whilst the latter could wear fashionable clothes including the more practical trousers if they so wished.

The 1980s decline in the British motor industry meant that the company had more and more spare capacity. With the closure of the Banbury factory in 1986 came an end of a unique way of life for those people who looked to AP for both work and leisure activities. It was also an end to an era that had seen company backing for town events such as Banbury Carnival.

Banbury Guardian 18 July 2013.

1.36: Paper & Publications, printers

In 1962 and again just recently a printing press made history. The early sixties arrival of the Goss machine would have been fascinating viewing for the casual onlooker. Its departure in 2002 was also noteworthy because of a destination close to the Chinese border of Uzbekistan. … Early sixties access to the site was by way of a substantial humpback bridge that spanned the Oxford Canal. Samuelson, the 19th century agricultural engineer had been well aware of this phenomenon, especially when heavy horses were required to draw a load across the surface. Taylors, the haulage contractors responsible for the transit of the Goss, clearly had quite a task to ensure its safe arrival. The picture of their lorry suggests that the last lap of its journey was not without a few nervous moments. Several men standing close to the bridge are seen watching the manoeuvre most intently. Compared with today's substantial industrial estate, the scene that confronted Taylor's driver was one of a considerable open space and rough ground. Paper & Publications, recipient of the Goss, were in the nature of pioneers in this part of Banbury. Their operation to receive the new machinery involved a great deal of hand excavation.

Once installed, the Goss units became the workhorse of the time. This was certainly the view of Les Chappell who acted as fourth minder when he first worked on it. Les had been a Stone's man in the widest sense. Apart from being on the payroll he found a place in their soccer team and has happy memories of inter-printer rivalries on the field. Stones v Cheneys was always a key fixture. Les Chappell's move to Paper & Publications did not involve a great distance as the Stone's factory had been on the site where today some of Morrison's shoppers hurry across the superstore car park. His new employer's decision to 'go Goss' became closely linked to another Banbury area development in the printing and publishing business.

An edition of the *Banbury Guardian* in 1964 was used by newspaper magnate Woodrow Wyatt as an opportunity to introduce colour to its pages. At about the same time, the *Birmingham Planet*, an ephemeral tabloid of the Wyatt empire also signalled its departure from presenting its material exclusively in black and white. Over a period of nearly 20 years Woodrow Wyatt developed Paper & Publications into WW Web Offset and there were many occasions when the presses and especially the Goss contributed to the fame and fortune of his business. The bubble of success sustained itself until September of 1982. On the third of that month, Maurice Weaver, industrial columnist for the *Daily Telegraph*, headlined his shock article '120 jobs lost as NGA rejects pay cuts to save printing works'. The message to the readers of that paper was that a single union, representing a minority of employees, has rejected a rescue formula that included pay cut proposals.

During the time of the rise and fall of this Tramway [Road] company Carl Yates, who is currently boss of Cherwell Valley Litho, had roles as machine manager and later works manager. When the end of the line was reached he was anxious to see what could be salvaged from the structure that had been created with the print needs of the *Banbury Guardian* as a solid core. With separate editions for Banbury, Chipping Norton and South Northants there had been print runs of some 14,000 to 15,000 copies in the 1960s.

In 2002 links with the *Guardian* are a matter of past history. The arrival of the Goss meant a journey into the world of colour. Now with the machine's departure full colour productions have come to the fore. The talk is about property presentations, industrial tabloids like *UK Coal Scene* and *Transco News*, in-house police news such as *Nene Beat* and football publicity specials, in particular West Bromwich Albion's news and views entitled simply *The Baggies*. Amongst the most interesting printing forays has been that into the business of party political fliers and news sheets. Recent Liberal Party attempts to win in marginal seats like Romsey have brought substantial work to Cherwell Litho.

Two weeks separated the closure of Wyatt's company and the formation of this new firm. At one time Woodrow Wyatt had been ahead of his age in the printing and publication of these newspaper. Today as the old Goss unit heads for an extended life in Uzbekistan, new generation presses are creating tomorrow's history. Carl, Les and their colleagues aim to be at the forefront of a demand which is all about long runs, glossy presentations and publications which bring readers closer to the action, be it law and order, political dominance or Premiership glory.

Banbury Guardian 24 October 2002.

1.37: Get on board the double-deckers.

Saturday, June 30, was a day for lovers of all matters nostalgic. Shoppers in Banbury's Market Place could not have failed to catch a glimpse of one of the many superb hobby horses. Morris teams were in close attendance and so the familiar sound of accordion music came floating on the air. Later that same day another bit of local history was enacted. This time I suspect comparatively few people were aware of what was happening.

The departure of Stagecoach 510 service to Farnborough at 3.50 would scarcely have raised the eyebrows of passengers waiting for buses on other routes. As Barry Anderson turned left out of the station he was commencing the final run of PUK 627R. Leyland Nationals, like the one which returned to the garage for the last time, were first introduced into north Oxfordshire 25 years ago. They were a joint development between Leylands and the National Bus Company and became the standard vehicle type for fleets owned by NBC. The first five of these, fleet numbers 502 to 506, were used to inaugurate a new pattern of town services. At the same time they replaced the double-deckers which had been a familiar sight in Banbury since the early 1960s.

The Birmingham and Midland Motor Omnibus Company (the Midland Red) had their own construction works at Bearwood. In 1976 the last two of these D9 vehicles were withdrawn and Banburians had to retune to the whine of a Leyland engine. When these engines had to be replaced, residents of the bus route areas had to adjust to more of a growl than a whine after DAF became the name printed on the working parts. This happened in about 1988.

Coinciding with the arrival of Leyland Nationals there was a major reorganisation of both Midland Red and Oxford South Midland bus services in the Banbury area. Included in this revision was a brand new route from Coventry's Pool Meadow bus

The early days of bus services in Banbury – a bus owned by an unknown operator waits to leave North Bar. The card was posted in 1930.

Hall and Bridge Street, Banbury.

Another of the first buses to operate in Banbury calls at the Town Hall, amidst varied horse-drawn traffic.

station to Oxford. It was called X59 and replaced certain journeys along a line from Claydon through Banbury and Deddington and on to Oxford. A new inter town service of that time was numbered 510 and linked Banbury with Leamngton Spa. The final journey of PUK 627R on the last day of June was clearly a residual of a once longer route.

Banbury had been connected with Chipping Norton since Midland Red services first began in the 1920s, when a boneshaker ran from Hunt Edmund's *Leathern Bottle* to the Cotswold gateway town. In 1976 the revision of services locally incorporated the realisation that villages were being drawn within town catchments. Accordingly Swerford was re-orientated towards Chipping Norton, but Milcombe was offered an hourly bus to Banbury. Our town was sending out its suburban tentacles and a relatively new feature on the local plan was a Poets' Corner routing of services 487 and 488 which reflected this and travelled by way of roads including one commemorating the name of Robert Browning.

Sadly the word 'withdraw' was built into the pattern of change. Williamscot, Upper Wardngton, Wardington and Chipping Warden quietly slipped out of the published timetables and buses were to pass from the view of those who had previously waited at Charlton's *The Bell*, Evenley turn and Shalstone village. As it was, service 495 operated on Tuesdays only. More locally in Banbury itself, the planners' term was rationalisation, a process which affected B3, B5 and B18. One of the most popular services was usually operated with a Leyland National. The last bus on the B5 circular route on a Sunday was the 22.45 from the bus station, a service which must have raised eyebrows considerably when timetable planners came to examine passenger returns. After West Bar, the service more closely resembled a London underground train in the rush hour. Many of the Trades and Labour Club's regulars happened to live on the Bretch Hill Estate and the 22.45 was a public service lifeline. Invariably driver Eddie Turvey was at the wheel and it was not unusual in those days for the bus to go twice round Queensway roundabout before some 40 stops ensured that for all on board the journey was door to door.

Banbury Guardian 12 July 2001.

1.38: Fun on the buses with Sumners

On August 13, 1988, a Sumner bus left Castle Street Bus Station for the very last time. The 5.30pm service for Hanwell Turn, Horley and Hornton was driven by Roger Sumner and had two passengers. They were Glenny Griffiths and Avis Turner. The occasion was very much the end of an era that had begun just before the First World War when John William Sumner used a horse and four-wheeled covered van to provide a link between Hornton and Banbury. This carrier's cart service was listed in Cheney's Railway Guide for 1923 which indicated that the terminus of his Thursday and Saturday journeys was the *Bear* at the eastern end of the Market Place. At the same time a carrier called Grimston was based at the *Flying Horse* and Gilks could be found at the *Plough*. These men were part of a long tradition amongst carriers from Hornton. Back in 1832 Verney went to the *Hare & Hounds* in Parsons Street whilst Gilks visited the *Flying Horse* at the top of the same street.

In 1912 John William Sumner, the founder of the business, who was originally from Marston St Lawrence, married Edith at the Railway Terrace Methodist Church in Rugby and the couple made their home in Horley. John established a weekly routine of collecting orders, doing the necessary shopping and generally ensuring that people got what they wanted. In round about 1926 John decided to invest in a Ford motor which was then given the necessary coachwork to convert it to a bus. This work was entrusted to Simons of Bridge Street. By upgrading his service John was able to serve more village people. He recorded orders in a black book and was even prepared to purchase a pair of shoes provided the size was specified. The 1926 bus had its drawbacks however. Notably there were the unyielding wooden seats and the fact that at every hill on the road passengers had to get off and walk alongside the vehicle.

Avis Turner has many happy memories of the journeys to Banbury. As a youngster it got her to Dashwood Road School. In her post school years when Avis worked for Spencers in Britannia Road the Sumner bus was again a lifeline. Occasionally, if there had been delays on the road, John Sumner would take her and other Spencer workers to the factory gates in Britannia Road. Throughout her years of using a Sumner's bus, Avis valued the time spent aboard because of the friendships that developed. As she said to me 'We had a good few laughs'.

During the 1950s the *Banbury Guardian* produced combined rail and bus timetables in the form of handy booklets. Table 76 gives an insight into the scale of the Sumner operation. Their schedule began with a 7.30am school run which terminated in Broad Street, Banbury, and ended with a late afternoon return service to Hornton. In between the availability of a bus depended on the day of the week. Thursday being market day there was a great demand, which the company was anxious to meet. On Saturday the two buses in each direction were timed to allow about two hours for morning and afternoon shopping. Apart from the timetabled services, a bus used to run to Banbury every Friday evening so that people from the villages could enjoy the silver screen presentations at the *Regal* in Horse Fair, the ABC *Palace* in the Market Place or the *Grand* in Broad Street.

When John retired the business was taken over by his son Vincent who came back from the 1939 war with renewed vigour and determination to expand the company's activities. This he achieved and extra members of staff were taken on. The firm became known as J W Sumner & Son. The post war period saw the evolution of school-related services as education for many children meant getting to Banbury. On Vincent's sad and early death in 1974 Roger took over and worked alongside Helen, Vincent's wife, so that the Sumner tradition could be maintained.

Banbury Guardian 19 September 2002.

1.39: Nesbitts of Banbury, removals

At a time when we are being exhorted to patronise locally-owned shops it is good to recall a family firm whose lorries were a familiar sight during much of the late 1950s and 1960s. Nesbitts of Banbury was synonymous with removals and the transportation of heavy goods. Ernest Nesbitt, who came to north Oxfordshire from Sunderland and was based at RAF Bicester, started the business. He acquired a lorry and worked for himself but as demand for transport services grew so a fleet of vehicles was needed and there was work for sons Ron, John and Tony Nesbitt as well. The impact of Nesbitts upon the Banbury area was much wider than I have indicated so far. Demands from the London Brick Company took Nesbitts' lorries to the Midlands and North while involvement with Cherry Orchard Brick Company brought about a link with the Kenilworth area. Nearer the town, Banbury Buildings in Fenny Compton required transport for their concrete garages and Lampreys and Watts, which was a leading corn merchant's, also made use of their services. Holiday times especially found Nesbitts on the road to and on behalf of the Hunt Edmunds and Hook Norton breweries.

The period when Nesbitts were operational will be forever associated with that phenomenon of town history, the two phases of overspill population movement. In the 1950s Banbury Borough Council entered into an agreement with London County Council. As a result families from the capital found themselves having to adjust to the measured pace of a Midlands market town. Bretch Hill became home to most of them. Almost ten years later West Midlanders were heading in our direction as more than 600 of the Alfred Bird workforce were persuaded to relocate from Deritend, Birmingham.

Both phases had many consequences, one of which was the need for removal services. Nesbitts was at the heart of that activity but found that in the 1960s an important internal change was the decline of Banbury's Victorian industrial district, namely the Cherwell area. Here, terraces of houses along the likes of Windsor Street were deemed fit only for demolition. Many of the residents were reluctant to leave but owed much to firms like Nesbitts who conveyed their furnishings and other effects to the Bretch Hill area to start a new life….

Movement of people in the mid to late sixties was further diversified by the arrival of Americans from France. Their destinations were the air bases at Croughton and Heyford but some became residents in private houses. Removal vans entered their lives and often the firm they used bore the name of Nesbitts who got accustomed to a pattern of work that involved container storage with subsequent unloading and ultimately transportation to the new homes. Ironically the earlier sixties were characterised by a weather episode that briefly impacted on the company schedules. The harsh winter of 1962/63 brought about an urgent need for fuel. Pre-packed coal in the shape of King Kole Cobbles was moved from Warwick and Water Orton.

The name 'Nesbitts' is now part of Banbury's yesterdays but I hope this article has revived memories of the part the company played during a decade which changed the town for ever.

Banbury Guardian 16 December 2010

1.40: Station's refreshment facilities, 1905

…The year 1905 marks a [significant] stage in Banbury's railway history. This town had become pivotally placed within an extensive network of lines. It is therefore not surprising that information about rail connections was locally and readily accessible within the pages of Cheney's railway guides. These continued to be available until 1923 when a disastrous fire at the firm's printing works in Calthorpe Street, Banbury ended its publication run.

Perusal of the guides reveals that travellers to London had no fewer than four routes including the so-called 'new route' – an express corridor via Bicester and Princes Risborough. The alternatives were the Great Western line by way of Oxford, the Great Central via Woodford Halse (GCR) and the London & North Western route into Euston. Only the GCR had no Sunday services. In addition Banbury had connections into East Gloucestershire along the Cheltenham line. There have been many milestones in the history of Banbury Great Western Railway station. Today's article focusses on one of these in particular, namely the provision of a refreshment room facility. The year was 1905 and the formal inauguration of it merited an especially long report in the *Banbury Guardian* for June 8.

The main thrust of the column was an attempt to identify the benefits that were expected to accrue from the development. Unsurprisingly the occasion merited a lunch reception which was held in the room designed for first class travellers. The guest list at the event included a strong civic representation headed by the Mayor Alderman Walkley and the Town Clerk Oliver J Stockton. As befitted his interpretation of editorship *Banbury Guardian's* William Potts made sure he was also present. The host was Mr S D Buott, chief of the Great Western company's refreshment department.

The new block at the station was designed to cater for the widest possible demand. In addition to separate provision for third as well as first class passengers there was also a private dining room. Support facilities included a kitchen and a capacious cellar. At the same time local builder W J Bloxham was asked to construct a station master's office and a book stall. The involvement of his company can be explained by previous experience of work for the GWR at Newport, Monmouthshire where he was responsible for the whole station when it opened in 1878.

At the conclusion of the lunch there were numerous speeches both from company officials and the Banbury-based guests. An especially interesting comment came from the Divisional Superintendent Mr J Murphy who remarked that in his recollection Banbury was now spoken about in terms different to those when it was judged 'a roadside place'. Mr Murphy saw the refreshment facility as part of growing involvement locally of the Great Western Railway. The outcome for Banbury was likely to be that the town's residential population would grow substantially and, even more than this, the town would acquire a sought after identity. At its most basic role the refreshment service would benefit travellers with time to spare before forward jouneys but not sufficient time to venture into the heart of the town.

In turn each of the principal guests had his say. The mayor was keen to attract business people who might add to the trade of the town especially when in addition

The GWR station at Banbury in 1935. The refreshment room opened in 1905 is behind the sign identifying Platform No 2.

the line to London via Bicester was opened. Both Alderman Walkley and William Potts saw Mr Murphy as a 'prophet of good for Banbury'. The expectation was that further rail-related growth at Banbury might come from the transfer of work from Oxford especially in the context of the town as an engine depot hub.

Banbury Guardian 6 December 2012.

1.41: Banbury – Ten years of the M40

In the ten years which have elapsed since the opening of the Banbury section of the M40 motorway, north Oxfordshire's rural retreat and market town has been converted into a modern staging post between London and Birmingham. This part of the British motorway network is the latest in a series of transport revolutions which have impacted significantly on the town.

Banbury was 'Mecca' for the village carriers and a key midway point for coaches rumbling along between the Midlands and South East England during the eighteenth and nineteenth centuries. The town secured access to cheap coal with the arrival in 1778 of the Oxford Canal but boat traffic gradually dwindled as the railway companies captured traffic from 1850 onwards.

Early in the life of the Banbury motorway corridor, the Cherwell M40 Investment Partnership was launched. The success achieved by this 1992 initiative can be gauged from the words of William Raynor printed in the *Independent* five years later. He noted that Banbury had changed from a market town 'into a magnet for distribution and high-tech firms'. A year after his article the town ceased to be the 'Stockyard of Europe' but strengthened vital links with motorsports. Unsurprisingly Banbury was no longer the South East's key unemployment black spot.

There is little doubt that the motorway has made it possible for more people to

So vibrant was trade in Banbury in the early twentieth century that some retailers, such as Robins Bros, ironmongers of Market Place, extended their displays on to the pavements and roads outside their shops.

access retail businesses in the town. The arrival of Debenham's store as well as the revival of the name of Woolworths within the Castle Quay shopping mall has taken Banbury into a new era of regionalism beyond Banburyshire. During the past ten years our town has been targeted for new homes, mainly in response to central government planning. For some farmers the final phase of the rotation has become an estate of houses often snapped up by people from outside Oxfordshire who have weighed up the economic and social advantages of the motorway.

Something Gate appears to be here to stay as the memory dims of the day when Michael Stevens, shepherd, herded his flock of sheep across an embryo surface destined for juggernauts. Back in 1989, Cllr David Cowan (Wimpy Bar manager) spoke about a small town steeped in history. The medieval street pattern is there and in part enhanced by a scheme of pedestrianisation which has incorporated eye-pleasing street furniture. Together with the tradition of cockhorse, cross and cakes there will be attraction for ever more visitors and this in spite of the fact that the location of a motorway services station at Ardley has dulled Banbury's image as the classic tea and wee stop.

Banbury Guardian 11 January 2001.

2. Localities

2.01: Grime and grind: Calthorpe Street

Castle Street North, Cherwell Terrace, Cross Cherwell Street and Globe Yard are residential locations that have disappeared from the road layout of Banbury. Back in the 1950s, James and Caroline Tobin occupied 8 Globe Yard, which was reached from Castle Street. There were three cottages here and at the top of the yard was a corrugated iron building which was the Toc H headquarters. In July 1957 the Tobins, both aged 82, celebrated their diamond wedding. They were married at St Mary's Church in 1897 (the year of Queen Victoria's Diamond Jubilee) just one month after a congregation of nearly 2,000 people had attended a service of dedication of the clock, chimes and bells. Canon C F Porter conducted the marriage and it is interesting to speculate on how aware he was of the severity of James' early upbringing. James Tobin was born in 1875 into a family who occupied a house in the yard of the *Catherine Wheel*, Bridge Street. The inn itself had existed since the 18th century when it was important in the coaching business.

James Tobin's earliest memories were very much linked to the basic necessities of life. They were about having porridge in Cheney's Yard and maintaining a tidy appearance in adequately warm clothing. His first school was Roman Catholic and this had the benefit that the nuns bought shoes for the children and he was one of those to benefit. James finished his education at the age of 14 and started his working days as a rope spinner near the Southam Road. There had been a rope works there since the mid-1830s when Jack Wall … founded the business. Mr Tobin's first wage was 2s 6d per week but when he was forced to rely on whatever work was available in the town, James received 1s 9d a day for helping to clear brooks and 2s 8d a day for holding horses. He later spent two years in the employment of the Great Western Railway Company. Perhaps his greatest excitement was to be at the station when Queen Victoria passed through on her way to London [or Windsor]. He actually flagged her train away.

James's bride, Caroline Brock, came from an Upper Heyford family and she had worked for a time at the *Globe* in Calthorpe Street. This would have been when John and Sarah Brain looked after the alehouse; he from 1885 to 1897 and she after his death from 1897 to 1900. After the birth of their eldest son, the Tobins moved from Calthorpe Street itself into Globe Yard. Here the rent level made it possible to effect a saving of 9d a week, sufficient to pay for bread to help feed their growing family.

However, it was not long before the spectre of unemployment loomed again. This time James did manage to find some work at the Green Lane brickworks. Here pushing wheelbarrow loads of bricks earned him a daily wage in marked contrast to fellow workers who were on piece rate terms. The work was physically very hard and often raised blood blisters all over his hands. Unsurprisingly one day James told the gaffer he was walking out on the job. Subsequently he joined Samuelson's Ironworks where he was employed for seven years on a 6am to 5.30pm working day but with not so much as a tea break. Banbury Corporation (for 39 years) and Hunt Edmunds for just a short period had him on their payrolls. His borough days were spent under no less than three surveyors, Messrs Dawson, Wrigley and Hilton.

The 1914 war had been a major interruption to his working life. Like many others he became a volunteer in the Oxfordshire & Buckinghamshire Light Infantry, which was under the direction of Lord North of Wroxton.

After the war James developed an interest in allotments, initially to supplement food but later for recreation. As he observed in 1957, his life had been very difficult at times which meant that any pleasures were real pleasures, for instance the taste of cheese at a penny for a quarter of a pound.

In July 1957 when James and Caroline celebrated 60 years of marriage, the nearby Toc H hut provided a very convenient location for a family get-together. Some six years later and Nos 8, 9 and 10 Globe Yard were just a memory. Ethel Usher of the Winter Gardens acquired the cottages so that she could expand her growing enterprise over the space that the demolition of the cottages created.

Banbury Guardian 25 September 2003.

- For the Tobin family of Calthorpe Street see B Trinder, 'Banbury's Victorian Lodging Houses', *C&CH* vol 16 (2004), 145-46.
- William North, 11th Baron North (1836-1932).

2.02: Castle Street in the 1940s & 50s

From time to time I receive letters from former Banbury residents who have interesting stories about their earlier years and where they lived. A recent example concerns Patricia Gibbs (née Mitchell) who is today in Sharnford near Hinckley in Leicestershire. Pat has sent me her recollections of Castle Street East during the 1940s and 50s following moves from Duke Street in Grimsbury – where she was born and later from Middle Barton. At the tender age of two, her family decided to return to Banbury and occupy part of 41 Castle Street East where her grandmother Lily Marshall was already a resident.

The new home was a terraced house fronted by railings with a cellar, front room and living room characterised by a black-leaded grate and oven. Stairs led to two first-floor bedrooms and there was also an attic room. Each of the bedrooms had a fireplace. On the ground floor there was a scullery with a sink, a brick boiler and a gas cooker. A rear door led to a yard with outside toilet and small garden area. Opposite this back door and supported by a hook was a tin bath with which she became familiar on a weekly basis. This part of Banbury had the great advantage of being close to the town centre. The rear gate provided a quick way of reaching Castle Street West, close to Hogben's watch and clock shop and the jitty… to Cornhill near the *Vine* public house and the St John Ambulance Hall.

A year on from coming to live with her grandmother, Pat began her school days at St Mary's School on Southam Road. The best route from the house to school was by way of Black Ditch and across a footbridge. To the right of the ditch were allotments where it was not uncommon to find pigs in huts. Further on and the marshes were reached, fields adjacent to river and canal. Periodically floodwaters were encountered and Pat and her friends enjoyed the opportunity to paddle. The reception class at St Mary's had both girls and boys who were required to have a nap every afternoon. Rush mats provided an appropriate surface for this. St Mary's was typical of the time in having an external toilet block and huts for school meals.

… Banbury was something of a safe haven during the Second World War. However, one of Pat's most vivid early memories is of German bombers flying so low that she could see the pilots and spot the swastika emblems. Realising that a raid was imminent, her mother pushed Pat under the dining room table. This was a testing time for the family as father was in the Merchant Navy.

One positive advantage of Castle Street East in the early 1940s was the large number of children. Typical girls' games were hopscotch, skipping, hide and seek, various ball games and activities that made use of cardboard milk bottle tops. In place of bicycles and scooters there were carts made out of old pram wheels and wood. November 5 was very special; a guy would be made and displayed to raise money for fireworks. As for a bonfire the site was the middle of the entrance to Alcock's builder's yard. Here and with the fireworks display over, fire embers were good enough to bake potatoes. Under the austere condition of rationing great use was made of local shops, especially Killpack's bakery at the end of Castle Street, and Adkins' grocery shop opposite Alcock's entrance. How right Pat is when she says 'It was not a materialistic society then as everyone struggled to make ends meet'. Even in the

Early nineteenth century houses in Castle Street West near the junction with Southam Road, awaiting demolition in 1962.

early 1950s large families meant sharing the good things such as Rocky Leach's sweets.

Looking back on her time in Banbury, Pat remembers the Castle Street area as offering a very friendly environment where no-one locked doors day or night. The spirit of the age was also evident in the application of skills learnt from parents or teachers. With stone floors in the houses, which might be covered with linoleum, a common pursuit in Castle Street was the making of peg rugs. These made use of old clothes that were worked into a hessian backing with a hook.

Pat Gibbs has strong recollections of the street parties, which marked the end of the war and celebrated the Coronation of our present queen. In 1945 Castle Street itself was the focus of activity. Trestle tables groaned under quantities of food and in the evening there was dancing to sound provided by Mr Buzzard of Parsons Street. The second of the street parties was held in Compton Street and a fancy dress competition and races for all age groups also marked the occasion.

After her early education at St Mary's School, Pat was successful in securing a place at Banbury Grammar. Sport featured strongly in her life there especially hockey. As a result of this involvement she had the opportunity to meet girls from elsewhere in the county. Hockey notes for the January 1957 edition of the *Banburian* magazine includes the following account of an away game at Milham Ford, Oxford: 'the forwards were playing much better and Pat Mitchell shot a lovely goal in the second half'.

Down the years memories of Banbury and especially Castle Street have remained clear. As Pat says in her letter to me: 'It is gratifying to know that some friendships formed earlier are still in my life today'....

Banbury Guardian 29 October 2009.

2.03: Starvation or the workhouse

It is always good to hear from people happy to reminisce about their days in Banbury. One such person is Audrey Dagger who has written me a long letter containing fascinating memories of the town in the 1920s and 1930s. She had an especially interesting childhood because of years spent within the Warwick Road workhouse where her parents Henry and Emily Peet were master and matron. His background was a military one whereas she had been matron of a services hospital at Tredegar in South Wales. Undoubtedly their combined experiences would have been more than useful when it came to running a small workhouse at Brecon.

In 1922 Henry and Emily moved to Banbury in order to take over responsibility for the larger local institution. Although there were inevitable constraints their efforts were directed towards making the place less formal and with fewer rules governing those who for one reason or another found that this was the only way of life open to them. Their style of management must have met with the approval of the board of guardians, a group of local people elected by the parishes in the union – originally 50 parishes crossing county boundaries.

At the time the Peets moved to Banbury the ultimate control was with [the] Local Government Board which became the Ministry of Health in 1919. Someone within that group who made an impression on Audrey was a Mr Bonham who lived in Cropredy and who used a pony and trap in order to reach the workhouse. Some of the residents were elderly and disabled and so unable to look after themselves. From 1870 the workhouse had an infirmary, which in the Peets' time was said to be one of the best buildings of its kind to be found attached to any institution of the size of that of Banbury. There was also a proportion of unmarried girls with their babies. Older children had their own home at Horley where they lived under the care of foster parents. Sadly room also had to be found for young ex-servicemen without jobs in post-First World War Banbury. Tasks were found for them both in the house and around the grounds and clearly this was a boon.

The young of the town also experienced difficulty in finding paid employment. For some of them the alternatives were stark: starvation or the workhouse. A fascinating episode that has embedded itself in Audrey's memory is the arrival of the Jarrow marchers who used workhouses as stopping points along the way to London, where they helped [hoped?] to influence government thinking about the plight of Tyneside shipyard workers. Audrey and her sister washed and bandaged the marchers' feet and then ensured that they were able to have a comfortable overnight stay. Tolerance and compassion were lessons learned from this experience.

Audrey's teenage years brought a whole run of new opportunities. There were dances at the Town Hall with the Ken Prewer Band and encounters here with service personnel from local army and RAF training centres made evenings great fun for girls like Audrey. The social scene widened to include places to be seen such as Brown's Cake Shop and Wincott's South Bar café. An equally vivid memory was of the Broad Street fish and chip shop opposite the *Grand* cinema. Here Charlie Charles, as he was known, cooked in a huge brick-built fryer. The fish and chips bubbled in an intriguing way, which doubtless today would be deemed unsafe and a health and safety hazard.

The workhouse in Warwick Road, Banbury. The oldest parts of the complex were built in the 1830s but this building is of later date.

Family life also changed in 1938 when the Peet family moved out of the workhouse (or Public Assistance Institution as it was renamed) to 4 Dashwood Terrace, a large and imposing residential block dating from Edwardian days. Henry and Emily remained there until their deaths in 1970 and 1971....

Banbury Guardian 28 October 2006.

2.04: Behind the bar with Nellie: the *Barley Mow*

In her study of the *Licensees of the Inns, Taverns and Beerhouses of Banbury*, Vera Wood begins consideration of the *Barley Mow* with a quote from some deeds housed in Oxfordshire Archives. These date back to January 1831 when William Bolton (1831-44) looked after 'All that newly erected storehouses, cottages and outbuildings'. By the time the Howe family gained possession in 1911, the location of this public house close to the junction of the Warwick and Stratford roads combined with a setting made more rural by its isolation from Banbury may well explain the beerhouse's popularity.

William Howe (1911-1920) appreciated all this, but in the wider context of an enhanced business opportunity, he established a dairy and drew upon milk supplies from many surrounding farms. His eight floats served several villages as well as Banbury. Upon William's death in 1920 his widow Ellen succeeded to the licence. She did so at a time when motoring beyond the built-up area was gaining in popularity and Banbury's importance as a market town was attracting draymen whose journey into the centre could be conveniently broken at 'watering holes' like the *Barley Mow*. Apart from other members of the family it is doubtful if many people realised the extent of Ellen's involvement in the activities of Banbury and district. During the First World War she was responsible for a milk round at a time when her husband William was indisposed while simultaneously helping at the restaurant for soldiers set up at Banbury's GWR station. Ellen's ability to run the *Barley Mow* was greatly enhanced by previous experience of bar work … both at the *Reindeer* (Parsons Street) and the *Coach & Horses* (Butcher Row).

Nellie Howe pulls a pint at the *Barley Mow*.

The *Barley Mow* inn near the junction of the roads from Banbury to Stratford and Warwick, probably in the 1920s.

With such a background it is unsurprising that she became a life-long member of the Banbury Licensed Victuallers' Association and for many years chaired the ladies' section. As if to maintain a link with the nearby village of Drayton, she also belonged to the Mothers' Union. During the years of Ellen's tenancy at the *Barley Mow*, Banbury's medical services depended greatly on a Workpeoples' Association which in turn relied on the sort of voluntary support she was able to offer to the Horton Hospital. In this instance much stemmed from her participation in an organised group known as the 'original barrel organ party'.

Most patrons of the Warwick Road public house regarded it as an alehouse but at some point it was inevitable that the question of alcoholic drinks other than beer was bound to arise. The nearest inns, the *Duke of Wellington*, the *Roebuck* (Drayton) and the *Hare & Hounds* (Warmington) – all Hunt Edmunds tied houses – were sufficiently far away to justify making provision for the sale of wine. Ellen's application of January 1928 was heard at the General Annual Licensing meeting held in the Neithrop police station [Newland]. A copy of her application was sent to the brewers Hunt Edmunds and prompted a letter from them to the effect that they would be willing to continue the sum of £9 10s 0d towards the beer licence…

Ellen died in 1951 and her daughter Nellie took over and remained licensee until the 'old' *Barley Mow* was closed and demolished in 1981. In her time the pub retained its original features of a snug, a main bar and a long room suitable for games. It was this layout combined with the atmosphere of a local that attracted lots of regulars, especially Alcan workers. Some patrons like Mr Lambert in the 1960s and 1970s brought their dogs and even did cellar work as well as garden maintenance. The beer was always in good condition and the large gardens colourful and well laid-out. As for Nellie herself, she ran a tight ship. Swearing was not tolerated and indeed any slip meant that money (for the Horton) had to be put in a special bottle. She never went away, the *Barley Mow* was her life. Unlike places like Grimsbury's *Prince of Wales* there were no Saturday night singalongs. However Christmas night was an exception.

The *Barley Mow* was very much a home to pub games especially darts and dominoes both played competitively within leagues such as Top of the Hill. A typical *Advertiser* report of 1956 was headed 'The Cup stays at home'. The award to the winning *Barley Mow* dominoes team was of the Ellen Howe Memorial Cup. They topped the Top of the Hill, a league many said would not be a success. Those people were wrong and no one could have been more delighted than Nellie.

As the original buildings came down in 1981 many memories must have died with them, even simple little habits like digging into your pockets for kitty money if you lost at darts. No wonder even a few police spent some time here on Nellie's last night. They knew it was to be an occasion never to be equalled. I'll bet that last pint tasted good.

Banbury Guardian 29 June 2006.

2.05: St Paul's Church

The *Banbury Guardian* issue for February 10, 1853 contains a main feature about the consecration of St Paul's Church. In it the building is described as 'plain but picturesque and an interesting object on entering Neithrop'. It was also a tribute to the zealous efforts of the Rev William Wilson, vicar of Banbury, that some of the more pressing needs of the area were met. Wilson was a courageous and determined cleric who addressed the most radical problem of the day, namely how to make worship available to the poor people, some of whom had turned for support to nonconformist chapels.

The labouring class accounted for close on 5,000 out of a total Banbury population of some 9,000 and formed a significant proportion of the residents of Neithrop, Banbury's westernmost suburb. In the days when a pew in the parish church had to be bought or rented, these people had been penalised by a lack of free seats in St Mary's.

In 1852 a plot of land for a church became available - Armitt's Garden near the Wroxton Road (now the Warwick Road). Keen observers of progress on the building were able to admire the design skills of Benjamin Ferrey from London and the practical interpretation of the grand plan by those who worked for Richard Claridge, a Banbury builder. Construction costs in the mid-19th century amounted to little short of £1,000. Even allowing for financial inputs by the Diocesan Building Society and the Incorporated Society for Promoting the Enlargement of Churches and Chapels, it was still necessary to raise £500 from private sources. A clear incentive was a fairly certain deadline date for completion of December 1.

The Rev Wilson's ambition of achieving a Chapel of Ease in Neithrop was a step nearer fulfilment when the foundation stone was laid by the Misses Wyatt of the Green in Banbury. On the stroke of three o'clock with the weather fine, their actions were keenly witnessed by 'a great many ladies and gentlemen assembled on the spot'. Appropriately their number was swollen by a considerable gathering of the poor of the area, as well as by children from Mr Cooke's academy, and several National Schools across Banbury.

The vicar then said a few wise words. He noted that within about 300 yards of the position of the stone there was a population of 1,700. All bar 200 of these folk were urban poor and had lost touch with the teachings of the church. His vision for St Paul's was that those responsible for services would endeavour to rectify the situation. At this junction he could not resist referring to the folly of pulling down the old St Mary's. As to ensure that no such act was repeated in Neithrop, the Rev Wilson made clear his intention to secure the building of a house close to the church so that a resident curate could work more effectively in the thickly populated district.

The weather on consecration day was far less favourable than on that previous occasion. However, despite this, support for the ceremony was again massive and included many Banbury tradesmen who were the leading civic figures of the day. The service was led by the Bishop of Oxford and so many people wanted to take communion that it was 4pm before anyone sat down to the lunch which had been provided by the vicar. The poor and the young were not forgotten. Two hours after

The church of St Paul, Neithrop, designed by Benjamin Ferrey and consecrated in 1853.

the meal, tea and meats were made more widely available and indeed meat was conveyed to many labourers of the area. The cost of this was met by Mr Webb of Wykham Park.

In 1853 St Paul's was at the heart of its district. More than 100 years later in the 1960s, first the Rev R P R Carpenter, who was vicar of St Mary's, and then the Rev David Evans, priest-in-charge of St Paul's, realised that the Warwick Road church had become fringe to a Neithrop where new estate growth was a response to the needs of overspill population. The former had discussions with the town clerk about the desirability of a worship centre near *Gould's Villa*. The latter had the pleasure of being part of the opening of St Paul's Church House on November 12, 1966. As well as Tuesday worship, the centre became home to a big Sunday school, a pre-school play group, and under-15s club and an infant welfare centre. David Evans had come to Banbury in 1964 and already made his mark because he helped Birds' Brummies to settle into the local community. On Sundays he ferried many of them to St Paul's Church.

This time of expansion was also characterised by social events that reached out into the community. Memories abound of garden fetes at Miss Barlow's in Broughton Road. These raised funds and generated family fun as did Christmas bazaars in St Paul's hall that featured performances by singers such as Peggy Gilbert's Beargarden Children's Concert Party.

The new millennium saw St Paul's becoming a parish church at the centre of its own parish. 2003 is another milestone in the history of an Anglican presence in Neithrop. On the long road to the anniversary it is good to recall that St Paul's has always been at the cutting edge of attempts to achieve social change and community integration.

Banbury Guardian 6 February 2003.

2.06: Neithrop Wesleyan Mission

[Neithrop] … township had a reputation for being a very rough area. William Wilson, who was vicar at St Mary's Church, reckoned that out of a total population of 1,700 in 1851, 1,500 were poor. A Board of Health Inspector painted a grim picture of life when he remarked that sanitary conditions, drunkenness and immorality were all much worse in Neithrop than in Banbury. It was against this background that Methodism first took root in the township in 1886. A Mission Band, which was made up of young people from Marlborough Road [Wesleyan] Methodist Church, organised open-air meetings especially on the Pound, the sloping part of Boxhedge Square. Ironically and appropriately, this space was close to one of the then notorious alehouses, the *Seven Stars* that belonged to the Banbury brewery company Hunt Edmunds. At this time the Boxhedge area of Neithrop was characterised by a patchwork of cottages. One of these provided an ideal base for enlarged gatherings initiated by the Band. These young people attracted ever-growing congregations and soon it became necessary to stagger services.

The man who came to their assistance was none other than William Mewburn of Wykham Park. Back in the 1860s he had orchestrated the move of Wesleyans from Church Lane to Marlborough Road. In 1887 more of his money was used to purchase two cottages along with their gardens. Demolition of these cottages and clearance of their gardens provided a site appropriate for a Mission Hall. On a bitterly cold December 27 of that year, Mr Mewburn laid the first stone and soon after pledged a further £200 towards building costs. Neithrop Methodist Mission Hall opened for services in April 1888. The occasion attracted so much attention that all seats were quickly filled and people had to be turned away. Undoubtedly part of the reason for the Mission Hall's success was that 'men and women would not feel out of place in their working clothes'. This may have been a factor in the raising of money by donation to cover outstanding debts at the time of the Hall's first use.

Sunday School activities followed quickly in the wake of the earliest services. In May 1888, there were some 100 scholars together with their 17 teachers. These numbers justified morning and afternoon sessions. As time went on the School developed its own pattern of life. On Boxing Day all participating children were given 'a useful gift of clothing and an orange'. In many cases the former would have been invaluable and the latter a real treat. A treat of a different kind was a summer occasion and happened first in Mr White's field and then later (after 1894) in one of the fields belonging to Josiah Lawrence Walker who was a farmer living at *Golden Villa*. Here children enjoyed tea and games and a brief opportunity to forget the harsh social conditions of the Neithrop Township.

An early deficiency of the Mission Hall was the lack of a font for baptisms. The lady who came to the rescue was the wife of the caretaker Joseph Jackson of nearby Chapel Cottage. She provided the slop basin from her tea service and subsequently this was used for every such occasion until Jubilee Year 1935 when a similar kind of basin was made available from the Chapel's own tea service.

A significant way in which Neithrop Methodists helped the area's poor was by the formation of a clothing club. Under the leadership of Sunday School staff people

The mission hall in Neithrop opened by the Wesleyan Methodists in 1888.

were encouraged to put something aside for vouchers that could be spent at selected shops in Banbury. Above all, an aim of Methodist activity was to try and inculcate a greater degree of sobriety. With the 2003 Banbury Fair in the offing it is interesting to note that a tea used to be organised for the second evening of the Fair in an attempt to divert attention from the brisk trade in the ale houses.....

… The Methodist Archive in Banbury is a highly important collection of documents. Among items relating to Neithrop Chapel is the minute book for the Sunday school that covers the period from 1902 to 1934. … Today it is my intention to select some of the minute book items that reflect life in a part of the town, which was seldom easy.

Unsurprisingly treats for the children figure prominently. The particular highlight of the year was the annual summer festival. This was always held in a field owned by Josiah Lawrence Walker who lived at *Golden Villa*, which today is surrounded by post-war housing developments, and is close to Woodgreen Avenue. The festival, which began at two o'clock, was usually exclusively for the Boxhedge Chapel children but in 1910 scholars and teachers from Adderbury were invited. Sports were held and a special focus of interest would have been Mr Castle's donkey. On the food side buns were always made available. The minutes for 1903 indicate that these were supplied by a Mr Jackson of South Bar and a Mr J Ratley. By 1914 fruit as well as buns were being preferred to lemonade and tea. That year a further sum of 5s 0d was made available for the purchase of cricket bats. Parents and friends were never allowed to come to the field before 6pm and even then they could only gain access on payment of 6d per head. It is interesting to note that the chapel teachers always arranged for a policeman to be on the gate, presumably to ward off gate-crashers.

Christmas was also a time of treats. Nearly always a tree was purchased and in 1903 the children were given a lantern show by the end of which each child had received a bun and an orange. Mr Boxold, a local nurseryman who had a shop in the High Street, provided the fruit, though in 1911 Miss Mold who lived in the Warwick Road also provided a quantity of oranges. By 1908 the gifts were more varied and consisted of a mince pie, a cracker and what was described as 'a useful little article'. Presentation of lantern slides was not confined to the Christmas treats. In 1903 slides from the Bovril Company were used as the basis of entertainment on Banbury Fair Night, October 15. The title of the presentation sounds very patriotic, *British to the Backbone*. Unlike most other occasions there were no refreshments for the children who were expected to attend rather than drift away to the fair. The youngest members of the Neithrop Sunday School appear to have been three or four years old in accordance with prevailing thinking.

Children of all ages inevitably posed some ongoing problems. These were highlighted at the meeting of December 13, 1906 when the issues for discussion were maintaining discipline, punctuality and regularity of attendances. The occasional expulsion gets a mention in the minutes and even teachers were sometimes late for classes. In May, 1908, news reached Neithrop of a teachers' preparation class in Banbury and those locally were advised to participate. In anticipation the committee agreed to purchase two copies of a book called *The Sunday School of Today*. It is clear that members of the committee at least were conscious of the chapel's role within an area that for long had been characterised by poverty and deprivation. One response was to support a clothing club but there was a need also to be proactive about rival organisations within the area whose missionary zeal was poaching some of their scholars. In 1903 there was much discussion about some of the Methodist Mission School children attending the Warwick Road Mission School. Mr Baker was authorised to write to a Mr Fox and request them to refrain from attracting these children away from the Boxhedge School.

Perhaps the biggest challenge for the Sunday school came at the time of the First World War. Several teachers enlisted for the army and navy and subsequently at least two lost their lives in the conflict. It says much for the spirit of those who kept activities alive that there was a strength post-war which ensured that by the time the chapel superintendent, Fred Mold, became mayor in 1930 the teachers and children were in good heart to celebrate the 150th anniversary of Robert Raikes who had founded the Sunday School movement way back in 1780.

Banbury Guardian 18 September/9 October 2003.

2.07: 1930s estates changed shape of town

Between the two world wars two new suburbs were added to the town, Ruscote and Easington. In Easington 528 houses were built (361 council) and in Ruscote 487 (160 council). Slum clearance and industrial expansion led to increased activity in Banbury but unlike today it was local firms and not national companies who were responsible for the estates. Some idea of the nature and scale of operations can be gathered from advertisements in the *Banbury Guardian* and *Banbury Advertiser*, but also more particularly an article in the *Advertiser* issue for March 30, 1939. Under the heading 'Private enterprise is filling a great need' the newspaper focussed on the developments helping to answer the call for houses at a time of town expansion.

Probably the most significant reason was the new wave of industrialisation, especially the arrival of the Northern Aluminium Company whose sheet metal business had been growing since its move to the town at the beginning of the 1930s. Housebuilders could also take advantage of the availability of land which was relatively cheaper in the inter-war years with fewer restrictions.

On the Grimsbury side of the town Messrs Wardyard & Co Ltd were developing their Manor Estate north of the 19th century working class housing which extended east of West Street. This land was described by the *Advertiser* as 'the most picturesque and healthy country surroundings' with no mention of environmental opposition to the new estate. Advertisements to entice customers to buy used the seasonal image of the Easter bride. The key slogan was 'make sure of buying the house SHE will be proud of'. With prices from £500 the company laid claim to the finest house value in Banbury so 'Why pay rent?' when a deposit of £25 and repayments of 12/11 per week secured your own house. As for the plots in Grimsbury Manor Estate a £5 reservation fee secured your choice of location. An added attraction was the show house furnished by F Roberts & Sons of 15 Market Place.

Shortly after the appearance of the *Advertiser* article, Messengers, whose base was in Oxford Road, decided to highlight its Orchard Way Estate with a whole page advertisement of the broadsheet issue of April 6, 1939. Central to their claim for attention was a happy couple who state the house they reserved was decorated exactly the way they wanted it. Messenger prices started at £450 with a £20 deposit and 11/2 per week payments. If the location had one key advantage over Grimsbury Manor it was [that] Banbury's topography around Orchard Way ensured they were built on high, dry ground. Buyers were guaranteed a large garden. An estate linked to the housing needs of the aluminium company was Hill View, close to Ruscote Avenue. Like the Orchard Way development the site was deemed 'high and healthy' but accessible by public transport, a 1d bus ride with Midland Red.

Timms & Son, building contractors on Newland Road, Banbury were also heavily committed to a house construction programme on the southern edge of Easington. Their advertisement was also full of quotes from satisfied buyers, 'I've found the home I've been looking for' and 'a house that comes up to expectations'. The Timms advertisement also stressed the size of gardens and convenient bus links to the town. Location may have had something to do with this as the development was bounded by the elegant Oxford Road and the rural attractions of the Salt Way. Interestingly

Grimsbury Square, part of the Grimsbury Manor estate construction of which was suspended in 1939 and resumed in the autumn of 1945.

the company also offered 'a few delightful detached houses with garages at Second Bodicote Turn'.

The 1930s suburbanisation continued the progress away from the core area of the medieval town. Unlike today's extensions into the surrounding country the estates do not seem to have posed a problem for nearby villages with their concern for retaining unique identities.

Banbury Guardian 7 March 2019.

2.08: Tom Pickston's memories of Grimsbury

Thomas Henry Pickston was born in Altrincham in 1909. Soon after he was brought to Banbury and lived for most of his life in Gibbs Road, Grimsbury. He died in 1992 aged 83 but not before he had filled several books with his memories of people, places and events during a boyhood spent in the Grimsbury suburb. Today's article and the following one in this Memory Lane column are a digest of these recollections together with my reflections on his writing.

In recent years many people have commented to me about the remarkable self-sufficiency of this neighbourhood. Mr Pickston confirms this view. In particular he highlights the diversity of trades including shoe repairers, a wood carver, a farrier and milkman (Mr Franklin), four bakers and a fishman (Ossie Brown) who was noted for his hard and soft roes. A Mr Slaymaker of West Street had a more unusual role which was responsibility for the street surfaces. He was expert at wielding a stone hammer. Other people who lived in the West Street/Gibbs Road area had significant jobs outside it. Typical were Mr Robbins, a guard and railway shunter, and Mr Barnes, horseman for Lampreys.

A building which meant a lot to Thomas Pickston was Grimsbury Manor. In the early 1920s the house was in a fine condition with attractive grounds. Fountains sprayed and peacocks strutted. A highlight of the year was a garden fete for St Mary's. Mrs Fortescue organised the event and Canon Jones made a speech, though not before a gun shot or two had silenced the local rooks. In those days the Manor sported a coachman and head gardener who lived in one of the cottages opposite. Behind these was a field called Thomson's Orchard. Here was where Mr Thomas, the North Street baker, kept his horse and looked after the ponies from the big house.

Equally memorable to Mr Pickston was Mr Field's Old Mill House which had gardens tended by a man called Carter who lived in East Street. People from the house went punting on the Cherwell and used boats maintained by Tooleys. The river was in fact quite a resource as at the canal end of Waterworks Lane there were osier beds which supplied materials for making washing, shopping and bakery baskets. One the corner of Manor Road and Daventry Road an old house was occupied by Councillor and Mrs Webb. Though Councillor Webb served only one term of office he appears to have established a successful way of airing issues. Local matters were argued over in the *Prince of Wales* and *Cricketers* pubs helped by a pint or two of beer at 4d or 6d a pint.

Mr Pickston has a lot to say about the use of leisure in Grimsbury, especially on what he calls Stroud's Field (the Moors). Here it seems the formal mixed happily with the informal. Cricket, football and tennis were played but additionally kites were flown. Interestingly most of these kites were the outcome of local enterprise. The frame was developed at the South Street Joinery which also acted as undertakers, whilst appropriate string was purchased from the tent shop [1.20] in the Market Place.

Overall life appears to have been a lot more relaxed in the 1920s than today. Certainly this seems the case regarding domestic livestock with no clauses about noisy fowl. Instead people in West Street used to remove bricks from a boundary wall so hens could peck free range and cockerels fatten for the Christmas dinner table....

The *Prince of Wales* public house at the junction of Centre Street and South Street on the Freehold Land Society estate in Grimsbury.

Thomas Pickston was educated at Grimsbury County School whose bell would be rung by the pupil with the best record of behaviour. Here children from different parts of the suburb mingled – yet those from the Causeway were never considered part of Grimsbury. Indeed if groups from that road or from further north strayed into each other's territory there was inevitably trouble.

After school hours and in the holidays youngsters sought vital pocket money especially to subsidise a 3d seat in the *Grand* Cinema on a Saturday afternoon. The main source of money was errands for parents and other people in the area. ... However the best money spinners were really tiring tasks like lugging gallons of paraffin from Broad Street or tar from the canal-side distillery.

Time came when Thomas and his friends left school and needed employment. Not surprisingly they all wanted to be engine drivers but the railway companies were closed shops unless there was a history of railway work in the family. The next best prospect was mechanical training under Sydney Ewins at £100 for five years or electrical experience under Joe Bustin costing £125 for seven years. Neither was a realistic prospect bearing in mind that the Pickston home in Gibbs Road had been purchased for £250!

Thomas and several of his friends ended up at Stones as trainee French polishers. Work lasted until 5.30 pm Monday to Friday and 8am to noon on Saturday. For this he received nine shillings a week. Later this increased to 12s 6d, but beyond that lay piece work with some jobs poorly paid... In his memoirs Thomas recalls the foreman called Bill Carter. As he says, whimsically, Bill thought more of his pigeons than he did his men. These were shown at fur and feather gatherings held at the *Unicorn* Inn in the Market Place on a Saturday night. The awards he received there were the only cause of happiness to him. Certainly at work Bill was a disciplinarian. Any boys involved in fighting or suspected of cheeking were sent home for three days without pay. ...

In recalling his youth and early working years Thomas Pickston does not neglect to consider life in general in the Grimsbury suburb. What impressed him so much was the extent to which the area had independence of the rest of Banbury...If Grimsbury pubs were lively there was no lack of street activity. Children all played outdoor games and marbles were very popular. In this they were copied by the railwaymen elders who brandished their steelies as these very special marbles were called. Thomas Pickston's books are a wonderful source of local history. .

Banbury Guardian 7/14 March 1996.

2.09: 125 years of St Leonard's

It is 125 years since St Leonard's Church was built on glebe land close to the Middleton Road in Grimsbury. Glebe was land held by an incumbent as part of the benefice or living. Prior to 1846 Grimsbury, despite being in Northamptonshire, was the responsibility of St Mary's Church. Someone from the area was appointed a churchwarden and served on the Parochial Church Council. Interestingly there had never been any attempt to include Grimsbury in the ecclesiastical parish of Warkworth.

In this article my main purpose is to discuss the built-up to the creation of an Anglican place of worship east of the River Cherwell. An excellent source of this material is a book entitled *The Banner of Faith*. In effect this is a bound together collection of monthly magazines issued by the Church Extension Association. Much credit must go to the Rev Graham Jones of Christ Church, South Banbury, who wrote enthusiastically about many activities which can be viewed as the foundations for development and ultimately led to the building of a permanent church. Amongst these was a Grimsbury Working men's Club. No less a person than Bernhard Samuelson, the industrialist, was a Vice President. Other well-known names were Goodway, Bennett, Adkins, Mousir and the Rev P Goldringham. Sadly not all club events had the same impact. A programme consisting of solos, glees, songs, readings and sketches attracted a disappointingly small audience.

Meanwhile Mothers' Meetings were a regular feature of Mondays and appear to have taken root in the *Prince of Wales* on Centre Street, which had a history of community-based activities. Older people appear to have supported what were called cottage lectures. These were popular in Old Grimsbury and Merton Street. When the former venue became unavailable an enthusiastic group leader saw to it that these talks could be accommodated in Cherwell Street (parish of Christ Church). Those who attended were in the main working-class people.

Before the building of the church, services were held in St Leonard's School but this did not diminish the need for a permanent church in Grimsbury. An initial meeting was held on May 27th 1889 and by June the prospect was fast becoming a reality. Cost of the proposed building was in the region of £2,000 and the number of seats was put at around 400. Most of the cost was met by public subscription and by November this had reached £1,260. Contributions came from both Diocesan clergy and people right across Banbury. When St Leonard's finally took shape in 1891 its status was that of a Chapel of Ease linked to Christ Church, South Banbury. From 1921 it was a parish in its own right. It has long outlived both Christ Church (demolished in 1967) and the Victorian schoolroom where the first services were held.

Since the 1970s as Grimsbury has expanded and become more multi-cultural, the church has become a focal point in the area. Recent vicars have worked hard to establish ecumenical links and dialogue with other faiths. Annual events such as summer fetes as well as special occasions such as the opening of the church's New Hall in 1975, the 21st birthday of the Women's Fellowship and above all centenary celebrations in 1991 were attended by young and old, lifelong members of St Leonard's and members of other faiths.

A fete at St Leonard's Church in the 1970s. To the right is the Revd Bob Rhodes,

In *Banbury Cross* (the magazine of the Banbury Team Ministry of which St Leonard's was part) for June 1978, Bob Rhodes dubbed Grimsbury the Cinderella of Banbury. However he also envisaged the area as of great strategic importance built on a foundation of proud village neighbourliness. Today all connected with St Leonard's have not forgotten his wise words. 125 years on from the building of this church local people should not be afraid to blow their own trumpets.
Banbury Guardian 16 June 2016.

2.10: Easington formed in the 1920s

In the edition of April 16, 1925 the *Banbury Guardian* described the emergency [emerging?] Easington estate as 'a little known district'. This did not stop Banbury Harriers Athletic Club from regarding their ground as offering 'a splendid view over the surrounding country' or, indeed, the Rev A L E Williams, vicar of Banbury, from appealing for financial support for St Hugh's Church Hall by giving a glowing account of the embryo suburb.

In 1932 Williams wrote to the people of Banbury along these lines:-

My Dear Friends,
As everyone interested in the life of the town knows, a great new residential suburb –
Easington – has grown up and is still growing at the south west corner of Banbury.
Some 2,000 people live there already and there are many of the amenities of a modern
town life, pleasant well-kept streets, a few necessary shops, a recreation ground, a
magnificently-equipped secondary school, but no single place of worship, no public hall
available for meetings, lectures, whist drives or social purposes.

The vicar's reference to the streets was clear from a map of 1925 which had been devised by Mr Wrigley who was Borough Surveyor. Springfield Avenue, Easington Road, St George's Crescent and Horton View combined to embrace and border the open spaces designed for public informal activity, cricket and tennis, and use by allotment holders.

These were in addition to the Harriers' ground which witnessed many exciting events. Not the list of these was the Athletic Sports Club's meeting of mid-summer

The church of St Hugh, Easington, consecrated in 1933, where Brian Little served as churchwarden and where for many years his local history class met on Wednesday afternoons.

Some of the shops on Horton View, 2019.

1925. Quite apart from the usual races which were watched by a huge crowd, there was the special attraction of a performer on the trapeze who used the profession names of Fitzroy and Katz. As the former he appeared in the guise of Tarzan's sensational flying ape doing loop-the-loop feats and in the latter role he did some amusing capers as a human Felix on the flying rings. The day came to an appropriate conclusion with a presentation of prizes by the Member of Parliament and his wife, Major and Mrs Edmondson.

The area of Easington shown on Wrigley's map had come together following the 1914-1918 war. Banbury Council acquired a site of about 90 acres. Roughly half of this was developed by 1919 but then the remainder was finished in 1923 and 1924. A total of 403 council houses was built but there was also private sector development of the west side of Oxford Road from the water tower to Grange Road. By 1932 there was even some discussion about constructing an infant school in Easington Road but after careful consideration the land was deemed inadequate.

The few necessary shops of Rev Williams' appeal were an early feature of amenity provision in Horton View, and according to Kelly's 1932 Directory, the St George's corner was occupied by bakers, Harris Bros, and next door by Percy Gilkes, the newsagent [who displayed] ... the typical external news boards. At that same date and almost opposite was the Easington branch of the Banbury Co-operative Industrial Society, and at number 22, Leonard Rider Withey, dairyman. Eight years later the baker and newsagent had turned into a greengrocer and the Easington sub-post office combined under the name of William Leslie Frost. Kellys for 1965 tells that the corner property was a grocery run by an F Knowles, whilst opposite Withey's enterprise had been superseded by J K Stainton, yet another grocer. The various directories indicate additional shop provision in Springfield Avenue at the corner with Ruskin Road but are less explicit about the activities. The name of Buzzard is however a recurrent one.

Once St Hugh's Church and hall got under way following successful fund raising

A van belonging to Harris Bros, bakers, in Horton View, *circa* 1930.

it soon plugged a gap in the social provision. The fete in the summer of 1937 was a good example and appears to have been a success despite the inclement weather. The occasion took place at *Springfield* in the Bloxham Road and featured many popular and notable side shows. There was bowling for a pig, a worthy animal which had cost St Hugh's social committee between £1 and £1-5-0d. Other bowling was exclusively for the ladies and their reward was a tea set. More elaborate still was a proposed tennis tournament; this was entrusted to a Miss Bernard Smith but sadly there were insufficient entries. A fancy dress competition was included. Entrants were required to parade at the church hall and then march to the fete ground headed by a band. At the end of the day and when the dust settled, the church found it had a profit of £41!

Banbury Guardian 4 September 1997.

2.11: Stephen Lake of Springfield Avenue, auctioneers' porter

On Thursday April 16, 1925, the editor of the *Banbury Guardian* decided to publish a street map of the Easington estate that had been compiled by Mr Wrigley who was the borough surveyor at the time. The reason given was that this developing estate was a 'little-known district'. By 1929 two people who had been attracted to Easington were Stephen Watson Lake and his wife. He was a native of Souldern whereas Mrs Lake had been born in Wigginton. They were married on January 12, 1879, at the curiously early hour of 8am. The ceremony took place in the Primitive Methodist Church located in Church Lane (the premises until recently occupied by the Swag Shop).

January of 1929 was therefore the golden wedding anniversary of the Lakes who were by then settled in Springfield Avenue. The occasion was an opportunity for Stephen Lake to recall his early life and working years. Although born and brought up in Souldern he appears to have received his limited education in the British School in Crouch Street. Sadly all he could remember of his years there was a Friday afternoon experience when he and other children listened to a story. 'I could tell you some of the goblin stories now', he said. It seems likely that his home background compensated for this insubstantial school experience as his mother was academically bright and helped villagers with their literary problems.

For part of his working life Stephen Lake was an auctioneer's porter mainly with Danby & Caless of Market Place, Banbury. Among his jobs was to leave bills advertising forthcoming sales in the bars of local public houses. This led him to become more aware than most people of the incredible number and variety of licensed premises in Banbury and the immediate district. In particular he was conscious of the pub-dominated character of Parsons Street. Apart from the *Reindeer* and the *Flying Horse* (now the *New Flyer*) he remembered that there used to be the *Hare & Hounds*, the *Shakespeare*, the *King's Arms*, and, in London Yard, the *Star*. In her study of inns, taverns and beer houses, Vera Wood notes that the last of these had been known as the *Eagle Tavern*. Other lost watering holes were the *Snapdragon*, half way between Banbury and Bloxham and the *Ship* in the High Street.

Another part of Stephen's role as a porter was to enter houses of people who were behind with the rent and seize goods to an appropriate value. On one such occasion after entry he found himself sat on the opposite side of a fireplace to a man who was brandishing a gun at him. In practice any person could carry out this process of seizure. The term for it was 'bumming'. It seems that even a fool could be taken off the street. Perhaps unsurprisingly the goods taken were often greatly in excess of the amount of rent owing.

A well-known 'bum' was Daniel Herbert. On one occasion Stephen Lake's grandfather discovered that this man had helped himself to £8 of goods when the rent owing on a property in Grimsbury was actually only £3 10s. Herbert was sworn at literally but unfortunately in the full hearing of James Cadbury who was opposed to such actions of violent language and excessive drinking. Cadbury, who was passing at the time, enquired into the matter. Subsequently he paid that tenant's arrears of rent, and demanded that the articles should be returned to the house.

On another occasion Stephen Lake visited the very house in Water Lane (Warwick Road) where he had spent part of his childhood. The purpose of his visit in his role as auctioneer's porter was to prepare the way for the selling up of the occupant's property. When the auctioneer himself arrived he expressed surprise that it was not possible to see out of the back of the house. Stephen's explanation was that there was a room above where they were standing and that it used to be reached by stairs in the corner. After tapping the wall the auctioneer produced a knife and cut away the wallpaper so revealing the door at the foot of the stairs. In the room above he found concealed £50 worth of goods.

The firm of Danby & Caless afterwards became Caless & Abbotts. As Henry William Abbots had the Corn Exchange in Cornhill, Stephen Lake got involved in setting out stalls for the sale of butter, cheese and corn on market days. The golden wedding anniversary of the Lakes in January 1929 was the perfect occasion for much reminiscing about his interesting life that had begun with youthful days filled with errands for a Banbury gardener by the name of James Butler and in mature years to be one of the early residents on the new Easington estate.

Banbury Guardian 1 September 2005.

- Wood, *The Licensees of the Inns, Taverns and Beerhouses of Banbury*.

2.12: The Fox fled to Easington

In December of 1929 the drought which had affected Banbury's suburb of Easington at last broke. The mayor, Coun(cillor) Mascord, in a gathering of civic and brewery representatives formally declared the *Easington Hotel* open.. Back in March of 1928 this looked the least likely outcome of local proposals and aspirations. True, out of 372 houses in Banbury's newest neighbourhood, 355 had signed a petition in favour but weighed against was a powerful lobby of property and landowners in the Bloxham Road combined with a formidable list of temperance groups. At the heart of the argument was the belief by some that the land at the junction of Springfield Avenue and Bloxham Road was the subject of a restrictive covenant ruling out licensed premises on Easington estate land. Indeed some people who had bought into the new properties maintained that they had been encouraged by the thought of a pub-less patch.

It cannot be denied that certain owners of large plots in the Bloxham Road might have had a case. Heading this list was Mr Joynson of the *Springfield* estate. His house was assessed at £131 and the adjoining 52 acres of land at £268 a year. As *Springfield* was directly opposite the site in question there was a risk of diminished value. In this argument he was supported by Robert Pursaill of No 41 who said he had lived there since 1922. The Judges of *Bidston* were additionally concerned about the possible busy charabanc trade.

Another interesting part of the equation was the ownership of the disputed land by Mr Morland. In a letter to the *Banbury Guardian* he denied that he had permitted this space to deteriorate. Rather he had allowed its use as a building operations store so that his Harriers scheme of development could progress. Mr Morland was clearly proud of his patronage of both a local workforce and Banbury area materials. The latter were used despite cheaper alternatives from elsewhere. So far as the *Springfield* land was concerned Mr Morland proposed to build a further five houses but in the end parted with the site to Hunt Edmunds for the sum of £250.

All along the brewers pressed their case in the courts and through the council chamber. They wanted licensed premises appropriate to the time – smoke room, bar, jug and bottle and club room. By their reckoning such a facility did not exist within the quarter mile and even at the half mile distance – there were only *The Case is Altered* and the *Constitution Tavern* brew-house.

In recognition of over provision in the town centre Hunt Edmunds proposed to transfer the license from the *Fox*, opposite the town hall, and also to close down the *Criterion*. The *Fox* landlord raised no objection and both the town centre houses were recognised as difficult to modernise. Such was the density of inns in Banbury centre that there was one for every 180 people in the centre (one for every 60 adult males).The final hurdle was surmounted at the Banbury licensing sessions held at the Police Court on Monday February 7, 1929. In favour of the granting of a provisional licence was a 10 to one support for the *Easington* from estate people, whereas still against were most of those from the nearest parts of the Bloxham Road. In mitigation Mr Eades stated that a referendum should be taken on the estate. At the

The *Easington Hotel* which opened, after much legal disputation, in December 1929.

One of Banbury's most distinctive suburbs, the Freehold Land Society estate in Grimsbury developed from 1853. This is the W side of Centre Street.

conclusion of a long session, the bench agreed to make the order paving the way for the Dents of Ross-on-Wye to be installed as the first mine hosts.

With the *Fox* licence released Colonel Stockton was able to toast the future of the *Easington Hotel* and its parent brewers with the facetious observation that 'now the Fox had broken cover and come out he was certain that there would be an enormous field on his tail'.

Banbury Guardian 10 April 1997.

3. Schools and Colleges

3.01: The last years of the British School, Crouch Street

Evidence of what life was like in a Victorian school comes to us through fascinating documents called log books. These record staffing, attendance, the nature of the curriculum, the effects of highlights in the local social calendar, views from the inspectors and the ravages of illness. This week I have been delving into Dashwood Road School's oldest log book which takes us back to the era of its roots, namely the Banbury British School for Boys in Crouch Street. The book in question covers the period from 1890 to 1900 when one Arthur Boulton was its headmaster.

Attendances at this school were peculiarly erratic, partly, it seems, because a proportion of the pupils were from rural areas. These could be cut off by snow as in November and December 1890, or subjected to flooding and lots of surface water on poor roads. Water was a problem in November of the following year after four days of rain in one week. Wet days seem to have had a very bad effect on presence at the school. Club meetings, shows – such as those for flowers and fatstock – as well as summer village feasts, all claimed the prior attention of the school's pupils.

Certain events were recognised by management and appropriate holidays were permitted. Chief of these was Banbury Fair but there were some occasions like Banbury steeplechase for which time off was agreed with huge reluctance. Illness claimed its victims. Colds are highlighted, but so too are those scourges of Victorian England, influenza, measles and scarlet fever. On February 1, 1893, the local authority forbade attendance by Grimsbury-based boys because of a serious outbreak of scarlet fever.

Compared with present day, school inspections appear to have been more frequent, indeed an annual affair. In the main their reports have been complimentary. For instance, in 1892, after visiting the school on February 1 and 2, they commented that, 'This school is in a creditable condition and there is evidence of good and careful teaching'. However, by 1894 boys in the fourth standard were found to be backward in all subjects. Sometimes the inspectors used terms which might seem a little strange today notably that the general character of the instruction is 'zealous and stimulating'. Towards the end of the decade the inspectors became very critical of the building and its ventilation and this may well have been a factor in its closure in 1900.

An interesting and unusual feature of each year is the listing of school songs. In the entry for 1889-90 is the amusing announcement of a patriotic song for the boys of Division II, 'If I were a Sunbeam'.

Songs for 1892-93 included the oddly named 'Wynken, Blinken and Nod'. Apart for some information on the curriculum there are references to occasional lectures. At 10.30am on April 2 1890, the boys heard about the dangers of alcohol and in November of that year the theme was to do with the Scientific Temperance Movement. Much more eventful than either of these was the impact of a thunderstorm during the afternoon of October 29 1894. Lightning struck and shattered the stone ball on the gable end of the roof. Fortunately no one was hurt.

Throughout the period covered by this early log book there seems to have been little or no back up when teachers were ill. It appears that the head endeavoured to cope. Appropriately he was the only person left in the building at 4pm on January 31, 1900. A sad note records that all the teachers had departed for the last time leaving the headmaster to contemplate his 21 years and four months of service.

Banbury Guardian 2 May 1996.

- For the earlier years of the British School see Trinder, *Victorian Banbury*, 104-05; for the transition from the British to the Dashwood Road School, see Potts, *100 years*, 80-81; for Dashwood Road see Milcham & Betts, *Dashwood School 1902-2008*.

3.02: Harriers' Primary School

On Thursday, May 22, 1919, Messrs Humbert & Flint sold by auction the 251 acres which comprised the very valuable freehold estate known as Easington Farm. This event took place in the *Red Lion* Hotel, Banbury, at 3 o'clock in the afternoon. There were four lots, of which the first included the farm buildings, together with enclosures of arable and pasture land amounting to just over 171 acres. Number 239 on the plan available to potential buyers was a rectangular pasture, some 5.3 acres. It was here that on July 21, 1949, Mary Cheney - Mayor of Banbury – officially opened Harriers Ground School.

Remarkably this was the first primary school to be opened in our town since 1912. Even more astonishing was the fact that the roads and houses of the Easington suburb had started appearing in the 1920s, a time when Banbury was heading off in new directions. By 1939 plans were in hand for a neighbourhood school but these were held in check when war clouds loomed. Six years before even that date the Borough Council had acquired the site that, in July 1949, caused many distinguished local area and country people to be on the platform of an assembly hall capable of holding an audience of about 200 people.

The summer of 1949 marked a post war period of pressure and innovation in the world of education. The country, and indeed Banbury, was gripped by a baby boom. Not only that but there were newcomers in the town linked especially to companies like Northern Aluminium, additional houses were appearing and there were anticipated effects of a raising of the school leaving age. County Education Committee thoughts were turning to aluminium as a school building material. It was said that the cost per pupil was much the same as for more traditional materials - £300. But how about durability asked Mr Woolgrove at a County Hall gathering. Amidst laughter, education chairman, Hermione Hitchens, remarked: 'I have asked the question myself and I was told to look at the statue of Eros in Piccadilly that has been there 60 years'. Hermione was on stage when Harriers opened but was able to celebrate traditional brick.

More importantly, the school was a step on the way to securing a primary and a secondary school in every neighbourhood in Banbury. For a school that had known so much delay to its appearance, circular number 7101 issued to prospective parents in July 1948 must have seemed the final blow. Collisons were not going to have the final completion until after the Christmas holidays. In the meantime embryo Harriers occupied the ground floor of Marlborough Road Methodist Church premises.

In this letter Mr A R Chorlton (director of education for Oxfordshire) took the opportunity to outline the new school's catchment. It included the Easington Estate, the area west of the main Oxford Road and that area south of a line, but including Town's End and Hilton Road. The Harriers of 1949 was designed for 250 children up to the age of 11. With its six classrooms there was also a dining room, a kitchen, a cloak room and a staff block. [Later] …a swimming pool was added.

The summer of 1999 provides an opportunity to open the archives and revive memories of faces. Hopefully the wonderful efforts of staff, pupils and friends will have achieved this. At the same time, it is worth remembering that cows once grazed the site, townspeople spent their pennies on a range of sideshows at major fete-like events and, above all, players of Banbury Harriers Football Club flitted to and fro in their efforts to overcome opposition as various as Oxford Gas and Osberton Radiators.

Banbury Guardian 1 July 1999.

3.03: Woodgreen secondary technical school

In August 1877 the British Association for the Advancement of Science had its 47th annual meeting at Plymouth. Professor Houghton presented an address to the geology section in which he claimed to have established by a new method that the length of the day was increasing. I very much doubt if such a formula and investigation was ever on the curriculum of the North Oxfordshire Secondary Technical School. However here was an institution with a distinctive pattern of education for boys and, latterly, girls.

Originally the Tech was housed in Grimsbury Methodist Church and was part of Banbury County School. The pupils wore the same uniform as their school-mates in Easington whose programme of studies was more academic. They were placed within Compton, Stanbridge and Wykham houses, and represented these at rugby, football, cricket and athletics. Integration was barely skin deep and Tech lads wanted their own identity. Success finally came their way in 1948 with the move to *Woodgreen*, family home of the Gilletts, a superb Victorian mansion on the edge of Banbury and undisturbed by the expansionist era. Like similar villas in the town, *Woodgreen* had extensive grounds graced by many fine mature trees. At the entrance to the long winding drive was a lodge housing Albert Taylor and his wife who did the caretaking and cleaning. However the limited facilities coupled with a teacher shortage meant

Pupils of Woodgreen Secondary Technical School who won prizes at the school's swimming gala in 1957 with the headmaster, Cllr Charles Emmott and the mayor of Banbury, Cllr Malcolm Spokes.

that a balanced curriculum could be achieved only by commuting to the Easington Campus for subjects like English, History and Geography and of course that incomparable moment of the day, the school dinner.

In 1949-1950 Woodgreen became independent of its parent organisation. This meant a board of governors and uniform. The head, Charles Emmott, wanted his students to have their say in the nature of the new identity. Competitions aided the decision-making process so that the outcome in September 1949 was smart blazers in navy blue with gold trim. All subjects were now taught at *Woodgreen*. Charles Emmott was the maths man and his deputy, Mr Merryfield was responsible for workshop crafts, geometry and technical drawing. Science was in the hands of Mr Mant. Then there were Miss Stanley (girls' head teacher and religious knowledge), Miss Kent (geography), Mr Barker (English), Mr Davies (shorthand and typing), Mr Bradley (Commerce) and Miss Ballard (history).

On the sports field soccer rather than rugby was the winter favourite …. Success came the way of the Tech team and they won the Banbury and District League in their first season. Many schools each year celebrate centuries of tradition. *Woodgreen* had to make its mark in a short time. That the Tech achieved so much says much for the spirit of the late 40s.

Banbury Guardian 9 April 1998.

3.04: Engineering: North Oxfordshire Technical College

Much attention has been drawn to Network Rail demolition of Banbury South Signal Box. Sadly much less publicity accompanies the gradual disappearance of E Block at Banbury & Bicester College. To the outside world this was better known as the Building and Engineering Department of 'the Tech', from 1958/59 North Oxfordshire Technical [College] and School of Art.

In 1976 Doug Golby of the *Banbury Guardian* turned back the pages of Further Education history to 1949 when Harold Jameson confronted the astonishing lack of provision of classes for those wishing to study in the evening. The little bit of engineering theory was tucked away above the public library in Marlborough Road. Harold had worked for the much more progressive Lancashire authority whose standards were far higher than Oxfordshire at that time. In a report to his new employer Harold recommended day release classes especially for building craft apprentices. The consequence was workshops in the North Bar area that covered plumbing, brickwork and painting and decorating. Carpentry was accommodated in Calthorpe Street drill hall, from where it was transferred to Stones in Swan Close. Stones had a furniture business as well as being well known for their fine printing.

In 1952 Harold was accorded Head of Department status and it must have come as no surprise that his personal target was to turn hopes into careers for young craftsmen. His own career took off with his appointment as chair of the heads of building and engineering for the Southern Regional Council for Further Education and he was also made chair of the North Oxfordshire Productivity Committee. Apprenticeship were central to the work of the Building and Engineering

Building apprentices under practical instruction at 'Banbury Tech'.

Department. It was these that cemented relationships between Banbury Tech and firms such as British Alcan, Automotive Products and, on the building side, Hinkins & Frewin. An especially interesting development was the pre-apprenticeship courses for prospective engineers and builders. The students came from a wide range of secondary schools and their curriculum included a distinctive liberal education element.

Popular images attached to B&E students. Their workshop safety footwear made a distinctive clatter betraying the approach of the 'Bath Road Boys' as they were dubbed by Jane Cowan, Head of Commerce. A more attractive image was of engineering apprentices arriving on the likes of 200 cc Triumph 'Tiger Cubs'. In the late 1950s these cost well under £200, 'a popular cheap and cheerful choice' according to former workshop technician Mike Cochrane. Students of this area of the college also had a ready wit. When teething troubles afflicted aluminium doors to the building housing the library it was a B&E apprentice who labelled their malfunction as 'another rough old job' naming one of the town's leading building firms.

Recently I had a conversation with Ian Davis who was a pre-apprenticeship builder back in the 1960s. Interestingly the aspect of the course that impressed him most was the way it kept his options open. He became apprenticed to AEI at Rugby where by his own admittance you came to learn the real meaning of commitment. Ian was from a farming background and this may explain his ultimate diversification into the butchery business, first with Clays of Buckingham and then Steve Betts in Church Lane, Banbury.

The activities of the Department covered a wide range of subjects as diverse as welding, brickwork and motor vehicle maintenance. These were taught in workshop environments. Throughout there was immense pride in jobs well done and this was fully reflected at the annual prize giving. New initiatives surfaced from time to time as in the 1970s when John Graber (a former inspector) praised a link between the college and Banbury School sixth form. When Harold Jameson retired in 1976 he was photographed surrounded by a superb team of colleagues who put into practice what he had preached from 1949. The Bath Road buildings were a monument to their achievements which welded education to local industry.

Banbury Guardian 18 August 2016.

- AEI: Associated Electrical Industries.

3.05: A Block: Banbury Further Education College

A fortnight ago I decided to take a final look at the fast disappearing A Block building of Banbury's Further Education College. Back in 1961-1962 this had been the long-awaited new accommodation after years of making do in a scattering of town locations. First on site was the commerce department together with the principal and associated administrative staff headed by the registrar Miss Linford. General and liberal studies soon filled space that was too small from the very beginning. A large proportion of general education still happened at Wood Green, the former Secondary Technical School. Its head Charles Emmott was close to retirement and saw out the final years keeping an informal eye on this college annex.

Liberal education in A block was given life and breath by Vernon Thomas, seen by Jane Cowan (Head of Commerce) as 'a bulky man, of medium height, with a fresh complexion, a bald pate fringed with brown hair and beetling eyebrows'. Vernon's office was close to the front door of the block. Jane, in her *History of Banbury Tech 1835-1972*, referred to him as a man of smoke and paper. The smoke issued from 'his many odoriferous pipes'. Papers were rarely filed so the piles rapidly gained height until they unbalanced on to the floor. During these early days liberal education entered the lives of everyone at the tech. One-day schools and one-week residential courses became the norm. Preceding the latter, students from whatever department had to prepare an initial piece of writing prior to departure for such places as *Thamesfield* (Henley). I well remember the occasion when apprentices from the building and engineering department clattered up the stone steps in A Block to be greeted somewhat scornfully by Jane Cowan as 'Bath Road boys of course'.

In these early days the college was small enough for the principal Norman Pratt to know the students individually by name. His general office staff occupied ground floor accommodation with a small reception area. Back in the sixties the familiar face of Irene Boscott could be spotted manning the office on a Saturday until 1pm – unheard of nowadays.

Amongst the quirky characteristics of A Block was the way in which sounds travelled from room to room and much was heard that was not for general consumption. Lessons in different areas could interact without that original intention. My geography room was above where typing classes took place. How I remember the wind-up gramophone that lost power temporarily and urged students into phrase 'carriage return'. On another occasion an all-girls class was gripped by hysterical laughter. The advice of the head of commerce to the colleague concerned was to walk out and leave them to subside of their own accord. By present day standards staff accommodation was inadequate and increasingly overshadowed by the arrival of much needed huts. Before that stage had been reached there was a pleasant view of the agricultural building and engineering buildings. The former's part-time courses included bee-keeping for which the public was given a direction notice which attracted the additional advice 'well buzz along then'.

A significant advantage brought about by A block coming on stream was that space could be made for a library with a worthwhile collection of books. The absence of book-shelves prompted an appeal to the building and engineering department who supplied planks of wood and bricks on which to rest them. Within two years more than 3,000 books had been acquired and Muriel Bennett appointed as part-time library assistant. The library soon developed into a multi-functional space. It was somewhere for governors and members of advisory committees to meet. Above all here was an area for extra-curricular lectures such as sex education. Unofficially this was styled talks with the 'sex woman'.

Down the years going up the Tech was as important as working down the Ally. For many it provided a logical progression from school to work training and for others a second chance of education.

Banbury Guardian 5 September 2013.

4. Pastimes and sports

4.01: Menu cards with a history lesson

One of the advantages of looking back over the engagements of a past mayor of Banbury is that it opens up a window on a range of local organisations. During any mayoral year most of these have held some sort of annual get together, usually in the form of a dinner. It is fortunate indeed that menu cards from these events have survived. In a few instances they have included some historical notes.

A more than usually informative card was produced by the Banbury United Homing Society for their gathering at the *Crown Hotel* on November 28, 1936. This meeting of pigeon fanciers was given a focus for competition by William Potts back in 1927. It was called the *Banbury Guardian* Challenge Cup. Entry fees made up a sizeable donation to the Horton Hospital. The first winner of this trophy was Ralph Tustain of Banbury. He was successful in 1927 and 1928. Later winners from our Banburyshire area were Mr W Pinfold of Clifton near Deddington (a 1930 novice) and Mr A Mold of Fenny Compton whose name went on the trophy in 1935.

Visitors to Banbury Museum and Tourist Information Office [as it was in 2001] may spot the date stone above the door (1900) but may be totally unaware that in the same year a small band of enthusiasts inaugurated the Banbury and District Licensed Victuallers Protection Society. It began with a mere 20 members but by 1962 had grown to 220. The card for the Fourteenth Annual Banquet and Ball of the Association notes that this body's main function was to help, advise and protect its members and to supply legal aid where necessary Their first prosecution was successfully defended in 1901, a matter of months after the foundation of the Association. Such action was reflected in a motto 'Defence not Defiance'. The Victuallers' Banquet and Ball of 1962 was held at Wincott's Café in South Bar. Brownie Lay and his musicians were on hand and adapted to the changing needs of the evening. During the dinner his Light Orchestra played Cole Porter and Jerome Kern melodies as well as Bing Crosby favourites. After the meal it was a case of 'over to you Brownie' for a programme of dances.

Many years earlier, Wincott's Café had been the scene of a very different function. In January 1937, Calthorpe Lodge No 5172 presented its Ladies' Festival. The toast to 'Members of the Fair Sex' was proposed by Sidney Ewins whose garage was a very prominent feature near the Cross. Musical items were presented by Mr and Mrs Greetham and Mrs Alcock and music during dinner and for dancing was in the very capable hands of Tommy Hutchings and his Futurist Dance Band. Tommy's versatility was evident once again when a month later Cheney's Piscatorial (Fishing) Club dined in style at the *Crown* in Bridge Street. I wonder if it was deliberate planning not to include a fish course. Pork and beef with all the usual trimmings prevailed.

If variety is indeed the spice of life it is also the hallmark of a mayoral year. In January of 1962 our leading citizen had to declare open the Annual Show of the Midland Whippet Club. The venue, popular for many events, was Church House in the Horse Fair. As in the world of horse racing, so with the canine occasion there was

The menu card for the Banbury United Homing Society's
annual dinner on 28 November 1936.

a fascinating array of dog names. I like especially Chorus Girl of Allways (a novice bitch), Test Dreamer of Allways (a puppy bitch) and Penny Farthing of Allways (a graduate bitch). Prizes for the various classes were only a modest £1 for first place, 10s 0d for second and 5s 0d for the third position. Fees were 5s 0d per dog in the case of members and an extra shilling if you did not belong to the club. ...

Banbury Guardian 28 June 2001.

4.02: Michaelmas still a fair old time in town centre

In last Sunday's *Nottingham Evening Post*, an article about the famous Goose Fair was headlined 'Fairground ride still a great turn'. The caption is a reminder that a major prime attraction used to be the Galloping Horses, originally steam-driven using coal. The carousel was also one of the highlights of Banbury Fair but the recently issued poster for Bob Wilson's annual extravaganza suggests that times have moved on and the technology of equipment has created rides that ensure sensational experiences such as reverse bungee jumping.

Showmen with long memories of travelling fairs are likely to recall with much affection the more traditional amusements. One such person is Johnny Biddle whose grandfather and parents were born into this world. He became involved in the running of a coconut shy and was responsible for picking up the balls. Apart from this particular sideshow he loved the Galloping Horses, which Lawrence Bishton is still featuring in Nottingham. In his own words the attraction is the music combined with the sound of steam engines. These offered a whiff of nostalgia. Johnny also spoke of the decline of certain sideshows, in particular one featuring the smallest woman or Sleeping Beauty surrounded by snakes.

A very special pitch used to be run by his aunt, a sweet stall with rock as a speciality. The rock was drawn out on a great hook and changed colour during the process. Nanny Curtis, as she was called, was located in Bridge Street at the railway end and she always parked her caravan behind the *Cricketers* in the Middleton Road, Grimsbury.

Our Michaelmas Fair has also changed in terms of its overall function apart from the ever present invitation to provide entertainment. Back in late Victorian times the emphasis was very much on the hiring of servants. The fair of 1884 had shows such as rifle galleries and swing boats but it is also the case that registry offices were crowded with potential servants and those in search of them. Press reaction to the fairground experience was not always favourable. The following year, a reporter penned these lines: 'there were as usual a large number of shows and stalls in the Cow Fair and Market Place and the din was appalling'. Articles of the day also stressed the reasons for police activity. In 1884 local bobbies, helped by Detective Sergeant Ashly of Birmingham, charged a Nottingham man with a felony. They discovered a peddler's certificate that had someone else's name on it. At the 1885 fair, a man was apprehended for stealing a watch five years earlier.

The fun of the fair was not held in esteem by every organisation or individual. It is therefore not surprising that the Salvation Army was much in evidence. Its band was heard on many of Banbury's streets and attracted some sympathisers though many more went in search of Bailey's Switchback, Gray's Flying Ostriches and Alf Bull's cinematograph exhibition.

The fair of Edwardian days had a further distinguishing feature. One Saturday evening the owners of many attractions offered portions of their receipts to local churches. In 1904 the overall total collected was £36 and just over £20 of this came from the Switchback, the Galloping Horses raised £4 and the Big Wheel £1 11s 0d.

Life on the last of these attractions could be more than interesting. In 1947 patrons

The 'Twister' under construction near the former *Crown Hotel* in Bridge Street for the Michaelmas Fair in 2014.

were stuck on it for over an hour on the Friday evening. That was a year when post-war austerity meant that the notice entitled 'the sensation of 1946' became the 'sensation of 1947' at the mere splash of a paint brush. Memories of the war also had an effect on people's reactions. At the Dive Bomber pitch, a customer was heard to say 'coming up in it chum?' 'No fear' was the response, 'It reminds me too much of a trip I made over Germany'. Enjoyment of the fair meant different things to different people. One person announced that a plate of whelks was essential to a good evening. Other people took away memories of encounters with the Turpin brothers at Gage's Market Place boxing booth. In the *Banbury Guardian* issue of October 23, 1947, the reporter of the day posed the question 'what are the chances of queuing outside the Town Hall for a five minute trip to the moon from Banbury Fair?' If the experiences of Oxford's St Giles Fair are repeated locally then the year 2002 could well be the time when the dream comes a little nearer to fulfilment.

Banbury Guardian 17 October 2002.

- Brian Little's article in the *Banbury Guardian* of 10 October 2002 describes Johnny Biddle's football career. He was a bustling forward who in the 1950s played for Bloxham, North Newington, Easington Sports and Banbury Spencer.

4.03: Behind the doors of the Masons

Banbury's *Red Lion* and *White Lion* inns have played a very prominent part in the history of our town. Both were hostelries on the coach routes, both were venues for sales and auctions and both were popular places for farmers' lunches. Possibly less well known are their links with the activities of Freemasons.

Modern Freemasonry is descended from an operative guild of masons that existed in the 14th century. The first Grand Lodge was formed in 1717, its members pledged to mutual help and brotherly fellowship. Locally it is recorded that in 1740 Lodge 181 was warranted at the *White Lion*. Other licensed premises also played a part in local Masonic gatherings and a later Lodge is said to have met at the *Cock & Greyhound* inn in Cornhill in 1807 and 1813. Here Nathaniel Goodwin would have welcomed the Brethren to his 17th century establishment.

Curiously, turning up on the right day and finding a way of reaching Banbury for 7.30 in the evening were early problems for some members of the Cherwell Lodge which was formed in 1852 and had its first few meetings at the *Red Lion*. In part, this problem was resolved by fixing meetings for the Monday nearest the full moon but the issue of transport was a more vexed one. Those village carriers who came to Banbury tended to arrive early morning and depart home in the late afternoon. Despite these teething troubles the formation of this Cherwell Lodge was greeted with huge enthusiasm. Here was an opportunity to pursue the basic and well-established principles of Freemasonry, brotherly love, faith and charity near to home.

Twenty-four of those who had paid for a dinner also indulged in lunch on the occasion of the consecration ceremony. Some were determined not to miss the occasion. A Mr Fowler ran up a bill of 10s 4d which was the cost of a carriage from the Great Western Railway station to the *Red Lion*. Undoubtedly it was all worth the effort especially when the culmination of the evening meal was a song called 'The Cherwell and her Crew'. Written and printed in Oxford, its versed provided a reminder of Masonic founders like the Rev Ridley who was also an important landowner in the town and area.

> *Come, now we've launched the Cherwell*
> *Let's toast our gallant crew,*
> *For never was a vessel mann'd*
> *With hearts more tried or true,*
> *Oh! Proud must be our admiral*
> *Who well sustains the fame*
> *Which Englishmen will e'er attach*
> *To Ridley's honor'd name.*

Amongst the regular attenders at subsequent Cherwell Lodge meetings were some very well-known Banbury personalities. They included traders like the grocer Perry and the draper Stutterd. Some notable members moved smartly up the Masonic tree. John Potts of *Banbury Guardian* fame was initiated in 1870, became Master of the Lodge in 1876 and Provincial Senior Grand Warden five years later. Tom Wilkinson Holland, who joined the Hunt Edmunds Brewery partnership in 1872, became a mason in 1876 and was made master in 1880.

The *Red Lion* in High Street which featured prominently in the history of freemasonry in Banbury, as painted by Maurice Draper. It was demolished in the summer of 1930 to make way for the Woolworth store which opened in the following year.

William James Bloxham, a builder who had given half a century of public service to the town, was described as a keen freemason in the *Banbury Guardian* tribute to him in the issue of June 24, 1937. Having been initiated in the Cherwell Lodge in 1904 and again in 1914, Bloxham's dedication took him further so that in 1915 he occupied the position of Provincial Grand Warden of Oxfordshire. A staunch Anglican who was politically Conservative and whose leisure interest was bowling for the Chestnuts all added up to a Banburyness which pre-dated the findings of that renowned sociologist Margaret Stacey.

Fourteen years before Bloxham entered into Lodge activities, a new meeting place was established in Marlborough Road. The foundation stone was laid by Prince Leopold, Duke of Albany, whose arrival in the town attracted thousands of spectators who lined the route from the GWR station. They were witnesses to a procession of brethren to the new site for which fellow masons W E Mills and J S Kimberley had been responsible for the design and construction respectively. The inauguration of the new building was followed by a banquet in the Cornhill Exchange and then, just before Christmas of 1882, a ball in the Town Hall made resplendent by masons in full regalia who danced to the string band of Sandhurst's Royal Military College. Despite all this ceremony and excitement, it was as early as the 1920s that the building in Marlborough Road was considered too small. An option to use reserve land was taken up and electric central heating ended an era of reliance on tortoise stoves that had warmed only those masons fortunate enough to be close to them.

There was talk of ousting Wincott's Café and Ballroom as the dinner venue but its popularity was all too clear. Masonic events were still being held there in the 1930s. A Calthorpe Lodge Ladies' Festival of 1937 was a splendid evening with Tommy Hutchings's Futurists topping the bill.

Late June 2002 is once again a time for celebration – the 150th anniversary of the Cherwell Lodge. In a span of time that has seen railway transport progress from open carriages of the early 1850s to the sophistication of the Virgin Voyager, local freemasons are anxious to show that they too have moved with the times and sought a greater public awareness of their role in upholding moral values and supporting worthy causes in 21st century Britain.

Banbury Guardian 27 June 2002.

4.04: **Rotary Club outlasts expectations with 75th anniversary**

Rotary District 1090 stretches from north Oxfordshire to north London. Interestingly the largest of the 62 clubs is here in Banbury where in 2010 members are celebrating the 75th anniversary of its foundation. The club was established in 1935, George V's Silver Jubilee year. Sidney Ewins, a prominent garage proprietor and the club's first president, was often hear to say 'when we started the Rotary Club they said it would never last. Nothing ever did in Banbury'. Subsequent events have proved that his friends misjudged the strength of the organisation. Evidence to the contrary is firmly embedded in the lives and roles of those men who became founder members. In all there were 18 whose combined interests and talents linked neatly with Dr Ted Brinkworth's comment within a talk to Banbury Rotary Club that 'history is about people'.

Most were leading figures in their particular business or profession. Prominent among these was Patrick McDougal who led the movement to set up Banbury Livestock Market under the direction of Midland Marts Ltd away from the town centre. On a suitable occasion he remarked to his audience 'By God we have made their town'. Flour miller Theo Clark was mayor in 1935 and therefore the town's leading citizen. William Potts edited the *Banbury Guardian* newspaper and was therefore in a position to ensure all Rotary affairs were brought to a wider public audience.

Forty year on from its foundation Rotarian Cyril Brownett delved further into the lives of the first president, Sidney Ewins, and the honorary secretary, Edgar Goddard. Sidney had a garage near the Cross and was often to be seen standing outside it. He was easily recognised because he favoured a charcoal coloured coat with matching trilby hat. As a garage proprietor his most remarkable characteristic was that he did not drive a car. A side of his life known only to friends and fellow Rotarians was his preference for kippers for breakfast at district conferences.

Edgar Goddard was apparently 'a firecracker' of a personality who was a partner in the accountancy firm of Thornton & Thornton. A keen Chestnuts bowler, he was a regular coffee drinker at Brown's Cake Shop in Parsons Street and also gathered with friends in various hotels, but especially the *Whately*. Many fellow Rotarians and especially Ewins would have looked askance at some of his driving antics. It is reported that on one occasion when returning from Oxford he rose from his driver's seat to shout at a passing motorist who did not return his salute: 'You are no gentleman' bellowed Edgar.

These two men with the other founder Rotarians, all prominent male members of Banbury society, were at the very heart of the first Charter Dinner of Banbury Rotary Club, which was held at the town hall on October 25, 1935. It was cooked and served by the staff of Wincott's café. William Potts gave the occasion page three coverage in the *Banbury Guardian* under the caption 'Large gathering at Historic Ceremony'. A total of 167 people were present that evening to see district chairman the Rev W Flint present the Charter.

An early activity of the Banbury club was the setting up of a free car service for hospital patients unable to afford transport. Such was its popularity it was found

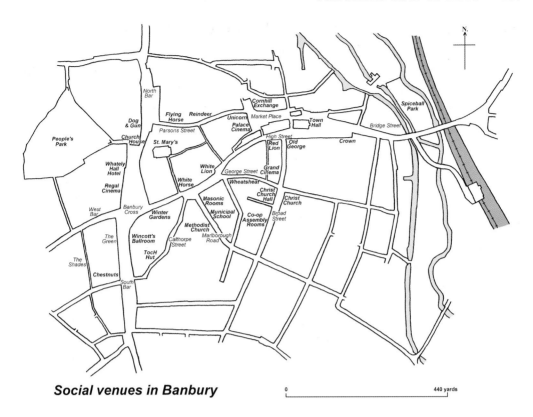

Social venues in Banbury

0 _____ 440 yards

necessary to attract additional drivers who were not Rotarians. This was achieved and the arrangement stayed in place until the onset of war. Most importantly the availability of cars was a great help to doctors and patients alike. The scheme could not have been a better example of the application of the club's motto which is 'Service before Self'.

Banbury Guardian 7 October 2010.

4.05: **Banbury's tartan army: the Caledonian Society**

On Saturday, December 2, the 52nd anniversary dinner of the Banbury Caledonian Society was held at the North Oxfordshire College in Broughton Road, Banbury. Like previous celebrations at St Andrewstide, it was an occasion to unite those whose origins lie north of the border.

Wincott's ballroom in South Bar was possibly the venue where the notion of a Caledonian group was first discussed. A young Scottish lady was participating in a version of the Gay Gordons when she realised how much she missed the dance styles of her homeland. Sympathisers were quick to identify themselves with these thoughts. They included Alex and Bill Rhind, Jock Laidlaw and Councillor Tom Auld. Before long all were meeting in Berrymore Road. The outcome of this inaugural get together was the planning of an advertisement to appear in the two Banbury papers, the *Banbury Guardian* and the *Banbury Advertiser*. The appeal was for Scottish exiles to gather in the Co-operative Assembly Rooms in Broad Street on May 7, 1949. This meeting place was very much the Mecca of the day, and with over 200 people in attendance, there was no doubt that the appeal had struck home.

Nearly two months later the society was being formalised at the *Wheatsheaf*, a Hunt Edmunds inn in George Street. Appropriately Tom Auld was placed in the president's chair and a programme of functions was arranged. During the 1950s

The Banbury Caledonian Society dinner in 1952. To the right of the speaker are the mayor and mayoress, Cllr and Mrs Harry Price.

President: MR KEITH McLEAN

The Society requests the pleasure of your company
at a Dinner and Dance to celebrate

St. Andrew's Night

to be held at

NORTH OXFORDSHIRE COLLEGE
BROUGHTON ROAD BANBURY

on

SATURDAY 1ST DECEMBER 2001

Reception at 6.30 p.m.

Dinner will be served at 7.00 p.m. prompt

Optional   Programme

NOTE: Under ballroom hire terms, dinner wine must be
purchased on the premises

The programme for the Caledonian Society's St Andrew's Night dinner on 1 December 2001, when Brian Little proposed the toast of the Society.

when the Caledonians were consolidating their position in Banbury's calendar of events, Margaret Stacey was directing a social survey of the town and its people which was to reveal a split between Banburians and those she termed aliens. More precisely she observed in her book *Tradition and Change* that 'to the Banburians the immigrants seemed foreign. They still referred to them as Scots, Irish and Welsh, with "those Northerners" added as a concession to the possible Englishness of some'…

Whether this was the case by St Andrew's Night of 1951, Caledonian bonding was even more in evidence at yet another traditional Banbury venue, namely the *Crown Hotel* in Bridge Street. Three years later the Society broke new ground by appointing its first lady president. She was Dr Margaret Ferguson who, amongst other things, secured the very first silver toasting cup known as a 'quaich'. By this time also members were in possession of cards with officers and committee members named.

The upper floor above this range of shops built by the Banbury Co-operative Society in Broad Street comprised the Co-op Assembly Rooms, the 'Mecca of the day' in 1949 when one of the first meetings of the Banbury Caledonian Society was held there.

A study of the menu cards for anniversary dinners reveals some most appropriate terminology. The event of the 40th occasion was characterised by a list of courses which was wholly identified with the Scottish palate. Diners were presented with cock-a-leekie soup, haggis, neeps and tatties, Scottish sirloin of beef, Caledonian Flammery and even assorted Scottish cheeses to accompany the biscuits. It goes without saying that cups of coffee had to be accompanied by shortbreads and the whole repast topped up with a wee dram, compliments of Johnny Walker.

Ten years later and the celebrations moved to the noble surroundings of Wroxton Abbey. Here the prelude to the 50th dinner was a performance in the ground by the Caledonian Pipe Band. After the meal Scottish country dancing both by the Acushla School and by society members occupied centre stage. This had been a lynch pin of the Caledonians since the local branch formed back in 1949. The first Saturday in December 2001, will be remembered by Scots and their guests as a fine celebration of all the traditional elements.

Banbury Guardian 13 December 2001.

4.06: Proud history of Banbury Harriers

Banbury Harriers Athletic Club was formed in September 1879. The motivation for the establishment of such an organisation was a desire to provide opportunities for physical exercise as well as somewhere for recreation after business hours. The target group was the young men of the town. A booklet of general rules dated 1882 makes it clear that recreation was interpreted as widely as possible and on an amateur basis only. Specific sub-sections covered participation in gymnastics, running, football and cricket. At this time the annual subscription level was 5s 0d but at least double this amount secured honorary status. Either way membership of the club entitled individuals to wear the badge, which appropriately was the sun in splendour as on the borough arms.

Public houses have always been popular haunts for committee gatherings. This club was no exception.

In 1882 business meeting were held in the Club Room of the *Old George* inn courtesy of the landlord who was Marmaduke George Hitchcox. This pub was owned by Hunt Edmunds and appears, according to Vera Wood, to have been a 'very class-related' inn, with rooms for different levels of society. Patronage by the Harriers may well have been highly regarded by brewer and publican.

A later copy of the club rules dated 1920 reveals that the Harriers' use of this

Members of the Banbury Harriers with a float ready to participate in a procession, probably as part of a hospital carnival.

A note from William, 11th Baron North, one of the Banbury Harriers' vice-presidents, thanking the club for remembering his 94th birthday.

hostelry had finished long before the *Old George* was pulled down (1932) and Barclays Bank opened on the site (1934). The new club headquarters was the *White Horse* hotel just below Church Passage in the High Street. This was a venue popular with several sports and social organisations and was also home to the Banbury Star Cycling Club and the Banbury Fishing Association.

Use of the gymnasium by its members necessitated the creation of no less than 13 specific rules in 1882. The final four of these are especially interesting as they had all been deleted by 1920. They relate to what might be termed good practice and 'sober' judgement. Weights and dumb bells have to be put down quietly and not thrown. Wrestlers were forbidden from catching hold of clothes, hair and flesh and must not kick an opponent. Boxing gloves had to be hung only in an approved place. Lastly alcohol was banned from the gymnasium.

Running was greatly encouraged by the Harriers. Saturday afternoons appear to have been popular with members, whether taking part in cross-country runs or paper chases. However, this did not prevent night runs when the club captain and sub-captain were responsible for approving pace-makers or, in the case of cross-country, hares and whips.

Although not as high profile in local soccer as Banbury Spencer FC became after its formation in the 1930s, the Harriers Club took great pride in uniformity of outfit. Members were expected to wear the chosen colours of blue and white. The other major concern was loyalty. There were fines for not turning up on time or at the specified location. Failure to appear at a home game in 1882 cost the individual sixpence. It was double this amount for what were termed out-town matches. An extant fixture card for the 1900 cricket season gives some insight into this side of Harrier activities. The opening match was a Married *versus* Single occasion but then the rest of the programme was made up of clashes with village teams like Adderbury and Bloxham, the Britannia Works side, Wroxton Abbey and St Leonard's Church in Grimsbury. A programme from 1934, which was printed by the *Banbury Advertiser*, is a reminder that this particular year marked the 50th anniversary of sports meetings organised by the Harriers Club. Since 1923, their ground had been on land at the corner of the Bloxham Road. This venue seems to have attracted quality athletes from clubs as renowned as Birchfield Harriers and Godiva Harriers.

Patronage of Banbury Harriers was an impressive aspect of its structure back in the early 1900s. People of no less standing than Lord North of Wroxton and the industrialist Bernhard Samuelson pledged their support and, at vice-presidency level, these notables were joined by the mayor of Banbury, the local Member of Parliament and the vicar of St Mary's Church. The fact that morning [evening?] dress was insisted on at the annual dinners is just one more sign that back in 1879 the founder members had established a club which was a beacon in Banbury Society.

Banbury Guardian 4 December 2003.

4.07: Easington Sports Football Club

It was the year of the golden summer, 1947. The sun shone and Dennis Compton established an English cricket record – 3,816 runs in a season. As memories of that glorious season were fading, Easington Sports Football Club played for the first time in the Oxfordshire Junior League. Sadly, September 13 was a black day, the side strolled out against Hornton at home and lost 11-1.

Home in 1947 was not the ground of today. It was a piece of rough pasture off Wykham Lane with a Nissen hut for changing and water only if you fetched it from a nearby stream. Whether these conditions influenced the pattern of play we will never now. However, we can be guided by the *Banbury Guardian* who accounted for the deficiencies against Hornton by saying 'Easington was unable to play its strongest team and there were weaknesses in defence'.

The bad start to league status extended over several matches. An away fixture with Banbury Boys' Club brought a 4-0 drubbing. Mollington then added to the discomfort with a 5-2 reverse. The appearance of Northend on the Wykham piece finally bought joy. Gordon Fivash netted five in a 6-2 win. This turned out to be the solitary success until the third Saturday in November when Mollington succumbed 5-3. All the league matches of season 1947-1948 were played in section C of the Banbury Division of the Oxon Junior League. Nearly all the teams were villages but there was one company, namely Switchgear. Those who attended the 1947 meeting of the local division at the *Dog and Gun* learned that Easington was one of three new sides, the other two were Northend and 251 Pioneer Company at Marlborough Camp.

By season 1954-1955 Easington had aspired to senior league status and achieved huge success. Their team finished second to Thame United with whom they had six encounters. Only the final one of these was successful, a 4-2 win in the final of the supplementary cup. The ninth annual dinner of the club was held at the *Easington Hotel* on Thursday, June 9, 1955. Everyone raised a glass to a most successful season. It was clear to the honorary secretary and legendary goal poacher Gordon Fivash, that a new ground and clubhouse was required. His eye was on some land at Addison Road and Easington president, Councillor [Charles] Hunt, promised help, including financial support.

In time for season 1959-1960, Easington Sports adopted Grimsbury Old Boys and ran them as an A team in the Oxon Intermediate League. The seconds enjoyed senior league status and the first team moved into the Warwickshire Combination. Coached by the ex-Spencer Doug Woodward, they started badly, losing 4-0 to Sterling Metals, but finished the season in style overcoming Rootes Athletic, 2-1 and Coventry Amateurs, 3-0. On the occasion that Wolves A were visitors to the Addison Road ground, the famous Ron Flowers was on duty for the team. Easington later re-joined the Oxfordshire Senior League and remained there until Hellenic League status was sought and gained in 1970. Successful entry was dependent on getting the ground into prime condition. With a touch of guile and a deal of fertiliser, Terry Horley produced a greensward fit to satisfy the inspector of grounds. Some 27 years on the club still enjoys Hellenic League status albeit in a division whose composition is decided largely on the basis of an absence of floodlights.

Welcome to Addison Road, said the match day programme for the last game of the 1996-1997 season. I felt more than welcome, but of the handful of spectators who braved a wet afternoon, how many knew that we were there not just to cheer on the men in red and white stripes but to be thankful for that brave decision in 1947 to do battle for league points on a cow pasture.

As team manager, Jimmy Hay wants to invest in youth. His heart is with the club, after all he played here in the 70s. If the young players of tomorrow can learn something of a guile fashioned in Scotland and sharpened at Wycombe, the next 50 years look assured. Terry Horley and the other club workers may not be around then, but they will know that their enthusiasm has been worthwhile. Happy half-century Easington Sports from a Milton United fan!

Banbury Guardian 8 May 1997.

- The munitions depot CAD Kineton was built from October 1940, and was known for many years as Marlborough Farm Camp.

4.08: Centenary of Central Bowls Club

H Hewer, A H Cowell, C Crisp. This is no ordinary list of names; instead these were sporting greats of the Banbury scene in the 1930s. Between 1932 and 1936, three players walked away from a town centre bowling green with a superb trophy. This was presented on behalf of the Banbury Central Bowls Cub for outright success in the Challenge Cup Competition. Their reward was a fine piece of silverware marked with a Pegasus, the winged horse. The probability is that this insignia was included because the green was located behind the *Flying Horse Inn* in Parsons Street (now *Ye Old Auctioneer*).

Sixty-five years on from the last award of this cup to A H Hewer in 1936, the Central Club is able to look back over a century of its history. The outcome of their endeavours has been a fine booklet printed and published to a very high standard. The slim volume opens with a few pages of fascinating history. So many events in our town have been instigated by retailers or licensees that it should come as no surprise that the Central Club was formed due to the efforts of Albert James Kilby who was mine host at the *Unicorn* in the Market Place from 1896 to 1904. His success in launching the bowls enterprise came in 1901, three years before he moved to the *Flying Horse*, where he remained in charge of the inn until 1913.

It is possible that A J Kilby's efforts in 1901 may have been a re-launch of an older club. A 'Day Book' ledger bears the date 1893 and was used by the treasurer who was appropriately a well-known retailer. His name was Arthur Pargeter … I featured Mr Pargeter of 56 Parson's Street when the *Guardian* published a photograph of a tailor's hat brush. The green identified by Kilby was situated behind *Trelawn*, originally home to the Bolton family and still offering a fine frontage in North Bar. It appears that the green had a marked hump at one end.

When Albert Kilby left the *Unicorn* for the *Flying Horse* he arranged yet another green to be laid down. Ironically the man who acted as overseer for the job, a Mr White, was groundsman for the Banbury Chestnuts at that time. According to a *Banbury Guardian* of the day this new green had 'pretty surroundings' and the enterprise in general seemed assured of success. At the outset there were some 30 members but there appears to have been a not uncommon problem of finding leading officers. It is recorded that A J Kilby had to be both Hon Secretary and Treasurer. Soon the size of the club grew to 63 members. Those who played parted with half a guinea, while those who did not strut the green had to submit five shillings (25p). It is appropriate that the Central Club won its first match which was against the Conservative Bowling Club. Later that year, on the evening of November 7, 1901, members were able to lift their glasses to this and other successes as they took part in the first and celebratory dinner which was held at the *Unicorn*.

Sadly 1929 saw the disbandment of Kilby's club. This arose because members could not agree a fixed tenure with Frederick Robert Lee who was landlord of the *Flying Horse*. Fortunately for the club members a new licensee took over in 1930. He was Walter Robert Sanders. Coincidentally the club reached agreement with the brewers who were Messrs Phipps & Co. Then years later, in 1940, local area clubs including the Central agreed to take part in a Hospital League. Proceeds were to the

Horton and sides competed for the Keyser Cup. After the war and in the Easter of 1946 superb spring blossoms appear to have greeted early bowlers.

By the mid-1950s ladies were gracing the green and paving the way for some notable events such as the Johns Trophy Competition. In 1959 Irene Townsend was President of the Oxfordshire Women's Bowling Association. Many enjoyable fixtures marked the years up to 1973 when the club lost its battle to stay 'central' and moved to Horton View. ... Congratulations to Central Bowls on so many fine achievements.

Banbury Guardian 19 July 2001.

4.09: Star shone brightly: Banbury Star Cyclists Club

Banbury Star Cyclists Club was formed in 1891. Forty-five years later a typical comment among members was 'anyone fond of cycling and good comradeship should give the joys and delights of club-cycling a trial'. In today's article I intend to demonstrate how club events of the 1930s revealed the truth of this remark.

An article about Banbury Star could focus on the programmes of rides out from the town but would miss the interest generated by certain critical decisions taken at Annual General and Extraordinary meetings. One of these was the agreement in 1935 on accepting lady members. At the Annual General Meeting of 1935 it was proposed that a women's section of the Star Cyclists should be formed. After early hesitation by some established men in the club attitudes changed and this was shown in a number of interesting ways. A subscription differential meant that ladies paid 2/- per year compared with 2/6d by the men. This move was quickly followed by the election of two ladies to the committee: they were Miss E Dale and Miss Baker. A year later and the presence of women was a factor in the organisation of a novel competition known as a 'fox and hound run'... Two very elusive foxes were Messrs J Russell and P Neal. It was reported that they 'led the pack a merry dance'. First at the 'death' were Miss E Wheeler and Mr W Adams. An incentive to be part of the occasion came in the form of prizes from notable business including Maycocks, the High Street hairdresser, Trinder Bros of Broad Street, and Cooks Tobacco store at the Cross.

Through much of the thirties membership levels fell but in 1937 the honorary treasurer was able to report an increase from 66 to 80, and that, out of the 80, 10 were women. Possibly encouraged by this change of fortune it was agreed to investigate the prospect of a clubroom, which could be used every night of the week. Such a winter facility would be invaluable at a time when runs were impossible in the evenings. During the 1930s there were several changes of venue for meetings and events. After the *White Horse* in the High Street came the *Dog & Gun* in North Bar where Albert Kilby a prominent club member was landlord. It was from here that enthusiasts set out for an annual road race.

In 1932 the day was very wet when 21 competitors began a ride through Northamptonshire. Sadly the first two home had to be disqualified because they took a wrong turn after Brackley and so cut a mile-and-a-half off the course. There were happier rides especially when 20 riders competed in a 25-mile road race from Bernhard Samuelson's Lodge to Sturdy's Castle. The best time was 1 hour 15 [minutes].

The thirties were also a time for reflection on the age of the Banbury Star Club. Some members wondered if it were the oldest of its kind in the country. There was a greater confidence about it being the oldest locally. Uncertainty was in the mind of Mr H Adkins (Chairman) when he stated that he had acquired a small medal inscribed Banbury United Cycling Club. Quite apart from the issue of age it was always being stressed that the club catered for the racing and touring cyclist. Colonel Edmunds, President of the Star Cyclists, raised a laugh when he commented that the club was 'a going concern' with 'a kick in it'.

In the background of the many away days for cyclists were contributions from local business leaders. Some loaned cars in order to help the work of marshals. Others like Stanley Ewins could claim 50 years in the cycle trade as well as support for the club…

Banbury Guardian 14 December 2017.

4.10: Vintage motor bikes: the Banbury Run

Last Sunday was the occasion of that eagerly awaited event for owners of vintage and veteran motorcycles known simply as the Banbury Run. It developed out of the Birmingham to Banbury Reliability Run that first took place way back in 1949. 'Thousands saw vintage motorcycles' was how the *Banbury Advertiser* captioned its report of the occasion.

The event was designed for pre-1930 machines but only two comprised the pre-1905 class. Their owners were allowed to by-pass Edge Hill. Seventy machines started from Sheldon and all but three arrived safely in Banbury's Horse Fair where they were greeted by marshals drawn partly from the local auto club and supervised by Captain Francis Jones of Farnborough, better known as 'Carbon' of the *Motor Cycle*. The first person to reach the town was Mr M F Walker of Harrow who was riding a

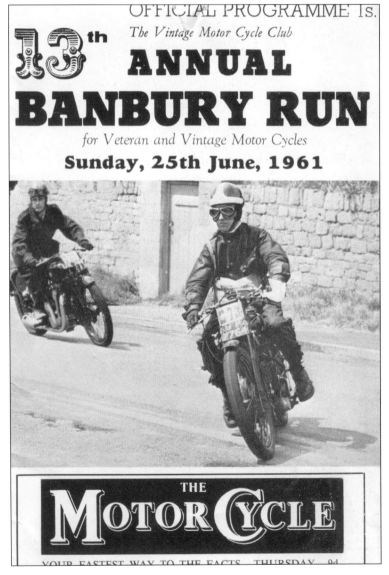

The programme for the 13th Banbury Run on 25 June 1961.

A competitor in the Banbury Run in the early 1950s.

1902 Clement Victoria. Interestingly, he arrived at the finishing line in Horse Fair at 12.00 noon, some 40 minutes early, which meant a deduction of 68 marks. Most rode their machines to the start of the race. Mr C Emmans brought his 1903 single-gear Kerry from Brighton but sadly on the run it broke down near Kineton; the culprit was an original exhaust valve. The most travelled machine in the 1949 run was the 1928 Norton owned by Mr J Masterman of Bolton. Not only had it seen 21 years of service but since 1933 had been to 19 countries within three continents. In 1939 it made London to Istanbul and back in as little as three weeks. Out of the 70 riders in 1949 only one was female – Mrs M Savage of Farnham. This did not deter her and she returned in 1950, once again with her 1913 Douglas.

The first run of the 1950s was routed in the opposite direction, from Banbury to the BSA Recreation Ground at Small Heath in Birmingham. It took place on Sunday, June 25 and attracted 122 riders. The first machines got away from the *Crown* yard at 10am and followed a route which took in Shutford, Sibford Gower, Brailes, Tysoe, Sunrising, Kineton, Gaydon, Harbury, Offchurch, Kenilworth and Knowle. In their midst was a 1905 Riley, thought to be the only one in existence at that time. Those people who saw the machines in the *Crown* yard or lined the route at Sunrising were treated to a remarkable sight of motorcycles that, in the words of the *Advertiser*, 'our fathers cursed, pushed and lovingly tended in the pioneer days of motorcycling'.

About 12 of them had been rescued from barns or sheds after years of idleness

The *Crown Hotel* in Bridge Street venue for many social functions in the 1950s. The yard to the right was the starting point for the Banbury Run.

gathering rust. One machine in particular had been in a field for 16 years. Another ridden by T Kirkpatrick of Carlisle was found in the ruins of a collapsed building and cost him just 20/- (£1). After the Banbury Run he re-mounted his bike and went all the way down to the Isle of Wight. For many machines the hill climb was a kind of return visit and Birmingham and Coventry bike manufacturers used to try out their machines on the Banbury Run circuit with Sunrising as the final test. Among these were a 1901 Beeston and a 1914 Alldays Matchless. Sadly the older machine ridden by C G Williams was passed triumphantly by the smoking Matchless whose owner D C Houghton must have derived much satisfaction from the performance. The Beeston was not the only one to struggle with the gradients as F A Bussey's 1912 Rudge TT model had to be pushed up the hill – his programme number was 13! By contrast a 1903 Humber Forecar negotiated Sunrising and afforded much interest as it was similar to machines used as motorised rickshaws in the Far East.

It is very clear from the remarks of entrants listed in this year's brochure that the challenge of Sunrising is still what inspires people, often from considerable distances, to want to participate even if, like George Gibbs of Banbury, they have had the experience of an impromptu exploration of a hedge at the bottom of the hill. One interesting bonus locally in 1950 was that the Saturday prior to the run the public could inspect the motorcycles closely in the *Crown* yard provided they bought a programme. They also had the satisfaction of knowing that half the proceeds of these sales went towards the cost of repairing the roof of Christ Church.

This year has been the 58th annual Banbury Run but perhaps equally important it has been the 60th anniversary of the Vintage Motorcycle Club (1946-2006). The

Diamond Jubilee of the parent club has been celebrated by a revival of the Festival of 1,000 Bikes held at Mallory Park and also by a bumper entry in the Banbury Run.

A brief note in the brochure for the 34th annual get together of enthusiasts (June 1982) conveys the true spirit of this remarkable event. For club members and area residents alike it is an annual opportunity to appreciate the engineering skill and vision of those who built the pioneer machines. Unsurprisingly the day is full of nostalgia about these machines that past generations rode when highways were far less cluttered with traffic than is the case today.

Banbury Guardian 22 June 2006.

4.11: Banbury Auto Club's TT thrill

On Tuesday, February 18 1947 some 150 members of the Banbury Auto Club were encourage to attend the club's first annual dinner, lured by the knowledge that they would hear and have a chance to meet Jimmy Simpson, an outstanding TT rider. It was also the occasion when W R Sewell, club chairman, remarked that Banbury Auto's prestige was fairly high in the sporting world and that 'members were establishing a tradition for the future'. Sewell's comments assumed significance later that year when the club held its last two grass track meetings of 1947.

The venues were Huscote Mill Field close to the Daventry Road and land in the vicinity of Hopcroft's Holt, on the Oxford Road. Both events were blessed with sunny, dry weather that ensured tracks were fast. In the case of Huscote, the *Banbury Guardian* referred to sweltering sun, which may have deterred some spectators. However there was every encouragement for enthusiasts especially as the Midland Red Bus Company ran a special service. The followers of the sport who went to Huscote were rewarded by the appearance of Arthur Flack of Amersham who could not make the subsequent meeting. If as a spectator you wanted spills as well as thrills, Arthur was your man. In the first heat of the 500 [cc] race he was thrown spectacularly through the air after his primary chain came off and jammed. Several other riders from around the country were at both meetings. These included Reg Lambourne of Worcester (JAP), Jim Cashmore from Leamington Spa (Martin, AJS and JAP), and Slough's Billy Newell (JAP). In the case of Hopcroft's Holt there were no fewer than nine competitors from Banbury and district, out of a total of 37 entrants.

One name shone like a beacon on each occasion. He was Charlie Wright (JAP). At Huscote his reward for turning up was success in every race bar one. During the Hopcroft's Holt meeting he went to the starting gate eight times and each time he rode the 500 cc JAP in a superb fashion. Unbeaten all day, perhaps Charlie's greatest triumph was in winning the Banbury Cross Cup. This he did despite being up against those who had been the most successful riders during the season – only the highest point scorers were invited to participate. He received the cup from Lt Col and Mrs Harcourt and then celebrated by doing a lap of honour holding the trophy aloft.

This alone must have been worth the admission money of 2/- (10p) and 1/- (5p) for children especially if you took advantage of the catering facilities provided by Mallets of Henley-on-Thames. I wonder how many spectators had their enthusiasm dampened by a 'no betting' rule. The programme was very clear on this point.

Even though Wright stole this particular occasion there were many other memories to warm departing hearts. Notably these occurred in the second semi-final of the Banbury Cup. The *Banbury Guardian* report reminded readers that there was a ding-dong struggle between Cashmore and Newell that kept the crowd on their toes and resulted in a dead heat for second place.

The programme for the Hopcroft's Holt races was well worth 6d (2½p) expended. Printed by the Advertiser Press in Banbury it provides good insights into the Banbury Auto Club. Apart from recording affiliation to the South Midland Central ACU some notes on the last page dwell on the club's aims and objectives. The author of these comments says 'we have tried to give both spectators and competitors good clean and thrilling sport and consider we have met with a certain measure of success but you can rest assured that we are making plans for bigger and better events'. The final comment says it all, 'if you would like to catch the infectious spirit of club life then the answer is to join the Banbury Auto Club.

Banbury Guardian 28 February 2013.

4.12: Legacy led to People's Park

In the late 19th century Banbury Council benefitted from a financial windfall in the form of a legacy from George Ball who, back in February 1844, had set up a pharmacy at 23 Parson's Street. The intention behind this sum of money was that the corporation should obtain land and so make provision for a public park which was to be called the People's Park. At first the search focussed on land owned by William Edmunds, Hunt Edmunds brewer. This was close to Dashwood Road and was the remnant of the extensive grounds which adjoined Calthorpe Manor House. The 1882 Ordnance Survey map shows that the park-like land then reached as far east as Newland Road and on the northern margin was delimited by a timber yard and roads called Calthorpe Gardens and Marlborough Place. However it was soon the case that progressive disposal of plots made what remained less appealing to the members of the town council who rejected the offer of sale made by Hunt Edmunds. The majority against purchase or lease for a public park was a large one and so the search for a more appropriate parcel of land was resumed.

In one sense time was on the council's side as Ball's legacy was a deferred one that would become legally available to the council in 1917. When *Neithrop House* and its grounds came on to the market, it was necessary for a syndicate to purchase the property. Public subscriptions then found the money which enabled the site to be secured and it was used as a public park under the management of the syndicate until the corporation was in a position to take it over. In this way it was possible to open the park in June 1912, when Mrs J W Bloomfield, Mayoress of Banbury, planted a tree to mark the occasion.

The Ball legacy duly became available in 1917 and the borough council was able to take the park under its wing. Lord North, High Steward of the borough, officially opened the People's Park in 1919, a ceremony which was regarded as part of the peace celebrations. The overall impression created by the park was than of pleasantly wooded rising ground. Much pleasure was to be had from a willow walk in the western corner where there was also a spring with a reputation for its mineral content. Samuel Pepys in his famous diaries wrote about Sir W Coventry going to drink Banbury waters. Bordering the corner of the park was Paradise Square (Lane). Here a once picturesque group of old cottages which had become a slum was cleared to provide additional land.

Three years after the 1919 opening of the park, another ceremony took place, this time the unveiling of the cenotaph, a memorial to the fallen. This cross of Celtic design was constructed by Cakebreads using Portland Stone, and was dedicated on Sunday, April 23, 1922. The cost was met through fund-raising efforts by ex-servicemen. The occasion was witnessed by several thousands of onlookers and was preceded by a procession of uniformed organisations from Banbury's Cow Fair.

One of the more bizarre scenes in the People's Park that same year must surely have been the time when sheep were present. The Francis Frith photographers were on hand to record this occasion. Curiously the *Banbury Guardian* issues for 1922 are silent on the matter. Were the animals seen as an option for keeping down the height

The People's Park with the memorial to the fallen of the Great War, dedicated in 1922.

of the grass? Had the council entered into a special agreement with a farmer for overnight pasturage prior to the animals moving to the weekly sheep market in nearby Horse Fair?

Although features such as tennis courts, a bowling green, an aviary and a children's playground and paddling pool were provided as attractions, it is worth a comment about a new bandstand that appeared in October, 1931, and replaced a more rudimentary structure. Sidney Hilton, borough surveyor, designed the stand which was capable of holding up to 40 musicians. The sloping ground in front of it formed a natural amphitheatre for a substantial audience.

By early November 1931 a local bye-law had banished livestock from the streets and Banbury had a park that was a credit to the town, especially since *Neithrop House* and grounds enhanced its attractiveness and value. Seventy years on it is good to hear that a new assessment has resulted in the award of a green flag of excellence. Perhaps this will be the first stage towards making our People's Park once again the green heart of the town to be enjoyed by all.

Banbury Guardian 8 November 2001.

4.13: Banbury Arts & Crafts Festival 1940s & 50s

During the final years of the Second World War, some people's minds in Banbury and district turned to thoughts of a possible arts and crafts festival. Notions became a reality in 1947 when Viscount Bearsted of Upton House accepted patronage of the week-long event and Alderman [R B] Miller, secretary to Hunt Edmunds brewery, became chairman. Other people well-known in the town who played a significant role in the early days included David Proctor and Joseph Ferrers, both influential in local education, and the sociologist Margaret Stacey. The aims of this festival, which largely based itself in the town hall, were clearly set out in the programme for 1951. Primarily the objective was to encourage study, performance and appreciation of music, dancing, drama and literary works and of various home crafts.

An added incentive for entrants was the exacting prospect of having their efforts commented upon by widely recognised and highly qualified adjudicators. Constance Grant who assessed the dancing in 1951 was also an adjudicator at dance festivals and especially the All England Sunshine Competition. It is possible that people of her calibre were encouraged to take part by the decision of the organisers to affiliate to the British Federation of Music Festivals. A gradual accumulation of cups for successful participants was a notable feature of this annual event. In 1947 there was just one piece of silverware for presentation – the Grut Trophy for the operatic music competitive class. A wartime evacuee from the Channel Islands had donated a cup. By 1952 there were 40 cups and medals and entries grew in response.

The crafts section alone had 198 entries in 1947, which had grown to 563 by 1951. It was this section that saw some exciting submissions such as when the 1st Grimsbury Scouts put together a plasticine model of the Pied Piper leading on more than 70 plasticine rats from the houses. At the same time Bodicote cubs made a matchbox model of Bloxham Grove windmill that incorporated no few than 300 matchboxes and had sails made of balsa wood.

By the late 1950s many people including regular participants were hoping for innovative ideas as there was an all-round feeling that the festival was losing its attractiveness. An *Oxford Mail* headline in its edition for December 13 1961 carried the dire warning 'Banbury Arts Festival faces a face-lift or extinction'. There was a clear need to attract new people into the competitive sections and also to give new images to what one newspaper columnist dubbed 'a sort of Oxfordshire Eisteddfod'. This journalist was Bruce Blunt. His message was very clear – 'put out more flags Banbury instead of the weary looking streamers above the town hall entrance'.

On that occasion he had listened particularly to a good rendering of 'All in an April evening' by the Marlborough Road Singers and it was his considered belief that they would have achieved as much success in a beauty contest as in the actual singing competition. This led Blunt to challenge the festival organisers to include a beauty contest in the overall programme. At the time this remark may have seemed somewhat facetious but clearly there was a growing need to breathe new life into the highlight of Banbury's May calendar. Several years later and closer to what appears to have been the final demise of the festival the adjudicator for the musical ensemble class suggested that jazz bands might be encouraged.

In his article about the 1964 event *Banbury Advertiser* journalist Ted Hanson espoused this idea when he added 'so in future perhaps Banbury will see jazz as serious music in the Festival'. Three years earlier the *Oxford Mail* had recorded declining attendances at the dancing competitions. It seems these were not attracting local schools, possibly because the festival had become stereotyped. Two brave attempts at innovation were made in 1961. La Fantasy of Banbury presented a fashion parade and there was a draw for a ballet shoe signed by no less a figure than the prima ballerina Dame Margot Fonteyn.

If the festival was destined to fail then major losers were going to be the many advertisers who bought space in programmes and linked their appeal to the nature of the event. Typical were Blinkhorns which proclaimed that they had been pioneers in arts and crafts for more than 60 years. The mid-late 1960s in Banbury in particular and the world in general saw the awakening of a distinct youth culture which was not mirrored by the organisers of the festival.

Banbury Guardian 10 May 2007.

- Walter Harold Samuel, 2nd Viscount Bearsted (1882-1948).

4.14: Banbury Steam Society

It is always exciting when an item of local memorabilia surfaces during a cardboard box rummage at a second hand bookshop. Recently I came across official programme No 2142 which had been purchased originally at the Banbury Steam Engine Fair held on Saturday and Sunday, June 26 and 27, 1971. This was the fourth rally to be held at Bloxham on land owned by Tom Smith. The event very much reflected the enthusiasm of members of the Banbury Steam Society who at that time were meeting monthly at the Railway Staff Concert Room located in the Middleton Road, Grimsbury. Amongst the officers of the Society was someone whose business was very close to this club room. Tommy Gascoigne ran Mumford's Garage and was the treasurer.

Some extensive programme notes compiled by the secretary W Upton, gave a good insight into the nature of the occasion. The key objective was to allow visitors to see engines performing tasks for which they were originally designed. In this way there was an opportunity to emphasise associated craft activities. With Banbury's history revolving around a combination of market town functions and 19th century industry, it was relevant to display engines involved in country work such as dredging. If there was a central focus for those people drawn to Bloxham then it must have been the versatility of steam traction. This characteristic would have set tongues wagging about unusual and heavy loads, as well as operational activities in difficult places.

Prime exhibits, as at previous rallies, were the 'Showmen's Engines' as exemplified by the five to seven tons Burrell and Garrett models and the much heavier (12-20 tons) Fowler and Burrell. Designed for haulage and electricity generation, the engines on display had received some interesting decorative treatment. Steam wagons were represented by the Sentinel types (relatively modern). Their role in town and country was very much to do with the delivery of flour, beer and coal, as well as other commodities. With Banbury close to some high quality arable land, the tractor was no stranger to North Oxfordshire life. This was an active part of the rally, and there was a trophy for annual competition donated by Mr J Hirons.

A memory of the time spent at Smith's Field will have been the sight of organs. Some had not been seen at Bloxham previously. An event of this kind was bound to attract owners of engines, rollers, wagons and tractors from all over the country. However, there were some links with Banburyshire.

Among the traction and general purpose engines was a 1908 Fowler. It had been restored by its owner who was E W Foreman of Deddington. The engine had been derelict for about 30 years from 1938. A portable roller presented for display by J H Russell of Chadlington had had one owner following its construction in 1890. Mr Hall of Hook Norton had put it to good service.

Interestingly among the caterers and traders there was very limited local input. G Parrauano of Banbury sold ice creams but old-fashioned gingerbread came from Malden in Surrey, rock novelties from Southport and brassware and wooden novelties from Wolverhampton. Among the adverts for Banbury area businesses was an imaginative half-page display from Trinder Bros, 'your two-wheeler dealer'. An accompanying illustration revealed that Fred was a happy man. The solution was simple, he had bought a moped. He would have liked a traction engine but as his wife said 'it wouldn't be any cheaper or quicker than the bus and where would he park it? Not under her stairs'.

It is good to note from other announcements that the Banbury Society for the Mentally Handicapped had taken a stall on the rally field. Visitors were invited to look out for gifts and novelties. Tradition rather than change was the keynote of the two days. Fairground attractions especially highlighted this feeling. Galloping horses, chairoplanes and swing-boats were side by side with hoopla and the fortune-teller's booth. ....

Banbury Guardian 8 June 2000.

4.15: Goodbye to a Grand venue

In 1996 the Post Office issued a commemorative stamp to mark 100 years of cinema-going in this country. Anyone locally who was aware of this stamp and its significance should have been reminded that these dream palaces have always played their part in ensuring that the silver screen has offered something for everyone. One such was the *Grand* in Broad Street, which opened on July 18, 1911. Specially invited guests were treated to dinners at the cinema but also in Banbury's premier High Street inns, the *Red Lion* and the *White Lion*. It was not long before the *Grand* was pronounced 'one of the most attractive theatres in the country'. Externally it had a very ornate frontage, internally the cinema was lit by electricity, warmed by gas, and provided with leather plush-covered seats for the best part of 500 patrons.

Short films dominated early performances but the management would always use the medium of advertisements to boast of any pictures. Several hundred people attended the opening ceremony when the management promised to seek films with themes that the *Banbury Guardian* of the day identified as mirth, morality, comedy and instruction. The last of these was well represented at the first showing. Opening the programme was a film about Zululand that focussed on African adventure. This was followed by a news miscellany – the king's return to Windsor, Boy Scout activities and colour pictures taken during the Paris fashion week. In complete contrast the first audiences were treated to what was billed as an amusing little story entitled *Priscilla's April Fool Joke*. The programme closed with shots of the review of the Fleet at Spithead.

The original *Grand Theatre* was not just a cinema but also a venue for stage events. One of these was especially notable. It was presented by children of the Cherwell Infants' School in June 1921 and enjoyed the patronage of Sidney James Mawle, who was mayor that year but whose family was closely associated with ironmongery. Those people who paid ninepence (4p) to two shillings and fourpence (12p) to attend the musical occasion would have been gratified to know that proceeds were going to the Horton Infirmary and Banbury Nursing Association.

Silver Jubilee Year, 1935, was an especially important time in the history of the *Grand*. After the final performances on Saturday, June 15, the theatre closed down so there could be a complete rebuilding as a modern super cinema. With an eye to the future, Edward Bagley, the then manager, announced an offer to patrons on each of the final three days – June 13, 14 and 15. This took the form of a free invitation to attend a showing of films in the new hall. In any case Banbury cinemagoers may well have wanted to be present at the final showings because of the appeal of the double bill. The main feature was *The Man with Two Faces*. In this film the lead part was played by Edward G Robinson and involved a character change. The movie was a baffling murder mystery with a plot that combined crime and hypnotism. By contrast the support film was *Big Hearted Herbert*, a comedy starring Aline MacMahon and Guy Kibbee.

Edward Bagley managed the *Grand* for ten years and impressed himself on Banbury's cinema-going public. Like many professional people locally his home life matched his status. In 1931 he and his wife Lena built a superb five-bedroomed house

Gerty and Percy Ashby tend the garden at *Coningsby*, Oxford Road, home of Edward Bagley, manager of the *Grand* cinema.

in Oxford Road, called *Coningsby* (named after Lena's Lincolnshire birthplace) which was rated the best-designed house of the year by the *Daily Mail*.

In her sociological study of Banbury and district, Margaret Stacey referred to it as a good example of a Rank One house. Its garden even had a novel feature, a custom-built mushroom growing building. Here Gertie and Percy Ashby ensured that the garden was always full of interest. In his manager's role at the cinema Bagley kept patrons informed about what was going on in Broad Street. He said that the site was to be extended so there was a much better building with seats for an audience of nearly 1,000, some of these in a spacious balcony. This drew a comment from the *Banbury Guardian* to the effect that nothing would be spared to ensure the new *Grand Theatre* would be the largest hall in Banbury and also one of the most up-to-date and luxurious cinemas in Oxfordshire, a real asset to the town. Sir James Edmondson MP performed the grand reopening on Wednesday, December 11, 1935 in the presence of the mayor who was Theo Clark. Bagley had gone for a scoop for his opening programme main feature. The showing of *Without Regret* with Elissa Landie was prior to London release. The support picture was a Bing Crosby favourite, *Two for Tonight*. Tickets were priced at from 6d (2½d) to 1s 6d (7½d) and this ensured big audiences. In their midst were many who admired the theatre's comfort, proportions, decoration and equipment.

The home of Edward Bagley on Oxford Road.

After 57 years of existence the grand showed its last film in 1968, *Where Were You When the Lights Went Out*? Local critic Ted Hanson gave the answer, 'playing Bingo'. No longer would eager youngsters queue along the length of Pepper Alley in order to guarantee themselves two hours of films. *Grand* days were over except for the new generation of enthusiasts waiting for their numbers to come up.

Banbury Guardian 14 May 2009.

- Albert James Edmondson (1887-1959), MP for Banbury 1922-45, created Baron Edmondson of Banbury 1945.

4.16: Methodists took to the stage 1939

In 1998 Church House presents a sad face of utter neglect. Back in April 1939, the Banbury Dramatic Society offered a very different appearance on the stage there. For two days only they entertained audiences with their version of the Jevan Brandon comedy *Passing Brompton Road*. The play had been performed in London's Criterion Theatre 11 years earlier. Just a few months before the hostilities of war, amateurs' spotlight illuminated yet again the drawing room of Mr Sloane's house off Broughton [sic] Road.

In this local version the casting was interesting and possibly unusual – all the players were Methodists. Their order of appearance was as follows: Mr Montgomery – Albert Chidzey; Veronica Sloane, Winifred Webb; Privett, Margaret Paxman; Dulti-tia Sloane, Irene Chidzey; Henry Sloane, Luke Coleman; George Harding, Randolph Webb; Miss Carruthers, Doris Bodman; Miss Pastel, Mable Field; Eric Sloan, Richard Paxman.

The programme for the two 8pm performances cost 2d and demonstrated just how much the society owed to Albert E Chidzey. Not only did he head the cast but he produced the play and moreover his orchestra provided the intervals. Chidzey was organist and choirmaster of Marlborough Road Methodist Church, had a shop at the top of Parson's Street and gave music lessons.

On Wednesday April 26, the substantial audience included a reporter from the *Banbury Advertiser* who picked up an interesting comment from the production. In thanking people for the warmth of their reception, Albert Chidzey stated that the show was the society's first full length play. The debut performance had been in 1938 when two short plays were on offer.

A year on and they had to be snappy about the humour and witty with the characterisation. It was the [Banbury] *Guardian's* view they achieved both. Maybe this is why graphic artist and cartoonist Hugh Evans sketched each member of the cast and achieved some remarkable likenesses. It seems that Albert Chidzey really got inside the part of Montgomery, a fashionable lawyer. The *Guardian* critic regretted that his appearance did not extend beyond Act One.

The cast also included a very notable husband and wife duo, Randolph and Winnie Webb. He was born in Hornton and devoted 50 years to the newspaper and print industry in Banbury. Randolph started as a journalist with Morland's *Advertiser* in Banbury. During the 1930s he became its editor and during the 1939-1945 war was the inspiration behind editorial matters. Randolph Webb was the fascinating link between Banbury Dramatic Society and Banbury Cross Players. He was their publicity manager for the first ever production, *Hay Fever*. His wife Winifred Doris had been an accomplished singer. In the 1930s she performed for the BBC as well as in many local concerts.

Banbury Guardian 12 March 1998.

- Jevan Brandon-Thomas (1848-1914), playwright,

4.17: Banbury Cross Players

This year is the 70th Anniversary of the Banbury Cross Players. It is an appropriate time to reflect on the fascinating origins of this society and to reveal how these were linked to the arrival of the Northern Aluminium Company in the 1930s. A prime mover within the process which the Players first appeared on the local scene was Peggy Knight who had moved from London with the Accounts Department of the Northern Aluminium Company. She had an intense enthusiasm and active love of the stage.

During the evening of December 15th 1944 Peggy gathered around her just sufficient people to read the parts comprising Noel Coward's *Hay Fever*. The meeting place was Peggy's flat close to the *White Lion Hotel* in High Street. Present were Olive Brown (NAC Director's secretary), Susan Penrose (daughter of Banbury's senior GP), Gwyneth Wilks (a founder member of the Players and secretary to Owen Reid, Banbury's Town Clerk), Richard Croucher (NAC office manager) and Clayton Wentworth who claimed that he had been a chorus member and dancer in New York musicals. This was the gathering that encouraged Neville and Nan Turner to add

A Banbury Cross Players pantomime presented to residents of Lincoln House, 1977.

Christ Church Hall in Broad Street, venue of some of the early productions of the Banbury Cross Players.

their voices to the play readers. They had not got very far into the play reading before Peggy said 'Let's do it'. Key roles then fell into place. Sholto Douglas (Bloxham School chaplain) was a logical choice as producer and Johnny Coombs with a background of Oxford stage experience was the man to manage affairs after curtain up.

Years on from these earliest decisions, Neville Turner has reflected on the parts he and his wife Nan were offered. His wife was assigned the role of Clara the maid whilst Neville was left to rue selection for the part of David Bliss (an age discrepancy issue). Formal identification of this emergent group had to await early 1945. It was then that sentiment overruled reason in Peggy Knight's mind when she conjured up names such as *The Good Companions* and *The Strolling Players*. The ultimate choice of 'Banbury Cross Players' came as a relief to Nan and Neville. More than that the agreed title may have been what attracted Peggy and Spencer Lester who joined in time to play the parts of Olive Peel and Gordon Whitehouse in *Hay Fever*. Rehearsals for the production, which was to be staged at Bloxham School, were mostly held in Christ Church vicarage at the top of Old Parr Road in Banbury. Neville records modestly that the group made up with enthusiasm what it lacked in stage experience. Fortunately help and guidance came from Sholto who had directed school plays.

Getting to Bloxham in 1945 both for actors and audience was more than interesting. Lack of cars meant out by bus and back on a late train along the Chipping Norton line. Most of the audience who lived in Banbury either walked or cycled. Friday and Saturday, 20th and 21st April will be forever imprinted on the minds of surviving members from the early days. Admission was free but the Horton Hospital benefitted from a collection. Memories of the production were recorded in a scrap book by founder member Gwyneth Wilks who was Honorary Secretary from 1948 to 1952. The Press congratulated the company on embarking on a production of the quality of *Hay Fever* and for performing it so ably. The scenery, dresses, make-up and lighting were all of an excellent standard. Owen Reid as Chairman of the Society acknowledged the reception and thanked the stage team of helpers. Saturday night bouquets were well-earned.

Seventy years on the BCP are still left to reflect on the 1948 comments made by Margaret Johnson, mayor of Banbury, at a *Crown Hotel* dinner when she stressed the need for a theatre in the town.

Since that time the Players have strutted their stuff on many different stages. Their needs are still to a degree unfulfilled. However the flame that Peggy Knight ignited in 1944 still lives on in members old and young …

… In January 1947 the venue was Christ Church Hall in Broad Street, a building that had started life as the parish rooms for the Anglican Church on the corner of George Street/Broad Street. On this occasion the production was a comedy in two acts entitled *How are they at home?* written by J B Priestley. The play was especially appropriate as its aim when written was to show British Forces overseas just how things might be at home in 1944. It was inspired by this very question put to the author when he was in the Middle East. The members of the Society taking part were Nan and Neville Turner, Diana Jones, Margaret Cowell, Herbert Chadwick, Barbara Stanford, Gwen Cox, Leslie Davies, Charles Huntriss, Spencer Lester, Gwyneth Wilks and Frederick Moir.

In the many reviews of the piece the essential ingredients of Priestley's play are revealed. The action begins in the lounge hall of Farfield Hall in the North Midlands. Lady Farfield (Gwen Cox) had abandoned the social life of the county for a wartime job in a nearby aircraft factory. She becomes a charge hand which is a cue for celebrations with work mates. The action then revolves around how various people with a military background interact with each other and with the factory operatives. There is of course the hall staff such as an old butler (Neville Turner) and a cook (Barbara Stanford). *How are they at home?* presented many challenges to the Banbury Cross Players., not the least that, unlike many subsequent productions, this one lacked a plot by which means the attention of the audience could be held. Instead much depended on the level of characterisation by the cast members. In achieving this, a limiting factor was the smallness of the stage….

The *Advertiser* newspaper summed up the generally held view of the Society's productions in Christ Church Hall when it stated that 'the town is fortunate in having so keen and successful a group as the Banbury Cross Players'. Public response can be gauged from the good houses on each evening of the presentation. Deservedly a party was arranged for the cast, other members of the Society and their friends. Apart from well-earned acknowledgements there was time for two amusing sketches by the Players themselves. ...

The programme for the production ...included some informative items. Some of these were gathered under the heading 'Titbits for our Patrons'. In this section it was revealed that the Players were in their second year and aimed to present four plays before 1947 ended. At the time of going to press the Horton Hospital had received £284 whilst £66 had been put towards the local Prisoners of War Fund. The Players were noted for their charitable activities. In the case of the hospital, money went towards specialist equipment. In the wake of early production such as *Hay Fever* and *How are they at home?* the society concentrated on broadening the spectrum of people involved.

The Tuesday social meeting had helped by focussing on play reading, marketing and lighting. This was perceived as a way of keeping people together and so creating a sense of continuous involvement and the 'always something on' feeling. In the society's 30th year, a 1975 newspaper review encouraged this approach. *A Lion in Winter* highlighted memorable performances which collectively led to the conclusion 'never before have I enjoyed a Players' production so much'.

Banbury Guardian 7 May/18 June 2015.

4.18: Centenary of the Girl Guides

In its edition of September 29, 2009, *Women's Weekly* magazine published an article under the title 'Let's hear it for the girls!' It was about the centenary of the Girl Guides movement and especially how this evolved out of Scouting. Agnes, sister of Robert Baden-Powell, was the instigator way back in 1910 but what she achieved may never have happened if it had not been down to the determination of a 'group of feisty girls carrying poles and haversacks' who joined 11,000 boy scouts at the Crystal Palace Rally of 1909. They persuaded 'BP' that there was a real need to provide something for the girls (also the title of Alison Maloney's official guide to the first hundred years of Guiding). His response, which raised their spirits, was 'you can take part in the march past at the end'. One hundred years on, ten million Girl Guides have representation in more than 140 countries.

At the start of 2009 in Banbury and the surrounding villages there were 693 members of Cherwell division of which 184 were guides. Down the years the movement has retained its appeal and popularity to the extent that those who wear the uniforms do so bearing in mind four key messages:

> We give girls and young women a voice.
> We provide a unique girl-only space.
> We promote equality and diversity.
> We're relevant to today's girls.

Several experienced Guiders have written about their memories especially those connected with being away from home. On June 30, 1923 the Adderbury Company visited Horley for 'a day in camp'. The occasion was especially notable as the girls were awarded full marks for a dinner they prepared that consisted of stew followed by fruit. Their reward was the district cup and a photograph, which included the trophy on display.

Julie Wood of the 1st Hook Norton Guides has highlighted her camp experiences at much more distant locations. In particular she recalled a 1970s visit to the Lake District where the site was flooded during a violent storm and her Guider, who was a Miss Rose, showed great determination in adversity. Hers was a disciplined regime and if bedrolls and wash stands were not right then they had to be done again. Another outstanding recollection was of a beef suet pudding steamed for hours over the camp fire.

Someone else for whom camp experience meant a great deal was Pat Gibbs (née Mitchell). She joined the 1st Grimsbury Guide Company in 1950 and has vivid memories of her first camp near Helston in Cornwall. The girls went by train to London where they joined the Cornish Riviera Express. The next part of the journey was part of the overall wonderful adventure. With eight girls in each compartment together with their kit, sleeping was an interesting experience. Two of the party tried luggage racks whilst the other six stretched between seats on either side. Kitbags bridged the gaps.

Memories of the 1st Grimsbury Guide come also from Eileen Shea. She was part of that company from 1942 to 1948. Her camp recollections are particularly vivid

Girl Guides and Brownies from Banbury at a parade in Spiceball Park in 1935.

because in 1947 Miss Wakelin hired someone with a furniture van to take the whole party all the way to Charmouth near Bridport, Dorset. Here the two weeks away were the first seaside holiday most of the girls had ever had.

Qualifying for badges has been as much a part of the life of Guides as parades for occasions such as Remembrance Sunday. The outcome was an accumulating of badges enabling Eileen Shea to secure her Little House emblem, which – in her excitement – was noticed by the Chief Guide during a visit to Oxfordshire. The 1st Grimsbury group was encouraged to aim high for Queen's Badge awards. Pat Gibbs was the seventh to be successful.

In her book *Something for the Girls*, Alison Maloney demonstrates how and why badges have changed. Girls today lead very different lives from those who were pioneers of the movement. 'Some of the first Guide badges such as Cook and Florist were rather more genteel than the Scout badges of the day'. ….

Aline Griffiths (née Ward Smith) has written about an unusual experience back in the late 1950s during Bob-a-Job week. She belonged to the 2nd Banbury (Methodist) Guides and was leader of the Fuchsia Patrol. She knocked on doors on the affluent Oxford Road and after undertaking the usual shoe cleaning type jobs she came to a small cottage. The door opened to reveal a distressed elderly lady. Using skills gained through Guiding, Aline was able to help her with a personal problem and as a result gained a donation to the guides and the lady's personal gratitude.

Locally those involved in the movement during the 1940s will recall Lady Baden Powell's visit to Banbury Town Hall in 1943 when the Guides sang patriotic songs and a nonsense item 'As I was going to Banbury'. In her address the chief Guide raised a laugh when she remarked that 'she always looked upon Guides as her own children and hoped that they looked upon her as their mother and grandmother'. The experience of the past 100 years suggests that the high standards of the movement will continue to be upheld. 'Something for the girls' in 1909 has become 'let's hear it for the girls' in 2009. Happy 100th anniversary!

Banbury Guardian 23 November 2009.

4.19: Banbury Sea Cadets

In Banbury and district 1953 deserves to be remembered not only as coronation year but also as the year in which a January headline in the *Advertiser* newspaper 'Banbury may have Sea Cadets' turned into the July caption 'Banbury Sea Cadets are Country's Furthest from the Sea'. First news of the proposal broke within Uncle Tom's Children's Corner. The Sea Cadet Corp was going to be the first ever in the town. A free regulation sailor's uniform awaited each recruit who would then be taught various aspects of seamanship and engage in a variety of activities including physical training.

In the vanguard of ex-Royal Navy personnel and joining with the clear intention of building up the organisation was 'Butch' Franklin of Bodicote. He was a male nurse at the Horton but had gained his early medical knowledge as a navy sick bay attendant. President Commander was the Earl Beatty who came from a very distinguished naval family and lived at Astrop Park in King's Sutton. He was instrumental in persuading villagers to share the profits of a 1953 fete at which his newly enrolled cadets, over 50 of them, gave a demonstration of drill. They had prepared for this moment in their 'borrowed' premises, the Oxford Road Drill Hall. On the strength of their fine display their president was able to use the press in order to appeal for several hundred interested members of the public to subscribe five shillings a year each.

Between 1953 and the present day cadets have known several different homes but especially space above A E Field's Church Lane shop and a canalside HQ which owed everything to the negotiating skills of that well-known public figure Harold Heath. The outcome of his efforts was a 25-year lease that started in 1971. Once again an eye-catching caption revealed the exciting news 'Sea Cadets set sail on a new course'. Their new home was a bit of Banbury's history – an old canal wharf.

At this time the original objects of the cadet force were recalled by people like training officer Jon Cox, who remarked that involvement with the corps was 'certainly better than hanging around outside the launderette'. He went on to say that 'youngsters who want something more out of life and relish learning the qualities of leadership in an adventurous environment should consider joining the Banbury-based TS *Harvester* (formerly TS *Lion*). The change of name was a link with 1941 when the town adopted this warship and raised money for the war effort.

In the Sea Cadets you really had the opportunity to live life to the full especially if you engaged in the wide range of activities on offer. Football alone attracted many cadets who strove for trophy success in regional competitions. In 1986-1987 an appearance in the soccer final meant a chance to run out on the green carpet of Villa Park, Birmingham, so there was every incentive to do well. A consistently outstanding feature of the cadet organisation has been its band which has held centre stage at a host of events. The chief of these have been area competitions in which musicians always acquitted themselves extremely well.

In 1966 they came third, one of many successes under Harry Parry (of George Mason and bacon slicer fame) who built up the band. The following year was perhaps the pinnacle of their achievement when in association with Coventry and

Cllr Malcolm Spokes, mayor of Banbury 1957-58, inspects the Banbury unit of the Sea Cadets in Marlborough Road. Behind Cllr Spokes is the town clerk, F G D Boys.

Nuneaton bands they appeared at the Royal Tournament, Earl's Court. It was an event that cost them nearly £100 especially as 25 of the boys needed new boots for the occasion.

The introduction of girls such as Ann Addison (née Finn) into the bugle band was a landmark and led to the occasional problem, such as when the Banbury Cadets took part in the Midland Area band championships at Hitchin, Herts. The organisers were insistent 'no girls' otherwise 'you're disqualified'. Camaraderie was intense in that group and the boys decided to go on strike as a token of solidarity with girls. After an emergency meeting, the girls told the organisers they would stand down – and this meant that Banbury was back in the competition. Despite a reduction to 12 players, the band achieved a creditable sixth place out of 11 and was also sixth out of 22 in the bugling competition. At the end of the day the boys and girls linked up to give a victory performance and received a huge cheer.

Many people with naval experience have been crucial to the success of the Banbury Cadet Force. Someone who especially deserves a mention is Bill Saunders who was commanding officer in the seventies. Bill had a fascinating background. He had been a gun trainer in the navy for seven years during and just after the Second World War. Probably his greatest moment was on board the *Belfast*, flagship of 10th Cruiser Squadron, when she sank the renowned German battleship *Scharnhorst*. 'We fired a broadside and registered the first hit. I would like to think that it was mine' he said.

Here was a first class person who in his post navy days took responsibility for the 40 boys and 12 girls aged 11-18 of the Banbury unit.

Perhaps the last word should remain a quote from Surinder Dhesi, a recent mayor of Banbury. She said, and how right she was, 'Belonging to the Sea Cadets is character-building for youngsters, giving them confidence and life-learning skills'.

Banbury Guardian 28 September 2006.

- David Field Beatty, 2nd Earl Beatty (1905-72), son of David Richard Beatty, 1st Earl Beatty (1871-1936), the naval commander.

4.20: Banbury Air Training Corps

Next Sunday a service will be held in St John's Church as part of the 65th anniversary celebrations for the Banbury Air Training Corps. It is, however, possible to trace the origins of a local unit back further to 1938 when a squadron of the Air Defence Cadet Corps came into existence due to the enthusiastic efforts of people like Banbury dentist Hubert Newton Peake. With storm clouds of war on the horizon there was a national movement to set up foundation (F) squadrons such as the one in our area that became known as 25F. The attraction of these was that they offered a taste of life in the Royal Air Force by providing basic training for young people. The first waves of cadets had to buy their own uniforms and this encouraged some to search for cheaper second hand clothing. One youngster spent ten shillings (50p) on a uniform too small for the first wearer. In the meantime Hubert Peake, with his great interest in youth activities, was setting up the infrastructure so that the squadron could function. A meeting hall was built on the side of his Warwick Road house, *Four Winds*, and a rifle range took shape in the grounds.

During 1941 the Banbury initiative, like those elsewhere in the country, was re-designated an Air Training Corps and ceased to be an ADCC Hubert Peake as commanding officer (CO) needed supported and received it from Bert Prescott and Percy Claridge. It was about that time that there were significant stirrings at Banbury County School. Douglas Rose, the headmaster who had commissioned status, decided to form his own 25F Squadron.

Interestingly an uneasy relationship developed between officers faithful to Hubert Peake and those who wanted Douglas Rose as CO. At this point Air Commodore Charmier was asked to intervene and he produced an alarming report that revealed all was not well in the local world of air cadet training. It was his view that there was 'a lack of snap and alertness'. He also highlighted incidents such as charging a cadet for the use of a former ADCC uniform that did not even fit him. The main outcome was the proposal that cadets from the original unit should be re-enrolled and added to the existing school contingent. Douglas Rose was to replace Hubert Peake as CO, a situation Peake never accepted. Indeed more than that he enlisted the help of several influential local people and continued to enjoy the loyalty of a substantial number of his former force.

Within a short period of time and despite the support of Norman Blinkhorn, Mr Rose found himself in a hostile situation. Worsening relations amongst officers especially led to a second intervention by Air Commodore Charmier. This produced an about turn and recommended the re-instatement of Hubert Peake though his responsibility was for a new 1460 Squadron that would function alongside 25F. However, whereas the new squadron went from strength to strength as flights were established in Deddington, Fenny Compton and Woodford Halse, the latter only lasted until just after the war. Early meetings of the 1460 Squadron were held in Banbury Town Hall but eventually in 1949 premises were found in the shape of the former Hunt Edmunds malthouse in Old Parr Road. In the same year another interesting development took place, a bagpipe band was formed under Willie Ledingham from Edinburgh.

A significant feature of life within 1460 Squadron has been a succession of visits to RAF stations. In the late 1940s and early 1950s cadets jumped off a training tower in Upper Heyford, encountered gliders in Abingdon and experienced flight aerobatics in Little Rissington. Lionel Drew (1948-53) felt that his ultimate experience was gained in a Tiger moth caught in the static electricity of a storm. During less turbulent years from 1949 to the present day, most COs have fostered links with Banbury itself. Someone especially who led from the front was Doug Todd (1966-76). His trips to Snowdonia involved climbs of peaks in excess of 3,000ft while the Malverns provided a training ground for participation in the annual Tour de Trigs. In 2004 Banbury Squadron was in the news again for the excellent reason that two cadets had flown with Polly Vacher of round the world fame.

Two years on and the Penrose Close HQ has many young people with ambitions that can only have been stirred by a squadron history that has put into practice the spirit of the RAF motto and seen ultimate triumph over early 1940s struggles to 'reach for the sky'.

Banbury Guardian 6 April 2006.

4.21: Winter wonders

With the New Year almost upon us, now seems to be an appropriate time to recall the place where so many people from Banbury and district spent the evening of the last day in December. I refer, of course, to the Winter Gardens. At the opening of this venue in 1956, Mayor Colin Taylor reacted most favourably to the enterprise which owed so much to Charles Hunt and his wife and to Ethel Usher. In his speech during the ceremony he said: 'They have built a hall fit for any occasion that might happen in Banbury'. His pride in the use of building materials bought locally inspired the comment: 'If you elect a beauty queen here certainly the ceiling will not fall in on her'.

The Winter Gardens was built on garden ground linked to property that originally belonged to the Gazey family in 1851, but which was sold to the Watsons. In 1944 Frank Watson sold out to the Hunt/Usher family. The new owners revamped the *Wine Vaults* in the High Street which was originally Gazey's *Wine and Spirit Vaults* and additionally developed the *Inn Within* which offered a range of snacks as a prelude to events and – in the days before the coming of the M40 with its service centre – travellers came in their droves for breakfast and lunch at the Winter Gardens. When the garden ground was developed as the Winter Gardens the initial leisure focus was on indoor bowls. This choice of activity was conditioned by Charles Hunt's love of the game. However it was not a financial success and diversification was clearly necessary. Dancing was part of the answer and in October 1956 the opening ball took place. Superintendent Buckingham introduced the Hunts and Mrs Usher who then declared the Winter Gardens open. Ken Prewer played, Pat Hustlebee (Miss Banbury) was in attendance and there was cabaret by the winners of the television programme 'Top Town' with Alan Course.

In its 150th anniversary supplement the *Banbury Guardian* noted that the town was described as the entertainment mecca of the South Midlands in the 1950s and 1960s.This was due in no small measure to the Winter Gardens where during the 'Swinging Sixties', Teddy Boys gathered – accompanied by girls in their beehive hair styles and dresses with many-layered stiff petticoats. For them the attraction was a series of pop idols with their backing groups. Typical of these was Dave Berry supported by the Cruisers. Teeny Boppers would go wild with delight and as one of them remarked 'who wanted to dance when Dave was singing'. This was in mid-December 1964. The tempo stayed high for the New Year's Eve dance when, between 8pm and 12.30am, all eyes were on the Frenzies and the Teen Beats.

Many of those who would have been thrilled by Dave Berry would have remembered the visit in February 1963 of Tin Pan Alley's top liners Jet Harris and Jimmy Justice. Jet was a fair-haired bass guitarist who had risen to fame with Cliff Richard and the Shadows. Hundreds of those in the hall stopped dancing and just listened. As the *Banbury Guardian* quite rightly observed, 'Jet had the fans in the palm of his hand right from the start'.

Equally popular with their supporters were the local groups. Then there were the big private occasions such as the Banbury Farmers' Ball. Sadly the weather was not always on its best behaviour for this start-of-the-year event; 1962 was no exception

The bar at the Winter Gardens.

but nevertheless 500 braved the conditions. On one New Year's Eve event, just before midnight, 400 people burst out into High Street and did a conga up to and around the Cross. Incredibly 700 folk returned to the Winter Gardens. Some 300 lacked tickets but the management were not worried – bar sales were boosted during the extended hours.

All types of music featured during any one year. This included strict tempo with such famous bands as those of Ted Heath, Joe Loss and Victor Sylvester. Invariably there was good local support from the likes of Brownie Lay. Chris Barber and Acker Bilk with his Paramount Jazzmen illuminated jazz occasions. Such evenings apparently were good for whisky sales.

For non-music customers there was boxing and wrestling. Support came from near and far, especially for famous wrestlers such as Big Daddy and Giant Haystacks, and of course Banbury's very own Jack Pallow who got the crowd going.

Ethel Usher will forever be remembered as Banbury's impresario. In 1982 she tried to find a new owner willing to don the mantle but in the end had to sell knowing that redevelopment was round the corner and Banbury lost an institution. Fans were devastated when they saw Keith Wood's headline in the *Banbury Guardian* 'the fight to save Banbury's leisure centre has been lost'. How we miss it, especially at this time of year.

Banbury Guardian 31 December 2009.

4.22: Wrestling with the past

In December 2009 I wrote about Banbury's Winter Gardens … [Their] popularity owed much to Ethel Usher who began her working life as a 'clippie' on her father's green buses. It was Ethel's determination to promote a diverse programme of events coupled with developing success as a businesswoman that ensure the Winter Gardens was Banbury's outstanding entertainment venue for over 20 years.

Wrestling ranked high in the popularity stakes. Dale Martin Promotions Ltd of London in association with Ethel Usher offered evenings of irresistible bouts. Famous wrestlers such as Big Daddy and Giant Haystacks were sometimes on the card but, curiously, it was often Banbury's very own Jack Pallow who got the crowd going. Individual wrestlers apart, it was the grunts and groans which worked up the crowd even if sometimes these were carefully choreographed and needed to be taken with a pinch of salt. The details of the roughly monthly shows appeared on hand bills published by Dale Martin Presentations and these were vital to the build-up to each evening. In October 1956 there was the meeting between Anglo-American heavyweight Buddy Cody (the Texan Tornado) and Black Butch Johnson. Later in the evening Australian 'Adonis' Gene Murphy met Francis St Clair Gregory and rounding off the show were Drop Kick sensation Jonny Peters of Ruislip and Winnipeg's Lew Edwards. Six years later in March of 1962 the Mexican Thunderbolt met Essex's Teenage Idol.

Fans were looking for entertainment as much as wrestling skills. Covering a wide age range they came from near and far. Fortunately there was always a hard core of support including a farmer called Hemmings from the Wykham Lane area. He and many others would dash to the *Inn Within* at the end of bouts in order to get the best seats for the next time.

On a good number of occasions there was something special about a particular contest. Just such a meeting occurred on March 10 1958. It was styled International Wrestling and included the first appearance at the Winter Gardens of world famous veteran of the mat King Kong Taverne. His meeting with 'Handsome' Ray Hunter was marked by 20 minutes of the usual grunts and groans but then Hunter ended the context with a kick under the jaw. Most of the crowd welcomed this as by that stage the end could not come too soon and Hunter was their idol. Additionally they were not impressed by a regular flow of unfortunate language from Taverne.

A report in *Wrestling Revue* for June 1973 features a most interesting example of a wrestler who combined his sport with a parallel career in the music world. British Middleweight Champion Brian 'Goldbelt' Maxine was also a singer of some repute. Having made a successful Long Player on the Starline Label which brought him two awards, he had nearly completed his second LP on the more expensive Columbia Label. On this second release Brian's theme was 'travelling' songs in the Country Style. Interest was generated by the news that he was backed by the local folk rock group Fairport Convention. In the wrestling ring Brian had successfully defended his British Middleweight Title twice heading the Review to suggest that he was 'the best wrestler in the country at his weight'. Unsurprisingly he was planning a Wrestling Musical Tour of Europe.

Evenings of boxing were also well supported. Ethel Usher became renowned as the only female boxing promoter in the country. A crowd 1,400 strong thoroughly enjoyed the bout between Irishman Tony Mulholland from Birmingham and Peter Heath of Coventry who punched viciously. The former lost on points but treated fans to a song which began 'no-one but you'. Cheering drowned the last few bars as did shouts of 'Nobbins', his adopted name. When the Winter Gardens closed in 1982 memories of wrestling and boxing were reflected in a *Guardian* headline which read 'Ethel plays it tough in a man's world'. Indeed she did!

Banbury Guardian 30 June 2016.

4.23: Pete Lay and Banbury Jazz Club

In the *Banbury Focus* for September 24 1987, Ted Hanson wrote in the following enthusiastic way: 'Next month Banbury Jazz Club will be 20 years old, so expect a real humdinger of a session on October 20'. This year the anniversary celebration is sure to be just as vibrant. In recognition of the occasions, even if smoke does get in their eyes, I am confident Pete Lay and all the regulars will be well and truly Stompin at the Savoy. During a recent visit to Pete I was left with no doubt about the extent to which he is indeed Mr Jazz of the Banbury scene.

The origins of this status can be traced to his father Brownie's huge encouragement but also to teenage experiences of the luxurious Flamingo Club in London's Wardour Street and, after 1969, at the initially less grand Gerrard Street home of the Ronnie Scott enterprise In each case, the nature of the premises, the quality of the musicians and the atmosphere generated all combined to produce a unique ambience. There is every good reason to think that Ronnie's sense of humour contributed to this. Typical was his advertisement in the *Melody Maker* for October 25 1959 which ran as follows:-'Ronnie Scott's Club, 39 Gerrard Street … Tubby Hayes Quartet, Eddie Thompson Trio and the first appearance of Jack Parnell in a jazz club since the relief of Mafeking'.

Out of these visits to the capital city, Banbury Jazz Club was born, first as a concept and then as a reality. 1967 was the year when the *Mount House* introduced Banbury public to the Pete Lay Quartet. Terry Mortimer played the piano, Eddie Jones supplied the bass effect and the late Ron Mole was drummer. Their performance was the outcome of initiatives by the Goodes who owned the hotel then. Their request for a regular music night started with a popular range from Glenn Miller to the Beatles but quickly gravitated to the traditional jazz front – everything from mainstream to be-bop. An early followers of the new Banbury musical fashion was Albert Dixon and it's good to know he is still a diehard supporter.

Once jazz was in the frame, the aim of the club was to represent local and midland musicians together with occasional top British and American recording starts. Four years into the life of Banbury Jazz Club and along came that sensation West Indian alto-sax Joe Harnett, sadly no longer with us. At the time jazz lovers saw in Joe shades of that legendary figure Charlie (Bird) Parker. The list of greats who appeared in Banbury is long, itself a tribute to the club and how it was perceived. There were trombonists and vibists, tenor saxists, and vocalists. Older members will recall names like Kenny Baker, Gordon Campbell, Kathy Stobart and Betty Smith. Out of these, Kathy from South Shields had a special place in this brand of music because she was 'the first musician to break the sex barrier in British jazz'. Among the performers who gave so much pleasure was Tommy Whittle and he will help to celebrate the anniversary this month.

Apart from Pete Lay's incomparable efforts, no review of the club's history would be complete without mention of the supporting cast. At the *Mount* (now the *Banbury House* Hotel) a succession of proprietors has been foremost among the key figures. First was Tony Goode, then John Fowlds and now Anna and Paul Galvin. Organisations have played their part as well, notably Jazz South (Oxfordshire's jazz federation) and Cheeses from Switzerland and spearheaded by managing director

Maurice Johnson. Pete also recognised the huge support of the Musicians' Union and of Cherwell District Council without whose grant support a jazz club could not have survived for long.

The members themselves have brought an infectious enthusiasm to the cause. Though jazz may be to a degree male orientated and the music attractive to the slightly older connoisseur, those who go hate to miss so much as an evening. In 1967 you could get in for 2/6d, today £4 is the going rate, or £2.50 if you qualify for a concession but the amount scarcely seems to matter. As Gerry Dibsdale's headline (one of many from a faithful follower) proclaimed to us back in 1986, those who go seek 'pure jazz enjoyment'.

The very evening that Anna and Paul Galvin took over the hotel jazz was in full swing and somehow it provided a hallmark for the new management. Since them there have been many great gigs, much to the pleasure of numerous hotel clients. Back in September 1987 Pete and Dee celebrated their silver wedding in some style. Ten years later there should be another of Ted Hanson's humdingers especially if Pete and his friends follow the wit of the waggish Scot. Congratulations and good luck Banbury Jazz Club, Pete Lay: the Millennium beckons.

Banbury Guardian 16 October 1997.

4.24: Dancing to Brownie's beat

The *Banbury Guardian* issue of March 28, 1985, included a photograph of the Futurists Dance Band. Their leader and pianist was Tom Hutchings. Three of the other players featured were Percy Allitt (sax), Ron Collett (violin and alto-sax) and Frank Howe (guitar and violin). Perched right above them all in this picture taken in the mid-30s was a 16-year-old drummer – his name Brownie Lay. Michael Blanchard has submitted a very fine appreciation of that drummer. Many of our readers will recall the days when the *Whately Hall* Hotel was under his direction and would want to echo the warmth of Michael's remarks about Brownie: 'The recent death of Brownie Lay will revive memories of Saturday night dinner dances held at the hotel in the 60s and 70s. During these decades, local patrons revelled in his band's strict tempo dance music, interspersed with some up-beat modern syncopation'. By 1988, the Brownie Lay band, sometimes augmented to orchestra status for special occasions, had played more than 1,000 times at the *Whately*. This achievement was officially recognised in June 1988 when Brownie, the sole survivor of the original 1960s combo, was guest of honour at a commemoration ball. All guests attending received an inscribed goblet marking the occasion.

While the band's style of music would have been matched in other hotels of the 50s, 60s and 70s, Brownie Lay's group had a measure of panache which was guaranteed to lift the tempo of any party or gig. This owed much to Brownie as leader and disciplinarian but also the personae of some splendid characters, notably Alfie Grant (pianist) and Jimmy Staig (trombonist). The Brownie Lay Band played at many more functions locally and further afield. Their reputation was very high throughout

Brownie Lay posing with admirers during the interval of a dance.

The Whately Hall Hotel where the Brownie Lay band played on more than a thousand occasions.

Oxfordshire and they always supported the big name bands playing at the old Winter Gardens on the High Street. These visiting greats included Victor Sylvester, Ted Heath and Cyril Stapleton, each of whose bands had a quality drummer much admired by Brownie.

Among the really notable occasions there used to be the outstanding Christmas ball events at *Penrose House*. Graced by the Horton ward sisters and supported by medical staff from a wide area, the Penrose parties appear to have been evenings (and early mornings) to remember. Grand events such as these must have seemed a long way from the late 20s when Brownie, at the age of ten, was going to Town Hall dances and helping with the refreshments. Some of the bands from those days caught his ear, especially the performances of the drummers.

In 1989 Brownie recalled some of these bands and mentioned especially those of Jimmy Newman (landlord of the *Old George* which stood on the site of Barclay's Bank), Fred Webb, Owen Sherwin Marshall and Fred Cleaver. Fred's group was called The Scarlet and Gold Band and on occasions gave free performances at the Warwick Road workhouse.

With so much to offer musically, it is easy to forget the many other reasons why we should regard Brownie as part of an elite group of people who have left their mark on the history of the town. Forty two years with the *Banbury Advertiser* enabled him to range from printer's devil to director, from tea boy to the top. During that time his huge interest in cricket emerged in the form of a weekly column written under the pseudonym of S T Ump. Brownie could write knowledgeably about the game because he had played it and been a member of key clubs locally. Some photographs of the Great Western Railway team feature Brownie but most notably he spanned the gap between Town and Twenty. In some jottings about the Futurists, Brownie gives a whole-hearted thumbs up 'What a fantastic line up in the musical heritage of the town. I've read many books on Banbury's history and never yet have I seen this wonderful musical family receive the credit due to them'.

Today's photograph was … taken … in 1975. The occasion was the presentation of silver tankards suitably inscribed to the band in recognition of 20 fine years playing at the *Whately Hall* Hotel. As Michael Blanchard says at the conclusion of his appreciation, 'Brownie's drum kit was Premier – simply the best'. A fitting epitaph to a man who illuminated the local scene so brightly and with such versatility.

Banbury Guardian 7 August 1997.

4.25: Ken Prewer's big band

A box advertisement at the foot of page 10 of the *Banbury Guardian* of Thursday October 27, 1960 contained the simple message, 'We regret to announce the retirement of Ken Prewer – the orchestra will continue to maintain the high standard presented for nearly 20 years'. In a simple and sincere manner this way of breaking the news summed up how so many people must have felt about the Prewer years. Today, and in next week's *Guardian,* I am going to explore the background to Ken's success and to show how much he has been missed by those whose lifespan coincided with the big band sound.

Though it is impossible to decipher the smaller print details on a poster located outside Ivy House, the Prewer family's residence, the eye can catch two pertinent words, 'Grand Dance' (see one of today's pictures). I was too late on the Banbury scene to appreciate their full significance but I am confident from experience of dance bands at Southampton and Nottingham that Ken's devotion to the world of entertainment ensured that every dance was 'Grand'. On occasions such as Rotary and masonic events, a disciplined approach might extend to a retreat from food and alcoholic drinks during the dance itself.

It is highly probable that Ken entered the world of dance music in the first place because of his father's influence. James Percy Prewer has been organist at Sunbury-on-Thames and Adderbury and ensured that Ken did plenty of piano practice. In later years James, who ran the Banbury Stamp Company, transposed a great deal of music for the orchestra's use. His son's understanding of music would have been helped by his time in St Mary's Church Choir.

Ken Prewer's band, with Brownie Lay on drums, at an event in Wincott's Café.

Dancers at Wincott's Café, probably at the same event.

The Ken Prewer years were divided into two parts by his time in uniform. In the early 1930s enthusiastic and very young musicians gathered under his leadership and met for regular rehearsals at Ivy House. Dick Wise (who was later to form a rival band), Tom Brinkworth, Frank Bolton, Ron Grubb, 'Hodgy' Perkins and Beryl Pewsey (pianist). The war robbed north Oxfordshire of the Prewer sound but nevertheless provided Ken with a whole range of new opportunities. He was drafted into the Grenadier Guards where his musical talents were soon spotted.

A surviving programme for Sunday, May 3, 1942, reveals his part in a Grand Concert put on at the Town Hall in High Wycombe. Among the members of the Dance Orchestra of HM Grenadier Guards was Corporal K Prewer, alto saxophone and clarinet, from Ken Prewer's Broadcasting Band, Banbury. In later years the way the programme was set out and the experience of taking part must have remained with him. His fellow Guardsmen included H Woods, who was dubbed King of the Burlesque, and T Parker who, with his ukulele, was rated a rival of George Formby. There was female support in the shape of Irisa Wills – the Blonde Venus – who was a singer of rhythmic songs, intoxicatingly vivacious. Particular highlights of Ken's years with the Guards Training Battalion were reserved for performances at Windsor Castle. He conducted the band at three royal command performances but was also involved in the provision of support music for pantomimes there such as *Sleeping Beauty* in which the royal princesses each played a part.

After serving overseas as a tank commander, Ken returned to Britain in 1945 and spent about 12 months until his demobilisation as a member of the *Stars in Battledress* show. Looking back on these war years it is possible to discern the makings of his post-1946 successes back in Banbury.

Ivy House, No 23 South Bar, home of the Prewer family and of the Banbury Stamp Co. To the right is Austin House, built as a Baptist chapel by the brewer, Richard Austin, in 1834.

The Grenadier Guards Dance Orchestra had been a high profile group. Not for nothing were patrons of a High Wycombe concert advised to book their seats without delay to avoid disappointment.

The late 1940s and 1950s were to be exciting times for dance devotees in north Oxfordshire. Wincott's Ballroom and the Winter Gardens, with a host of one night stand venues, were places to be seen… Ken moved ever closer to the strict tempo style so beloved of band leaders like Victor Sylvester….

…Throughout all his years in the dance band business there can have been few more unusual playing positions for Ken Prewer and his fellow musicians than a 1936 hospital fete float. This had been submitted by the management of the *Palace* Cinema in order to draw public attention to the forthcoming film musical of the year, *The Music Goes Round*. Ken's musicians had been hired to play at intervals on the way to the Horton Infirmary. Traction for the float was provided by Young's Service Garage located in the Warwick Road. The weather on fete day was not the best. A deluge of rain greeted the procession of floats but despite this hazard, a huge crowd assembled along the route, many of whom may well have been encouraged to see the hit musical as a result of Ken's rendition.

One of the legacies that the Second World War left in Banbury – the Cold Store alongside the railway in Grimsbury (now demolished).

Much more to his liking was the opportunity to play dance music in strict tempo style. In some advertising literature Ken set out his image with obvious pride. He stressed that the members of the orchestra had been 'specially selected for their wide range of experience', including over 150 hunt balls at which, invariably, he wore his Grenadier Guards red coat. A trump card was that he was able to state that his musicians had often acted as relief to such famous orchestras as that conducted by Victor Sylvester. It followed that Ken could lay claim to 25 years in the dance band business and still hold the finest connections in the Midlands.

The advertising worked. Ken Prewer and his orchestra were never short of work. Much of it came at either the Winter Gardens in the High Street or Wincott's Ballroom in South Bar. The latter became his home base until the decision to retire was made in 1960. Typical events of some calibre were a Sportsmen's Ball of December 1956 and a Masonic Ladies' Festival in 1959. The first of these occasions saw Ken share the dancing sessions with the Melochords and the Ken Martin Band. By contrast Alfred Lodge 340 booked the Prewer Ballroom Orchestra exclusively for dancing till 1 am. During the golden years at Wincott's Café, evenings were often diversified by competitions. On one unspecified occasion, the *Banbury Advertiser* recorded the details of a 'sweater girl' competition. The winner was a Hilda Green and she was caught on camera receiving a guinea voucher from the smiling Ken Prewer.

Most of his dance floors were a sea of faces – often of the young of Banbury letting their hair down. This made all the more poignant the news of Ken's retirement in October 1960. Regulars on the dance floor were left to treasure their memories of 'Who's taking you home tonight' and 'You're dancing on my heart'. Ken's retreat into the world of business with Goodenoughs was accompanied by the decision to hang up his saxophone.

Back in July 1959 Ken and his wife Pearl had been involved in Reginald Keep's 50th birthday celebrations. It was some event. The world famous Frank and Peggy Spencer formation gave a display and at a minute past midnight Victor Sylvester cut the cake. It speaks reams for Ken's popularity that the invitation card allowed for the possibility that he might be too busy to join those celebrating. On October 17, 1960 the *Banbury Guardian* carried the simple box message 'We regret to announce the retirement of Ken Prewer'. So too did a host of people in Banbury.

Banbury Guardian 5/12 April 2001

- Ivy House. 23 South Bar.

5. World War 2

5.01: Annie Meadows, billeting officer, 1939

At the time of the outbreak of the Second World War Banbury was perceived as a safe haven. It was for this reason that the town was called upon for implementation of the central government's Evacuation Scheme known as Operation Pied Piper. In early September 1939 Banbury expected 2,000 youngsters while a further 2,200 were destined for villages that formed part of the rural district council's area. The evacuees came from different parts of London and were accompanied on the journey by mothers and teachers. On the first train there were 800 children with 80 London County Council teachers. Their homes were in West Ham, Camberwell and Dagenham and so it was right for them to ask the question 'what sort of town will be ours until the war ends?' Many of the smaller ones with memories of Sunday school outings seemed to expect a glimpse of the sea. As if to prove a point a report for the *Banbury Advertiser* quoted the case of one youngster who was heard to inquire 'is this a seaside town, guv'nor?'

Collectively the children were easily identified as evacuees because of the combination of luggage labels and new gas masks in their boxes. The party went straight to a reception centre that was set up in the nearby former Andy's Garage. Here children received a bag of food before being put on the Midland Red buses that were to transport them to their new homes. When the second train arrived it was seen to be more crowded than the first. Even the guard's van had to be pressed into service. These children hailed from Bromley-by-Bow and Limehouse. Their foster homes were in Banbury itself and were reached either in private cars or the majority by walking with their teachers and billeting officers.

It would be wrong to assume that all evacuees [were] transferred from London under the government scheme. Some came privately and also had to be found accommodation by the 80 or so billeting officers, most of whom, like Annie Meadows, were teachers. These officers were called to a meeting in the council offices in Marlborough Road in late August 1939 and each was given a list of the streets they were to canvas in order to ensure sufficient places for the children. Annie was a teacher at Britannia Road Infants School and was well-known to many of the residents of Gatteridge Street, her allotted road, and so hoped this would encourage a greater willingness to participate in the scheme. This street had another advantage, namely that many of the houses were three-storied and so had four bedrooms. Despite these apparently favourable factors, Annie encountered a deal of reluctance until she let it be known that her own family in Castle Street were prepared to offer hospitality.

When the children arrived on the doorsteps in Gatteridge Street they received a warm welcome, though some of the older residents appeared worried by the fact that the youngsters were from an area of East London where hardship was common. This was reflected in the clothes worn by these children from Poplar. After finding accommodation for all the children in her charge, Annie finally returned home to Castle Street to discover that instead of the expected girls her family's evacuees were male, Peter Driscoll and Henry Adshead. After tea she escorted the lads to the town centre where they could post the prepared cards to their parents to let them know their address and spend 6d each had received. They went to Woolworths where the boys chose toy guns and Annie bought a supply of caps. The children arrived on Saturday, September 2, and war was declared on Sunday, September 3. The following Monday Annie arrived home at noon to discover that Peter had been whisked away to St Mary's School by one of his London teachers – not what she had expected, which was that the children would attend the re-located Britannia Road School based at Marlborough Road Sunday School. (Britannia Road School had been requisitioned for use as a gas decontamination centre).

It turned out that Peter had a small sister he had been parted from at the reception centre and they were moved in together. The Meadows agreed to take Henry's ten-year-old brother John who had been too ill to make the journey on September 2 and came ten days later.

In the rural district area causes for concern were overcrowding, as in East Adderbury, and a shortage of bedding especially blankets. 400 unclaimed blankets were obtained from the famous Witney Mill at 10/- (50p) each but then the government sent 2,500, most of which had to be put in store. Despite these hiccups, the reception given to evacuees impressed the London County Council party leader who remarked movingly 'may this adventure in comradeship outlast its evil origin and, as a shining light, 'illumine the paths of future generations'.

Banbury Guardian 30 September 2009.

5.02: Wartime child's fond memories

Last week the *Times* newspaper ran a series of articles with the title 'Was childhood so much better before?' comparing experiences of different generations from the 1940s to the present day, so it was good to hear from John Davies of Hemel Hempstead who has written down his memories of Banbury and especially Easington. Three cover the years from 1937-1951. Unsurprisingly wartime features strongly in his recollections. In 1941 part of Marlborough Road Methodist Church was home to some classes of Dashwood Road School. His teachers included the well-respected Annie Meadows.

Three years later it was time for John to transfer to the Newland site where one of the most memorable happenings was the post-war demolition of air raid shelters, which were close to the classrooms. In his own words, 'lessons were very difficult because of the pneumatic drills breaking up the concrete roof and there was dust everywhere'.

The final years of schooling were completed at Banbury Grammar School (the former County School) in Ruskin Road. The head was Alec Rose who lived on site in the specially built headmaster's house. At the rear of the house he kept some lambs, goats, chickens and ducks. As for the curriculum John had a particular fondness for what were known as 'Special Activities'. These were fortnightly and included a history club, swimming and also outdoor sketching with the chance to enjoy Crouch Hill. This was also the area where spent bullet cases could be collected as childhood trophies, a consequence of the Home Guard shooting at the Butts.

During 1944 the presence of tanks along Horton View was a reminder of the approach of D-Day. A particular attraction was an American Sherman tank opposite the Co-op on which John and his friends often played. Unsurprisingly, the tank tracks did a great deal of damage to the roads. Home life and diet at this time was very much influenced by rationing and there was encouragement of any activity that helped to supplement resources. John and his friends went gleaning for ears of corn (destined for chickens) in the fields beyond the end of Ruskin Road. They also paid visits to Salt Lane, where in autumn rosehips would be gathered and subsequently sold to Thompsons the chemist near the *Palace* cinema to be turned into rosehip syrup, a useful source of vitamin C. In John Davies's time edible fungi could be found locally in fields leading towards the Sor Brook.

Early years in Easington were as much as anything about using the local environment beyond the built-up area as a playground. Bales of straw in the fields were converted into tunnels for chasing games, the Sor Brook was just right for fishing and swimming and Salt Lane was ideal for camps and bird nesting. Sticks, especially from privet, could be shaped and with the aid of cardboard flights turned into what were called Jack Arrows. Nearer home, streets were safer then than now and so it was possible to fly balsawood gliders bought from Trinders and to play miniature cricket with twigs for stumps, a piece of wood for a bat and a marble as the ball.

Further afield and during snowy winters Crouch Hill became attractive for sledging probably on the north side where the slope towards the Broughton Road was more challenging. An alternative location would be found behind the present

Sainsbury's superstore. Here there was a very steep slope known as the rapids…
Equally absorbing and not seasonal was the craze for collecting cigarette packets. In
Easington during wartime the place to look was Reg's Café in Oxford Road. With
Americans camped on what is now the Sainsbury's site, the greatest triumph was the
spotting of packets originating from the States and much swapping took place.

If there was one day of the week linked to a specific ritual it was Saturday,
otherwise known as 'Chums Day' at the *Palace* Cinema in Banbury Market Place.
Especially favoured films were those about Flash Gordon and his space adventures.
Each morning began with a song from which the following lines are extracted:

> *Every Saturday we line up*
> *To see the films we like to see*
> *And every Saturday*
> *We shout aloud with glee*
> *We like to laugh and have our sing-song*
> *Just a happy crowd are we*
> *We're all pals together*
> *We're minors of the ABC.*

I feel sure that John would agree with the final comment in the *Times*, 'I don't think
I'd swap my childhood. It makes you what you are, doesn't it?'

Banbury Guardian 31 January 2008.

5.03: Flying high in Wings Week

This month sees the 60th anniversary of a very special Wings Week that appears to have claimed public attention in a quite remarkable way. The main objective was to raise £250,000 to provide 10 bombers and 10 fighters – an ambitious sum of money being in mind the size of the town (population 18,000 approximately, together with another 12,000 in the rural area) and wartime levels of hardship within families. Central to this occasion was the erection of a Wellington bomber in the Horse Fair. A footbridge enabled people to reach the cockpit and greatly facilitated appreciation of the exhibit. It can only be a matter for speculation whether or not the aircraft was the same Wellington bomber (F for Freddy) that had been positioned in Northampton market place immediately prior to the Banbury Wings Week.

The mounting of this static display was but one aspect of a very busy week, which was given an official start by Squadron Leader Sir Alfred Beit, Bart, MP. He was accompanied by a party of notables that included the Lord Lieutenant of Oxfordshire, Lord and Lady Bicester, Sir James Edmundson (the local MP) and his wife as well as the mayor and mayoress of Banbury along with members of the rural district council. The ceremony took place on the steps of the Horse Fair cinema theatre, which was then known as the *Regal*. Coincidentally, a procession of relevant organisations started within the grounds of the People's Park. There were detachments of the Royal Air Force, the Women's Auxiliary Air Force, Women's Land Army, National Fire Service, Civil Defence Services, Cadets, Air Training Corps and also many other bodies. Musical accompaniment was provided by several bands including that of the Home Guard. The route of this procession took in most of the town centre and so provided an extended opportunity for money raising to boost the RAF Benevolent Fund and help support the work of the Horton Hospital. Getting amongst the crowds lining the route was in the capable hands of members of the Workpeople's Hospital Association. As a body of willing volunteers they were very well known in Banbury and district. Northern Aluminium Company members conducted a mile of pennies in the town centre.

An attractive exhibition of aircraft equipment and accessories must surely have drawn numerous visitors to Christ Church Parish Hall in Broad Street. Opening hours ranged from 10am to 9pm each day and there was the added attraction of the chance to purchase savings stamps which could be stuck on a bomb case. Alongside the display of military hardware and safety appliances, there were some fascinating photographs loaned by Armstrong Siddeley Motors. Two of these depicted war incidents. Both were Avro Anson reconnaissance planes in action, in one instance guiding a destroyer to a raft sheltering survivors of a merchantman that had sunk. From Broad Street it was just a short step to the Market Place where organisers of the overall event had located a full size inflated dinghy on a circular water tank. The challenge to the public was to throw sufficient coins aboard to sink the dinghy.

Wings for Victory Week was not just about symbols of war. Leisure and Sports featured within a comprehensive programme that included dances, cricket matches, a boxing tournament, whist drives and a swimming gala. For connoisseurs of brass music, a must was the appearance of an RAF military band at the *Whately Hall Hotel* on the Sunday. Even filmgoers were not forgotten and the *Grand* in Broad Street secured some special savings features. Those who went to the *Palace* cinema in the Market Place discovered an interesting display of fragments of bombs that had been dropped on the canal wharf and the GWR goods yard.

Despite the incredibly varied programme for Wings Week 1943, the central task remained that of raising £250,000. In an effort to stimulate public interest, a savings indicator was erected on the town hall and this made it possible to chart the flow of money from the numerous sources. Each day a local person of some note was responsible for declaiming the interim position. On the Wednesday this responsibility was in the hands of the secretary of the Northern Aluminium Company. The final result was given on Tuesday, June 1 by Theo Clark (chairman of the savings committee). Amazingly the target was exceeded by nearly £100,000. Apart from this superb outcome, a significant reason for remembering the week was that the mayor, Councillor Deacon, presented a savings certificate to every baby born in the borough during the week. Nothing like catching them young!

Banbury Guardian 22 May 2003.

- Sir Alfred Beit MP, 2nd Bt (1903-64).
- Vivian Hugh Smith, 1st Baron Bicester (1867-1956).

5.04: Fires lit to mark end of the war

This year marks the 60th anniversary of Victory in Europe Day (VE Day). Back in 1945, Tuesday May 8 was the particular day that the nation celebrated the end of the war against Hitler and his European allies. Although mainly a joyous occasion, for some people it was a more subdued affair because of family involvement in the continuing hostilities in the Far Eastern theatre of war.

The first signs that Banbury was getting ready for VE Day became evident early on the Monday previous when flags and bunting appeared at scattered points across the town. By bedtime that day and in the knowledge that the Prime Minister, Winston Churchill, was going to address the nation at 3 o'clock on the Tuesday afternoon, the town was 'beflagged from end to end'. In common with previous periods of celebrations such as the Silver Jubilee of George V in 1935 and the Coronation of George VI in 1937, certain parts of the town made outstanding contributions to the overall Banbury response. According to the *Advertiser* newspaper, the Cherwell Street district was expected to 'come out with an amazing show'. Possibly the especially close-knit nature of communities had something to do with this. Calthorpe Street and parts of Neithrop were determined not to be outdone and it was reported to the *Banbury Advertiser* that residents in some streets had been paying into a club in order to meet the cost of flags and materials for decoration.

Some industrial firms also entered into the spirit of the occasion. The Northern Aluminium Company dressed its buildings with the flags of the Allied Nations, while the Braggins family of timber yard fame planned a massive 'V for Victory' sign at the top of a tall crane. Several businessmen and property owners in the centre of the town were very involved with enhancing their surroundings.

Norman Blinkhorn, whose photographic studio was in South Bar, added flood-lighting to the fine trees on the approaches to the Cross, the *Whately Hall Hotel* was a mass of coloured lights and radio engineer Thomas Luckett dressed his High Street window in a way which attracted much attention.

All these preparations for VE Day would have meant a lot to those people who remembered the town of the 1930s, but it is also interesting to gauge the reactions of children. A newspaper reporter asked a happy youngster from the Grimsbury area what he thought of it all. Back came the response: 'All right so long as we don't have to write a composition about it'. A long standing Banbury tradition on occasions such as VE Day was a formal gathering in the Cow Fair (the part of Bridge Street near the Town Hall) for the purpose of hearing speeches from the balcony of the Town Hall. At 3pm on Tuesday, May 8, a huge crowd appeared here in response to the news that there would be loudspeakers to relay Churchill's address. After this broadcast, Alderman Mascord, Mayor of Banbury in 1945, said a few words and echoing Churchill's speech ended with a call to action: 'Go away and according to your desires be joyful'.

Later in the day people were more than happy to oblige, they wanted to let their hair down. Banbury folk danced until midnight, cheered any passing military vehicle and a few even stayed on for a night-time vigil. Elsewhere after dark bonfires were focal points for local gatherings. Two were lit in the vicinity of the aluminium works and many others could be spotted from the top of Hardwick Hill. The tallest fire, all of 50 feet, was near the Great Western Railway station. It was reported that the glow from this was so bright that anyone standing on the bridge would have been able to peruse a newspaper in comfort.

Readers of both the *Guardian* and the *Advertiser* may well have been surprised to see formal statements by Associated British Cinemas who owned the *Palace* in the Market Place and by the Midland Motor Omnibus Company. These were contained within formal box advertisements and congratulated service personnel and senior commanders for such a wonderful outcome to the war in Europe.

During the following weeks there were numerous street parties at which consumption of teatime goodies to which most would have contributed was followed by dancing to music provided by Albert Boote and his Banbury Sound. Children especially received gifts; in the case of Crouch Street this amounted to an ice cream and an orange. Presentations were made to the mayor and mayoress who had endeavoured to attend as many events as possible. Sheila Robinson of Upper Windsor Street was a mere two-and-a-half when she handed a bouquet to the civic couple. Just as the tempo of events appeared to be winding down, a Victory Fun Fair opened on the Easington Recreation Ground.

As if to demonstrate a new kind of beginning, advertisements for the fair promised 'all clean up-to-date amusements'. Hard times lay ahead in Banbury but for the moment this fair was a chance to cling to the hope that the period of celebration would never end.

Banbury Guardian 5 May 2005.

5.05. The election of 1945

[This] … article is about the 1945 election that resulted nationally in a landslide victory for the Labour Party. This was an outcome which was the very opposite of what would have happened if everyone had heeded the message in the local Conservative candidate's advertisement. It read 'Thank Churchill' (General Election 18th June 1945), YOU will be thanking Churchill by working and voting for Dodds-Parker. In the event 23,777 did just that but 21,951 supported the Labour candidate and so the Banbury seat became a Conservative marginal.

Neither candidate was local. Colonel Arthur Douglas Dodds-Parker had his roots more in Oxford than in the north of the county. His father had been a senior surgeon at the Radcliffe Infirmary from 1905 until 1927 and he himself enjoyed a public school and Oxford University education followed by military service in many theatres of war. Resumption of peace in Europe found him still a bachelor at the age of 36 and with a home in Chesham, Buckinghamshire. His marital status caused much amusement at a meeting of the women's branch of the Banbury Conservative Association. Lady Edmondson, wife of the retiring MP, reminded him that he had once remarked, 'If elected I might also find a wife in that part of the country'.

His only opponent was the Labour candidate Richard Brian Kerry Roach, a staunch trade unionist who lived in the Moseley area of Birmingham. His principal supporters in the constituency were from Warwick Road in Banbury. Oxfordshire as

Arthur Douglas Dodds-Parker, MP for Banbury 1945-59.

a whole did not follow the trend for a significant swing to the Labour Party. However, at a pre-election rally, the former secretary of the Holborn Labour Party made an interesting observation when he said 'Banbury was no longer a small town isolated in the middle of England for it was affected by what happened in Russia, India and Abyssinia'. In terms of policy there was more than a hint of nationalisation, especially of the Bank of England and all forms of transport.

Unlike most recent elections there was no Liberal candidate. The *Banbury Guardian* of the day carried a letter about the possibility but nobody came forward. Instead a prominent local Liberal, Harold Early of Witney, wrote to the newspaper to explain why he would be voting for Brian Roach and not for Dodds-Parker. His reason was summed up as follows: 'Mr Churchill is a big man, but he is not wide enough to hide the "old gang" who are sheltering behind him'. This was a reference to what he felt was the unsatisfactory nature of pre-war Conservative rule. Colonel Dodds-Parker undertook a heroic programme of meetings in town venues and village halls. By contrast Brian Roach favoured gatherings at works such as outside Stone's factory in the Cherwell area. These were occasions to parade party slogans, notably, 'We are ALL for Dodds-Parker this time' (Conservative) and 'Now is the time to strike a blow for progress' (Labour). 'Big guns' turned out to support the candidates. Conservatives booked the town hall for Earl Beatty, Parliamentary Secretary for the Air Ministry, while a great Labour rally in People's Park was addressed by Arthur Deakin, the assistant general secretary of the Transport & General Workers' Union. He spoke enthusiastically of a Labour win and added 'Your future depends on it'.

Later and in a final advertisement the Labour message promised 'better and literally more and better houses'. This was to be combined with a square deal for all workers. Overall Labour had the pre-election pledges but it was local Conservatives who celebrated with a victory dance in the town hall. The outcome prompted Dodds-Parker to buy *Grey Stones* in Great Rollright….

Banbury Guardian 29 April 2010.

- Colonel Arthur Douglas Dodds-Parker (1909-2006), MP for Banbury 1945-59.

5.06: Vital roles of those left behind

In a year in which we are looking back to times of war and their aftermath, it is good to recall the involvement of a company with a strong local base. During the dark days that stretched out from 1939-1945 the Northern Aluminium Company (NAC), whose successor Alcan occupies the same site and some of the same buildings, 'played no small part in the defence of our country during the critical time of the Battle of Britain and helped to make possible the mighty offensive action directed by the Royal Air Force against Germany's industries which hastened the end of the war'. These words first appeared in a victory edition of the Northern Aluminium Company's in-house publication called *Safety First*. They were penned on behalf of the management by Mr E L Ashley who went on to pay tribute to the 'many women in the Works who contributed so much to our War effort'.

Their efforts were critical because conscription and the act of volunteering resulted in a serious loss of men from the workforce. At first the solution was to draft in older men whose previous occupations were less essential to the war effort. Typically they had been shop assistants, hairdressers, bus conductors, building workers, printers and wood workers. Channel Islanders who had escaped the German occupation and also many refugees of the Blitz in London and south-east England diversified their ranks.

Initially only a few women came through the company's Southam Road gates but their numbers soon increased to the point at which it was clear that they would be filling jobs previously regarded as the prerogative of men. Inevitably some had husbands who had been called up. There were also mothers and grandmothers who turned themselves into shift workers to enable them to combine war work with the care of their homes and children and ensuring that they had food. Many of these women and older men did not live in Banbury so a huge fleet of buses brought them from villages within a 20-mile radius. Shift changeover times were particularly periods of unease. Apart from these fleets of buses, Southam Road was filled with bicycles and a few cars whose lights would have made them very visible from the air.

However the works were well camouflaged and there was also a decoy factory in nearby Bourton. Apart from its height this closely resembled the actual factory. Clearly it deceived the pilot of a raiding aircraft on October 3, 1940. Following an attack on the gas works and the GWR station, a stick of bombs hit the dummy building. Had this been the actual works it has been estimated that the emergency services would have been confronted by as many as 300 casualties. NAC had its own ARP organisation whose efforts were vital to the defence of the real factory. Interestingly the compilers of Safety First for October 1945 estimated that, throughout the whole of the war, production was stopped for a mere 17¾ hours by the need for total evacuation.

A fascinating section of the magazine was devoted to revelations about the effect of war effort on the production line. Under a banner headline, 'Now it can be Told', the employees of the Banbury and Adderbury works were able to learn that from 1939-1945 the Banbury works' output was half the country's sheet, strip and extrusion

Change of shift in 1952 at what was then the Northern Aluminium Company's Banbury factory, with buses waiting to take home workers who lived in the countryside, and extensive sheds sheltering the bicycles of Banbury-based employees. The scene was very similar during the Second World War.

output. The significance of this outcome of an 'all-out' production effort was that back to September 1939 Britain was ill-equipped in all branches of the services but especially the Royal Air Force. Aluminium from Banbury ensured that our forces in the air could be built up into an efficient fighting machine.

War efforts were not confined to the factory alone. As well as setting up their own Home Guard unit (300th troop) employees were encouraged to become involved in the likes of the fire service, the St John Ambulance Brigade and the British Red Cross. Inevitably all this activity left little time for leisure but the company's athletic association did manage to keep going. The various sports sections were hampered by the fact that many clubs in Banbury and district ceased to play. Fixtures were hard to come by and in any case there was a lack of transport to get players to away venues. This may partly explain why one of the chief aims of the athletic association was to give games to service teams in the district.

Elsewhere in the magazine the company reported that many men from the works were still involved with armies of occupation. This is why it is so important that in 2005 we remember VJ Day just as much as we celebrated the rejoicing that characterised the earlier VE Day, and also that there were many still serving their country after peace had been declared.

Banbury Guardian 7 July 2005.

5.07: A great war effort

On Sunday morning, September 3, 1939, the people of Banbury and district learnt that a 'state of war' existed between Great Britain and Germany. With obvious pride both the *Banbury Guardian* and the *Banbury Advertiser* reported that the area had made and would continue to make a fine response to war-time responsibilities. It is interesting to reflect on the many and various ways in which this response was achieved. Particularly noteworthy was how this area coped with evacuees, especially from London. The scale of the operation was itself remarkable. In early September and in the course of just a few days more than 2,000 children stepped on to the Great Western station platform.

Billeting of these youngsters was in the hands of local teachers such as Dashwood School's Annie Meadows. It says much about local hospitality that few wanted to return to London. Subsequently parents were able to come on day visit, for instance, when Mr A R Taylor, Air Raid Warden for Bow, arranged for their conveyance by a fleet of charabancs. Local newspapers made much of the 'fine sight all over town when children with parents and foster parents enjoyed lovely weather and seeing the sights of Banbury'.

On a later occasion Bow children were highly delighted when the swimming bath was made available for their annual gala that under normal circumstances would have been staged at Poplar Baths. A further feather in Banbury's cap came when Banbury [County] School absorbed girls from Fulham School. These pupils had been at Thame but the Easington site was perceived as having more adequate educational facilities.

During the early days of the war the town was fortunate in having excellent civic leadership. This had one interesting consequence, namely that the mayor, Horace Lester, agreed to continue for a further term. He had displayed a keen interest in the welfare of the town and also played a full part in the development of the local ARP organisation. His wife was equally active and highly successful with appeals for the likes of boys' clothing, perambulators and push chairs as some of the evacuees had come with very little. A similar role was played by Mrs Berkeley of Hanwell Castle who was the Chief Billeting Officer for Banbury Rural District Council.

Observation of blackout arrangements was of a very high order. However it was not long before the *Banbury Advertiser* ran a front page headline, 'First local Black-out Prosecution'. An Oxford Road resident was fined £1 for failing to properly obscure lights. Purposely this was less of a punishment and more of a warning of severe responses in future and similar cases. One of the biggest impacts on daily life was brought about by reduced shopping hours for both shops and the produce market. Shift workers benefitted from different closing times from day to day. Local residents accustomed to doorstep deliveries of bread and milk also had to be prepared for change and possibly inconvenience. Robert Pursaill and Henry Lay wrote on behalf of local bakers to say that they would endeavour to supply and deliver quality bread for as long as possible. Banbury and district dairymen could only promise one milk delivery per day.

If the morale of people locally was to be maintained during the wartime conditions it was deemed important for everyone to have some opportunities for leisure pursuits. In this respect football played a significant part. Most leagues were suspended or curtailed but friendlies involving district teams were encouraged. Matches required police agreement and at the final whistle spectators had to disperse quickly. Early examples of such matches were Northern Aluminium Company *versus* Early Closers and Banbury Spencer against Oxford City.

Perhaps the epitome of local determination to help the war effort was a Thursday working party at the Bluebird in Bridge Street who, instead of attending keep fit classes, knitted and sewed for hospitals and military establishments.

Banbury Guardian 3 October 2013.

5.08: Alderman W G Mascord, wartime mayor

In her sociological study of Banbury called *Tradition and Change*, Margaret Stacey analysed the Labour/Trade Union connection. The resultant diagram fits superbly the life of William George Mascord. Born locally in 1888, William came from solid working-class stock. His father, Alfred Josiah Mascord, was for many years general outdoor foreman for Kimberleys the builders in Britannia Road. This may well have influenced William's career choice as he fashioned a workshop at 6 Bridge Street and plied the trades of carpenter, joiner and undertaker.

An issue of the *Banbury Guardian* for February 1961 includes the very important comment that he 'has a particular place in local history'. My article today is an attempt to explain this and to show how William was an excellent example of what today we would call 'old Labour'. This title stemmed from the way in which his political allegiances connected with the Co-operative movement, the activities of local trade unions and Friendly Societies. As indicated in Professor Stacey's chart, he had strong church and sport connections. His youthful membership of St Mary's choir was followed by a commitment to the role of sidesman. In the local world of sport, and apart from a keen soccer interest, he was secretary of the Banbury Harriers Whit-Monday Sports Committee.

In 1912 he married Margaret Ann Morrison and they made their home at 7 Compton Street, which was a small, close-knit working-class community near the town centre (demolished to make way for the Castle Shopping Centre). Seven years later William was elected to Banbury Borough Council for the first time. This was the beginning of a long and distinguished career in local politics. A moment of huge personal significance came in 1929 when he became the first Labour mayor. He succeeded Alderman Collingridge, a difficult act to follow. However at the time of his nomination Alderman Theo Clark had every confidence when he expressed the hope that William Mascord would not 'lose his wicket however varied the bowling'.

On the day of his installation large crowds gathered to watch the Mayoral procession from the Town Hall to the Masonic Hall where the Mascords held their reception. Appropriately, refreshments were arranged by the confectionary department of the Co-operative Society. This was followed in the evening by the Mayor's banquet laid on by that High Street favourite the Lorna Café. During his time as Banbury's leading citizen William had the huge satisfaction of helping the effort that led to the construction of the outdoor swimming baths in Park Road.

Now Alderman Mascord, he was mayor again in 1943 and for part of 1945 after Theo Clark had sadly passed away. It was during the last of his Mayoralties that he and Margaret took great pleasure in attending all the street parties and religious services that marked the end of World War II. The party aspect alone was a great undertaking. In many instances the Mascords opened the events and presented special keepsakes. *Banbury Guardian* reports summed up their dedication when they wrote of the Golden Villa Estate party that this was the 36th Banbury celebration for VE Day that the couple had attended.

In 1949 his council career ended. It seems that he had got out of step with the local Labour Party and the only way he could continue was to stand as an independent.

A VE-Day children's party in East Street, Grimsbury.

He was beaten by ten votes and for a further ten years he continued working as a carpenter. Sadly retirement in July 1960 left him with little time to pursue leisure interests. He and his beloved Margaret passed away at the Horton Hospital in February 1961 within two days of each other. So ended a life of dedication to the town of his birth and there could have been few more fitting tributes than when the Borough Council agreed three street names, Mascord Road, Mascord Close and Margaret Close.

Banbury Guardian 26 April 2012.

Bibliography

Anon [R B Miller], *Hunt Edmunds & Co 1896-1946* (Banbury: Hunt Edmunds, 1946).

Banbury Central Bowling Club: Centenary 1901-2001 (2001).

Beere, A, *'I'm going down to vote': a history of the Labour Movement in Banbury 1945-97* (London: Reflective Hedgehog, 2011).

Beesley, A, *A History of Banbury* (London: Nichols, 1841).

Beeson, C F C, *Clockmaking in Oxfordshire 1400-1850* (Banbury Historical Society, 1962).

Bowen, C J, *Catholicity in Banbury since the Reformation* (Birmingham: 1898).

Brinkworth, E R C, *The Borough of Banbury 1554-1954* (Banbury Borough Council, 1954).

Brinkworth, E R C, *Old Banbury* (Banbury Historical Society, 1958).

Claridge, J, *The Shepherd of Banbury's Rules to judge of the changes of the weather* (London: Thomas Hurst, Edward Chance & Co, 1827).

Clegg, B, *The man who made Littlewoods: the story of John Moores* (London: Hodder & Stoughton, 1993).

Cowan, J, *Banbury Tech: a brief history 1835-1972* (Banbury: North Oxfordshire Technical College, 1987).

Davis, B, & Little, B, *The Changing Faces of Easington* (Witney: Robert Boyd, 2000).

Davis, B, & Little, B, *From Banbury Cakes to a Bushel of Sweetmeats: A look at trades and trademarks* (Witney: Robert Boyd, 2011).

Gibson, J S W, ed, *An Alphabetical Digest of Rusher's Banbury Directory to Trades and Occupations 1832-1906* (Banbury Historical Society, 2014).

Gibson, J S W, *Banbury and the Origins of the Coventry to Oxford Canal 1768-78* (Banbury Historical Society, 2015).

Graham, M, *Oxfordshire at School* (Gloucester: Sutton, 1996).

Graham, M, & Waters, L, *Banbury – then and now* (Stroud: The History Press, 2011).

Greenwood, M, *Pilgrim's Progress Re-visited: the Nonconformists of Banburyshire 1662-2012* (Charlbury: Wychwood, 2013).

Harman, C L, *Cheers, Sir! From the Vicarage to the Brewery* (Cheddar: Challis, 1987).

Harrison, B, & Trinder, B, *Drink and Sobriety in an early Victorian country town: Banbury 1830-69* (Longman, 1969).

Hartland, G, 'The Britannia Works from Living Memory', *C&CH* vol 4 (1971), 194-95.

Hartree, R, 'The Banbury Aluminium Works 1929-2009', *C&CH* vol 20 (2015), 3-30.

Herbert, G, *Shoemaker's Window: Recollections of Banbury .. before the Railway Age* (3rd edn, ed C S Cheney & B Trinder, Banbury: Gulliver Press, 1979).

Hodgkins, V, & Bloxham, C, *Banbury and Shutford Plush* (Banbury Historical Society, 1980).

Holmes, G, Portergill, J & Smith, J, *Fifty years of service* (Banbury Rotary Club, 1985)

Jones, H, *The Chiltern Railways Story* (Stroud: The History Press, 2010).

Kelly's Directories Ltd, *Directory of Banbury* (London: Kelly, 1950).

Kirkham, B, *Our World Was New* (Banbury: privately published, 2012).

Lester, M, *Memories of Banbury* (Banbury: privately published 1986).

Lester, M, *These Golden Days* (Banbury, privately published, 1992).

Lickorish, W H, *Our Jubilee Story or Fifty Years of Co-operation in Banbury and the Neighbourhood* (Banbury Co-operative Society, 1916).

Little, B, *The Changing Faces of Banbury* (Witney: Robert Boyd, 1998).

Little, B, *The Changing Faces of Grimsbury* (Witney: Robert Boyd, 1999).

Little, B, *Banbury: a photographic history of your town* (Salisbury: W H Smith, 2001).

Little, B, *Banbury: a History* (Chichester: Phillimore, 2003).

Little, B, *Banbury: a Century of Change* (Derby: Breedon, 2005).

Little, B, & Shadbolt, D, *The History of Banbury Spencer Football Club* (Witney: Robert Boyd, 2013).

Maloney, A, *Something for the Girls* (London: Constable & Robinson, 2009).

Mann, M, *Workers on the Move: the sociology of relocation* (Cambridge University Press, 1973).

Mileham, R, & Betts, D, *Dashwood School 1902-2008: A Souvenir History* (Witney: Boyd, 2009).

Mitchell, V, & Smith, K, *Didcot to Banbury* (Midhurst: Middleton, 2003).

Northover, K, *Banbury during the Great War* (Witney: Prospero, 2003).

Parry, T, *Scouting for Banbury's Boys* (Witney: Boyd, 2009).

Potts, A, 'Ernest Samuelson and the Britannia Works', *C&CH* vol 4 (1971), 187-93.

Potts, W, *Banbury Madrigal and Glee Union 1891-1930* (Banbury Guardian, 1930).

Potts, W, *Banbury through one hundred years* (Banbury Guardian, 1942).

Potts, W, *A History of Banbury* (Banbury Guardian, 1958).

Rolt, L T C, *The Making of a Railway* (London: Hugh Evelyn, 1971).

Rusher, J G, *Rusher's Banbury Lists and Directories* (Banbury: Rusher, 1798-1906).

Sherwood, J, & Pevsner, N, *The Buildings of England: Oxfordshire* (Harmondsworth: Penguin, 1974).

Stacey, M, *Tradition and Change: a study of Banbury* (Oxford University Press, 1960).

Stacey, M, Batstone, E, Bell, C & Murcott, A, *Power, Persistence and Change: a second study of Banbury* (London: Routledge & Kegan Paul, 1975).

Stanley H B, *Banbury and the Country of Shakespeare* (Banbury: privately published, *circa* 1900).

Steatham, T, *Memories around Edge Hill 1922-39* (Banbury: privately published, 1996).

Symonds, A S, *Oxfordshire People and the Forgotten War* (Witney: Boyd, 2002).

Taylor, A M, *Gilletts: Bankers at Banbury and Oxford* (Oxford: Clarendon Press, 1964).

Tempest, E, & Kendall, B, *Banbury: a history and celebration* (Salisbury: Frith, 2004).

Townsend, S, & Gibson, J S W, *Banbury Past through Artists' Eyes* (Banbury Historical Society, 2007).

Trinder, B, *The History of Methodism in Banbury* (Banbury: Marlborough Road Methodist Church, 1965).

Trinder, B, *Banbury's Poor in 1850* (Banbury Historical Society, 1966).

Trinder, B, *Victorian Banbury* (Banbury Historical Society/Phillimore, 1982/2005).

Trinder, B, 'Fifty years on', *C&CH* vol 8 (1981), 117-137.

Trinder, B, 'Banbury's Victorian Lodging Houses', *C&CH* vol 16 (2004), 138-57.

Trinder, B, 'Banbury: Metropolis of Carriers Carts', C&CH vol 18 (2011), 210-43.

Trinder, B, ed, *Victorian Banburyshire: Three Memoirs: Sarah Beesley, Thomas Ward Boss, Thomas Butler Gunn* (Banbury Historical Society, 2013).

Trinder, B, *Junctions at Banbury: a town and its railways since 1850* (Banbury Historical Society, 2017).

Utechin, P, *The Trumpets Sounded* (Oxford: Robert Dugdale, 1996).

Victoria History of the County of Oxford, vol X, Banbury Hundred (Oxford University Press, 1972).

EW [Edward Walford], *Pathways of Banburyshire* (Banbury: Walford, *circa* 1900).

Walton, J, *Fish & Chips & the British working class 1870-1940* (Leicester University Press, 1992).

Williams, A L E, *From A to B (Antrim to Bermuda),* Sherborne: Dorset Publishing, 1972)

Wilton, G, *The Saxon princess and her infant saint* (Banbury: Four Shires, 2004)

Wood, V,   *The Licensees of the Inns, Taverns and Beerhouses of Banbury* (Oxfordshire Family History Society, 1998).

Index of personal names & businesses

Abbotts, Henry, auctioneer, 141,

Adams, W, cyclist, 174,

Addison, Ann (née Finn), Sea Cadet, 199,

Adkins, F J, shopkeeper, 117,

Adkins, H, cyclist, 174,

Adshead, Henry & John, evacuees, 218,

Albany, Prince Leopold, Duke of, 160,

Alcan, see Northern Aluminium.

Alcock, Harold, builder, 30-31,

Alcock, Percy Reginald & Co, builders, 30-31, 117,

Alcock, Mrs, 155,

Allen, A E, architect, 40,

Allen, Dorothea, factory owner, 98-99,

Allen, Nick, soldier & local historian, 12,

Allitt, Percy, musician, 209.

Amos, Irene, shop assistant, 55-56,

Anderson, Barry, bus driver, 105,

Andy's (Andrews') Transport, 37, 217,

Anker, Frederick, insurance agent, 82,

Aplin Hunt, solicitors, 28,

Ascoli, Mrs -, of Southam Road, 76,

Ashby, Gertrude & Percy, gardeners, 189,

Ashley, E L, aluminium factory manager, 227,

Ashley, Nigel, hairdresser, 43-44,

Ashly, -, police sergeant, 157,

Auld, Cllr Thomas, 164,

Austin, J B, chemist & mineral water manufacturer, 24

Automotive Products, 16-17, 101-02, 152,

Baden Powell, Agnes (1858-1945), 196,

Baden Powell, Sir Robert (1857-1941), founder of Boy Scouts, 196,

Baden Powell, Lady Olive (1889-1977), Chief Guide, 197,

Bagley, Edward, cinema manager, 188-90,

Baker, Miss A, 64,

Baker, Kenny, jazz musician, 207,

Baker, Miss -, cyclist, 174,

Baker, -, Sunday school secretary, 129,

Baker, -, outfitter, 55,

Baldry, Sir Tony (b 1950), politician, 71,

Balfour, Matthew, draper, 67-68,

Ball, George V, chemist, 172,

Ballard, Miss, teacher, 150,

Banbury Buildings Ltd, 110,

Banbury General Motor Co, 86,

Banbury Stamp Co, 212-14,

Barber, Chris, band leader, 204,

Barker, -, teacher, 150,

Barlow, -, 126,

Barnes, -, horseman, 132

Barrows, engineers, 99,

Barton, Neil, haberdashery salesperson, 44,

Baylis, Cyril J, ironmonger's salesman, 52-53,

Beale, Violet, confectioner, 36,

Bearsted, Walter Harold Samuel, 2nd Viscount (1882-1948), 184-85,

Beatty, David Field, 2nd Earl Beatty (1905-72), 198, 200, 226,

Bedlow, 'Knacker', foundry worker, 92,

Beit, Sir Alfred, MP, 2nd Bt (1903-64), 221,

Bell, Professor Colin (1942-2003), sociologist, 16,

Bennett, Muriel, college librarian, 154,

Berkeley, Joan, billeting officer, 229,

Berry, Dave, band leader, 203,

Betts, S, butcher, 152,

Betts, William, Switchgear & Equipment manager, 97,

Bicester, Vivian Hugh Smith, 1st Baron (1867-1956). 221,

Biddle, John, fairground showman & footballer, 157-58,

Biddlecombe, Terry (1941-2014), jockey, 71,

Big Daddy (Shirley Crabtree, 1937-97), wrestler, 204-05,

Bilk, Acker (1929-2014), band leader, 204

Bird, Alfred & Co, 78, 110, 213,

Bird, -, co-operator, 40,

Birmingham & Midland Motor Omnibus Co (Midland Red), 105-07,

Blanchard, Michael, hotel keeper, 209, 211,

Blinkhorn, Norman, photographer, 75, 185, 201, 223,

Bloomfield, Mrs J W, mayoress, 182,

Bloxham, W J, builder, 111, 160,

Blunt, Bruce, journalist, 184,

Bodman, Doris, amateur actor, 191,

Bolton, Frank, musician, 121,

Bolton, William, publican, 121,

Bone, R A, steel fabricator, 24,

Bonham, Elias, 46,

Bonham, -, poor law guardian, 119,

Boot, Henry, builder, 30,

Boote, Albert, sound engineer & foreman, Switchgear & Equipment, 224

Booth, J F & Son, builders, 30,

Boscott, Irene, college secretary, 153,

Boss, Susan, Automotive Products worker, 101,

Boulton, Arthur, headmaster, 145-46,

Boys, Frederick, town clerk, 27, 199,
Boxold, H, gardener, 129,
Bradley, -, teacher, 150,
Braggins, G F & Co, timber merchants, 17, 80-83, 222,
Braggins, George Frederick, timber merchant, 80,
Braggins, Ald George Donald McCleod, timber merchant, 80-83.
Braggins, James (1818-73), timber merchant, 80
Braggins, James Henry, timber merchant, 80,
Bradshaw, Mary Jane, 50,
Bradshaw, Nelson, seed merchant, 50,
Bradshaw, Roger, seed merchant, 50,
Brain, John & Sarah, publicans, 115,
Brandon, Jevan (1848-1914), playwright, 191,
Bridge Motors, 86,
Brinkworth, E R C, historian, 162,
Brinkworth, Thomas, musician, 213,
Britannia Works, ironfounders & engineers, 17, 91-92, 98-99, 115, 169,
Brook, D T, founder of Automotive Products, 101,
Brooks, Kenneth, solicitor & photographer, 28,
Broughton & Wilks, ironmongers, 22, 69,
Britannia Works, ironfounders & engineers,
Broughton, E B, founder of Automotive Products, 101,
Broughton, Mrs E B, 102,
Brown, E W, baker & confectioner, 24-25, 98, 119, 162,
Brown, Olive, secretary & amateur actor, 182,
Brown, O, fishmonger, 132,
Brownett, Cyril, 162,
Browning, Robert (1812-89), poet, 106,
Brummit, R & Sons, toy dealers, 55, 69,
Buchan, Charles (1891-1969), footballer & journalist, 78,
Buckingham, Ralph, police superintendent, 203,
Buggins, Peter, outfitter, 60,
Bull, Alfred, fairground showman, 157,
Buott, S D, railway manager, 111,
Burgin, -, retail manager, 76-77,
Burrow, E J & Co, guidebook publishers, 26, 98,
Burton, Montague, outfitters, 43-44, 61,
Burton, William, 45,
Bussey, F A, motor cyclist, 178,
Bustin, Joseph, electrician, 22, 133,
Butler, A J, fruiterer, 37,
Butler, Edward, grocer, 40,

Butler, James, gardener, 141,
Buzzard, M W, shopkeeper, 136,
Buzzard, -, sound engineer, 118,
'By the Fire', shop, 73,

Cadbury, James, 140,
Cakebread, George, stone mason, 32-33,
Cakebread, Thomas, stone mason, 32-33, 182,
Caless & Abbots, auctioneers, 141,
Campbell, Gordon, jazz musician, 207,
Carpenter, Revd R P R, 125,
Carter, Christopher, gardener, 32-33,
Carter, George, stone mason, 32-33,
Carter, William, foreman French polisher, 133-34,
Cartwright, Jack, timber yard worker, 82,
Cashmore, James, motorcyclist, 180,
Castle, -, donkey owner, 128,
Chadwick, Herbert, amateur actor, 194,
Chapman, Bros, furnishers, 76,
Chappell, Leslie, printer, 103-04,
Charles, E A J, fried fish dealer, 119,
Charmier, John A (1883-1974), RAF officer, 201,
Cheney, Cllr Mary, 147,
Cheney & Sons, printers, 84, 103, 108, 111, 155,
Cherryman, Maureen, 76,
Cherry Orchard Brick Co, 110,
Cherwell Litho, 103-04,
Chidzey, Albert, musician, 40, 191,
Chorlton, A R, director of education, 147,
Chowins, -, retail manager, 76-77,
Christoforu, Andrew, James, Mary, Peter, fish & chip shop owners, 70-71,
Churchill, Winston (1874-1965), statesman, 223, 225,
City Motors, 86,
Claridge, Alfred, stone mason, 32,
Claridge, Percy, ATC officer, 201,
Claridge, Richard, builder, 124,
Clark, Ald Theodore, miller, 162, 189, 222, 231,
Cleaver, Fred, musician, 211,
Clegg, Barbara, biographer, 76,
Cluff, J E, boat dealer, 37, 98,
Clutterbuck, stone mason, 32,
Cochrane, Michael, college technician, 152,
Cockerill, Robert, cabinet maker, 34,
Cody, Buddy, wrestler, 205,
Colebrook & Co, fishmongers, 75,
Coleman, Luke, amateur actor, 191,
Coles, George, carrier, 34,
Collett, Ron, musician, 209,

Collingridge, Ald John, 93, 231,

Collison, W & A, builders, 147,

Compton, Dennis (1918-97), cricketer, 170,

Cook's Tobacco Stores, 22, 174,

Cooke, Henry James, co-operative manager, 17, 39, 45,

Coombs, John, stage manager, 193

County Garages, 72, 85,

Course, Alan, 203,

Coventry, Sir William (?1628-85), politician, 182,

Cowan, Cllr David, 113,

Cowan, Jane, lecturer, 152-53,

Coward, Sir Noel (1899-1973), playwright, 192,

Cowell, A H, bowls player, 172,

Cowell, Margaret, amateur actor, 194,

Cox, Gwen, amateur actor, 194,

Cox, John, Sea Cadet officer, 198,

Crisp, C, bowls player, 172,

Cronk, -, builder, 30,

Crosby, Bing (1903-77), singer, 155, 189,

Croucher, Richard, office manager & amateur actor, 192,

Curtis, 'Nanny', fairground showperson, 157,

Dagger, Audrey (née Peet), 119-20,

Dalby & Co, builders' merchants, 34-35,

Dale, Miss E, cyclist, 174,

Danby & Caless, auctioneers, 140-41,

Davies, Ian, builder & butcher, 152,

Davies, John, wartime scholar, 219-20,

Davies, Leslie, amateur actor, 194,

Davies, -, teacher, 150,

Davies Bros, slate quarry owners, 34,

Dawson, -, borough surveyor, 116,

Dayman, Rev Charles, 34,

Deacon, Cllr J A, chemist, 222,

Deakin, Arthur (1890-1955), trade union secretary, 226,

Dean, Thomas, newsagent, 22, 78-79,

Dean, -, founder of Switchgear & Equipment, 96,

Debenhams, store, 113,

Dent family, publicans, 143,

Dhesi, Surinder, mayor, 200,

Dibsdale, Gerry, jazz enthusiast, 208,

Dixon, Albert, jazz enthusiast, 207,

Dodds-Parker, Arthur Douglas (1909-2006), politician, 225-26,

Dods, Archibald, cabinet maker, 34,

Douglas, Malcolm, outfitter, 62,

Douglas, Revd Sholto, school chaplain, 193,

Drew, Lionel, 202,

Drinkwater, John, hotel keeper, 34,

Driscoll, Peter, evacuee, 218,

Dumbleton, -, 34,

Dudley, Sir William 1868-1938), co-operative administrator, 42,

Dunn, -, shoe dealer, 35,

Dutton, -, retail manager, 76,

Eades, -, solicitor, 143,

Early, Harold, blanket manufacturer, 226,

Eaves, George, canvas merchant, 22, 67-68,

Edmondson, Major A J, 1st Baron Sandford (1887-1959), politician, 138, 189-90, 221,

Edmunds, Richard, ironmonger, 52

Edmunds, William, brewer, 182,

Edmunds & Kench, millers, 50,

Edwards, Lew, wrestler, 205,

Edwards, W S, carrier, 34,

Ekins, Henry, outfitter, 57,

Ekins, William, outfitter, 57-59,

Emmans, C, motor cyclist, 177,

Emmott, Cllr Charles, headmaster, 149-50, 153,

Emmott, William, founder of Automotive Products, 101,

Evans, Revd David, 125-26,

Evans, Hugh, artist, 191,

Ewins Garage, 83, 85,

Ewins, Sidney, garage proprietor, 83, 85-86, 133, 155, 162, 175,

Export Packing Ltd, 57,

Fairfax, 'Foxy', foundry worker, 92,

Fairport Convention, 205,

Ferguson, Dr Margaret, 165,

Ferrers, Joseph, School of Art principal, 184,

Ferry, Benjamin (1810-80), architect, 124,

Field, A E & Co, clothiers, 198,

Field, Mabel, amateur actor, 191,

Field family, millers, 132,

Fivash, Gordon, footballer, 170,

Flack, Arthur, motorcyclist, 180,

Flint, Revd W, 162,

Flowers, Ronald (b 1934), footballer, 170,

Flowers & Son, brewers, 21, 65,

Fonteyn, Dame Margot (1919-91), ballerina, 185,

Foreman, E W, steam engine owner, 186,

Formby, George (1904-61), comedian, 213,

Fortescue, E C, solicitor, 26,

Fortescue, Mrs, 132,

Fowlds, John, hotel keeper, 207,

Fowler, -, freemason, 159,

Fox, -, Sunday school secretary, 129,

Franklin, A E, milkman, 132,
Franklin, 'Butch', Sea Cadet officer, 198,
Franklin, Samuel, 34,
Franklin, -, 45,
Friswell, Cllr James, iron merchant, 26,
Frith, Francis (1822-98), photographer, 182,
Frost, W L, shopkeeper, 136,

Galvn, Paul, hotel keeper, 207-08,
Gardner, R H, co-operator, 41,
Garrett, Lynne, shop assistant, 77,
Gascoigne, Thomas, garage proprietor, 86,
    186,
General Foods, 28,
George V, King (1865-1936), 85, 162, 188, 223,
George VI, King (1895-1952), 52, 223,
Giant Haystacks (Martin Ruane, 1946-98),
    wrestler, 204-05,
Gibbs, George, motor cyclist, 178,
Gibbs, Patricia (née Mitchell), 117-18, 196-97,
Gilbert, Peggy (née Coleman), 126,
Gilbert, Wallis & Partners, architects, 98,
Gilkes, P, newsagent, 136,
Gilks, -, carrier, 108,
Gill, -, ironmonger, 54,
Gillett family, bankers, 149,
Gloucester, Alice, Duchess of (1901-2004),
    25-26,
Goddard, Edgar, accountant, 162,
Golby, Douglas, journalist, 151,
Goldringham, Revd P, 135,
Goode, Anthony, hotel keeper, 207,
Goodenoughs Ltd, corn merchants, 215,
Goodman, R J, chemist, 21,
Goodwin, Nathaniel, publican, 159,
GPO Telecommunications, 28,
Graber, J, college inspector, 152,
Grain, Pauline, 43,
Grant, Alfie, barber & musician, 209,
Grant, Constance, dance adjudicator, 184,
Grant, -, of Fenny Compton, 34,
Great Central Railway, 111,
Great Western Railway, 66, 89, 91, 97, 111-12,
    115, 121, 211, 224, 227,
Green, Hilda, 'sweater girl', 205,
Greetham, -, 155,
Gregory, Francis S, wrestler, 205,
Griffin, Aubrey, footwear salesperson, 44,
Griffiths, Aline (née Ward Smith), Girl Guide,
    197,
Griffiths, Glenny, 103,
Grimsbury Motors, 86,
Grimston, -, carrier, 108,
Grubb, Ron, musician, 213,

Grut, -, 184,

Hall, Matthew, contractor, 57, 59,
Hall, -, steam engine owner, 186,
Hankinson, Thomas, butcher, 28,
Hanson, Ted, journalist, 184, 190, 208,
Harlock, J, draper, 55,
Harnett, Joe, jazz musician, 207,
Harris Bros, bakers, 136-37,
Harris, Jet, band leader, 203,
Hartrop, -, co-operator, 41,
Hartwell Motors, 87,
Haskins, Ald Thomas, trade unionist, 81, 94,
Hay, James, football manager, 171,
Hayes, Tubby (1935-73), jazz musician, 207,
Hayward, Brent, quarry manager, 33,
Heath, Harold, Sea Cadet supporter, 198,
Heath, Peter, boxer, 206,
Heath, Ted (1902-69), band leader, 204, 210,
Hemmings, -, farmer, 205,
Henrys, outfitters, 61-62,
Herbert, Daniel, bailiff, 140,
Herbert, Henry, foundry worker, 91,
Herbert, Henry, timber yard worker, 81,
Herbert, Joseph, foundry worker 91-92,
Hewer, H, bowls player, 172,
Higham, Ellen (née Goode), coal merchant,
    72,
Higham, Harold, coal merchant, 72.
Higham, Mary (née Humphris), coal
    merchant, 72-73,
Higham, Robert, coal merchant, 72,
Higham, Cllr Rosemarie, coal merchant,
    72-73,
Hilton, Brian, ironmonger, 54,
Hilton, Sidney, borough surveyor, 26-27, 116,
    182,
Hinkins & Frewin, builders, 152,
Hirons, J, steam society supporter, 186,
Hitchcox, Ann & David, outfitters, 57-59,
Hitchcox, Marmaduke G, publican, 167,
Hitchens, Cllr Hermione, 147,
Hitler, Adolf ((1889-1945), 223,
Hogben, A G, watch repairer, 117,
Holland, Thomas W, brewer, 159,
Hollowell, Edward, carpenter, 34,
Hood, S & H, ironmongers, 15, 3738, 51-54, 69,
    83, 98,
Hood, Edward Henry, ironmonger, 51,
Hood, Stephen, ironmonger, 51,
Horley, Terry, groundsman, 170-71,
Hornton Quarries Ltd, 33,
Houghton, D C, motor cyclist, 178,
Howe, Ellen, publican & dairywoman, 121-23,

Howe, Frank, musician, 209,
Howe, Nellie, publican, 121-23,
Howe, William, publican & milkman, 121,
Humbert & Flint, auctioneers, 147,
Humphrey, Rowland, tool room worker, 96-97,
Humphris & Sons, builders & stone masons, 32, 46, 57,
Hunt, Cllr Charles, 23, 170, 204,
Hunt, Thomas, brewer, 46,
Hunt, -, carrier, 34,
Hunt Edmunds, brewers, 21, 24, 45, 47, 72, 106, 110, 115, 122, 143, 182, 184, 201,
Hunter, Ray, wrestler, 205,
Huntriss, Charles, amateur actor, 194
Hustlebee, Patricia 'Miss Banbury', 203,
Hutchings, Thomas, musician, 155, 161,
Hyde, Leslie, cabinet maker, 23-24,

International Tea Co, 77,

Jack family, farmers, 57,
Jackson, Joseph, chapel keeper, 127,
Jackson, W J, baker, 128,
Jakeman, Clare, 53,
Jakeman, Elizabeth, 53,
Jakeman, Kenneth, ironmonger, 53,
Jakeman, , Stephen, ironmonger, 53,
Jameson, Harold, lecturer, 151-52,
Johnson, Ald Margaret, 194,
Johnson, Black Butch, wrestler, 205,
Jones, Arthur W, 55,
Jones, Diana, amateur actor, 194,
Jones, Eddie (1919-97), jazz musician, 207,
Jones, Capt Francis, motor cyclist,
Jones, Revd Graham, 176,
Jones, Harold, wine merchant, 67,
Jones, Michael, wine merchant, 65,
Jones, Sidney Herbert, wine merchant, 21, 64-66,
Jones, 'Stodger', foundry worker, 92,
Jones, Revd Canon, 132,
Joynson, -, landowner, 143,
Judge family, 142,
Justice, Jimmy, band leader, 203,

Kearns, Michael (b 1950), footballer, 78,
Kent, Miss, teacher, 150,
Kern, Jerome, composer, 155,
Kerridge, Mrs, café proprietor, 69,
Kibbee, Guy (1882-1956), film actor, 185,
Kilby, Albert, publican, 21, 172, 174,
Killpack, G E T & Son, bakers, 117,
Kimberley, A T, Ltd, builders, 99-100,

Kimberley, J S, 160,
King & Co, mineral water manufacturers, 24
Kirkpatrick, T, motor cyclist, 178,
Knight, Peggy, accounts clerk & amateur actor, 192-94,

La Fantasy, fashion shop, 185,
Laidlaw, John, 164,
Lake, Stephen, 140-41,
Lambert, -, customer at pub, 122,
Lambourne, Reginald, motorcyclist, 180,
Lamprey & Son, seed merchants & brick makers, 49-50,
Lamprey, John Barrett, seed merchant, 49, 110,
Lamprey, William, seed merchant, 49,
Landie, Elissa (1904-48), film actor, 189,
Laverick, -, founder of Switchgear & Equipment, 96,
Lay, Henry, baker, 229,
Lay, Henry Brown (Brownie), musician & printer, 155, 204, 207, 209-12,
Lay, Peter, musician, 207-08,
Leach, 'Rocky', confectioner, 36,
Ledingham, William, ATC officer, 201,
Lee, Frederick R, publican, 172,
Lees, Gwen, shop assistant, 76,
Lester, Cllr Horace, bookmaker, 229,
Lester, Peggy, amateur actor, 193,
Lester, Spencer, amateur actor, 193,
Lickorish, W H, co-operative manager, 39-43,
Lido Service Station, 86,
Lidsey, W R, farmer, 93,
Linford, Miss, college registrar, 153,
Littlewood Stores, 16-17, 76-77,
Lo Cost, grocers, 70,
London & North Western Railway, 89,
London Brick Co, 110,
London, Midland & Scottish Railway, 89,
Lorna Café, 231,
Loss, Joe (1909-90), band leader, 204,
Lovell, Samuel, 46,
Luckett, T C, electrical engineer, 223,
Lundie, -, brewery manager, 47,

McDougal, Alexander Patrick (1880-1959), managing director, Midland Marts, 89-90, 162,
McIlroy, William, Ltd, outfitter, 55,
McLean, Keith, 165,
McMahon, Aline (1899-1991), film actor, 188,
Maloney, Alison, author, 196,
Mander, Robert, stone mason, 32,

Mansfield, Frederick R, leather goods dealer, 62-63,

Mant, -, teacher, 150,

Marks & Spencer, 176,

Marshall, Owen S, musician, 211,

Mascord, Alfred J, builder's foreman, 231,

Mascord, Ald William G (1888-1961), carpenter, 16, 46, 143, 222, 224, 131-32,

Mascord, Margaret, 231-32,

Mason, Frederick J, butcher, 37,

Mason, George Ltd, grocer, 198,

Masterman, J, motor cyclist, 177,

Mawle, Cllr S J, ironmonger, 188,

Maxime, Brian, wrestler & singer, 205,

Maycock, H B, hairdresser, 174,

Meadows, Annie, teacher & billeting officer, 8, 217-19, 229,

Merrett, Commander, aluminium factory manager, 94,

Merryfield, -, teacher, 150,

Messenger, R W, builder, 130,

Mewburn, William (1817-1900), financier & philanthropist, 127,

Midland Marts Ltd, 17, 57, 69, 89-90, 162,

Miller, Glen (1904-44), band leader, 207,

Miller, Percy, ironmonger, 52, 54,

Miller, Ald Raymond B, brewery company secretary, 47-48, 83,

Mills, W E, architect, 160,

Milne, Elsie, hairdresser, 44,

Moir, Frederick, amateur actor, 194,

Mold, A, pigeon fancier, 155,

Mold, Frederick, gardener, 129,

Mold, Miss, 129,

Mole, Ron, jazz musician, 207,

Moores, Sir John (1896-1993), entrepreneur, 76-77,

Morland, R B, printer, 143,

Morrison, Dennis, stone mason, 33,

Mortimer, Terry, jazz musician, 207,

Moss Bros, outfitters, 61,

Mulholland, Terry, boxer, 206,

Mullis, Nancy, shop assistant, 74-75,

Mumford's Garage, 86, 186,

Mumford, George, 86,

Murphy, Gene, wrestler, 205,

Murphy, J, railway manager, 111-12,

Myers, -, engineer, 94,

National Provincial Bank, 75,

Nationwide Building Society 31,

Neal, P, cyclist, 174,

Neale & Perkins, ironmongers, 22,

Needle's Fish Restaurant, 70, 72,

Nelson, John, stone mason, 32,

Nesbitt, Anthony, Ernest, John, Ronald, haulage contractors, 110,

Newell, William, motorcyclist, 180,

Newman, Jimmy, musician, 211,

Nicholson, A F, 90,

North, William, 11th Baron (1836-1932), 168-69, 182,

North, William, 12th Baron (1860-1938), 116,

North Bar Tool Co, 24,

Northern Aluminium Co, 24, 57, 93-96, 122, 130, 147, 152, 154, 192, 221, 223, 227-29,

Oakes, G H, borough accountant, 93-95,

Orchard, Ernest Walker, ironmonger, 51,

Orchard, William Stephen, ironmonger, 51, 53,

Oxley, Arthur, founder of Switchgear & Equipment, 96-97,

Pallow, Jack, wrestler, 204-05,

Paper & Publications, 17, 103-04,

Pargeter, Arthur, tailor, 172,

Parker, Charlie (Bird, 1920-55), jazz musician, 207,

Parker, T, musician, 213,

Parkin, Joan (née Plumb), 67-69,

Parkin, Thomas, canvas dealer, 68,

Parnell, Jack (1923-2010), band leader, 207,

Parry, Harry, Sea Cadet officer & grocer, 198,

Parrauano, G, ice cream seller, 186,

Partridge, Cllr Frank, draper, 27, 94,

Paxman, Margaret, amateur actor, 191,

Paxman, Richard, butter manufacturer, 191,

Peacocks, market traders, 36,

Peake, Humber Newton, dentist & ATC officer, 201,

Peet, Emily & Henry, workhouse matron & master, 119-20,

Penrose, Susan, amateur actor, 192,

Pepys, Samuel (1633-1703), diarist, 182,

Perkins, F J, tobacconist, 22,

Perkins, 'Hodgy', musician, 213,

Peters, Jonny, wrestler, 205,

Pewsey, Beryl, musician, 213,

Phipps & Co, brewers, 172,

Pickston, Thomas H, French polisher, 18, 132-34,

Pinfold, W, pigeon fancier, 155

Plester, -, blacksmith, 54,

Plumb, Mark B, rope & canvas merchant, 67-69,

Plumb, Mary Eliza (née Thornton), 68-69,

Porter, Cole (1891-1964), composer, 155,

Porter, Revd Cann C F, 115,

Potts, John, newspaper proprietor, 159,

Potts, William (1868-1947), newspaper proprietor & historian, 22, 97, 111-12, 155, 162,

Powell, Samuel F, postmaster, 168,

Pratt, Norman, college principal, 153,

Prescott, Albert, ATC officer, 201,

Prewer, James P, stamp dealer & musician, 212,

Prewer, Kenneth, band leader, 119, 203, 212-15,

Price, Cllr Harry, 164,

Priestley, J B (1894-1984), writer, 194,

Proctor, David, headmaster, 184,

Pursaill, Robert, baker, 229,

Queensway Fish Saloon, 70-71,

Raikes, Robert (1736-1811), founder of Sunday schools, 129,

Ratley, J, baker, 128,

Raynor, William, journalist, 113,

Reg's Café, 220,

Reid, E Owen, town clerk, 26-27, 98, 192, 194,

Rhind, A & W, 164,

Rhodes, Revd R, 159,

Richard, Cliff, singer, 203

Ridley, Revd, 152,

Riedel, glass manufacturer, 66,

Roach, Richard B K, parliamentary candidate, 225-26,

Roberts, Edward, 71,

Roberts, F & Son, furnishers, 130,

Robbins, -, railway guard, 132,

Robinson, Edward G, (1893-1973), film actor, 188,

Robinson, Sheila, 224,

Rose, Alexander Douglas, headmaster, 201, 219,

Rose, Miss -, guider, 196,

Russell, J, cyclist, 174,

Russell, J H, steam engine owner, 186,

Rutter, Dolly, confectioner, 36,

Sainsbury, J & Co, supermarket proprietors, 28, 220,

Salmon, A F, confectioner, 36, 40,

Samuelsons, see Britannia Works.

Samuelson, Sir Bernhard (1820-1907), politician & ironmaster), 80, 91-93, 103, 115, 135, 169, 174,

Samuelson, Ernest (1856-1927), foundry master, 92,

Samuelson, Francis (1861-1946), foundry master, 92,

Sanders, Walter R, publican, 172,

Sansbury, Walter Richard, bookseller, 51,

Saunders, William, Sea Cadet officer, 199-200,

Savage, Mrs M, motor cyclist, 177,

Saye & Sele, viscounts, 32,

Scott, Ronnie, jazz club host (207), 207,

Sewell, W R, garage proprietor, 179,

Shea, Eileen, Girl Guide, 196-97,

Shilson's Wool Yard, 23,

Shires Motor Co, 86,

Shropshire, Worcestershire & Staffordshire Power Co, 46-47,

Simmons, John, draughtsman, 94,

Simmons, Olive (née Watton), typist, 94,

Simons, -, coach builder, 108,

Simpson, James, motor cyclist, 180,

Simpson, -, of Eydon, 34,

Slaymaker, -, road worker, 132,

Smith, Bernard, draper, 55-56,

Smith, Betty 1929-2011), jazz musician, 207,

Smith, John, 55

Smith, Thomas, farmer, 186,

Smith, William, solicitor, 69,

Smith, Miss -, 137,

Spencer (Banbury) Ltd, 16, 98-100, 108,

Spencer, Frank & Peggy, dancers, 215,

Spencer, Jack, market trader, 36,

Spokes, Cllr Malcolm, 149, 199,

Stagecoach Ltd, 105,

Staig, Jimmy, musician, 209,

Stainton, J K, grocer, 136,

Stanford, Barbara, amateur actor, 194,

Stanley, Ada, ironmonger, 52,

Stanley, Frederick, ironmonger, 52,

Stanley, Richard, foundry worker, 92,

Stanley, Miss, teacher, 150,

Stapleton, Cyril (1914-74), band leader, 210,

Stevens, Michael, shepherd, 113.

Stewart, Douglas, landowner, 67,

Stobart, Cathy (1924-2014), jazz musician, 207,

Stockton, Arthur, town clerk, 93, 111, 142,

Stockton, Oliver, town, clerk, 111,

Stockton, Colonel, 143,

Stone, Henry, printer & 'box' manufacturer, 99, 103, 133,

Stroud, family, 86,

Stubbs, Jonathan, 77,

Sturley, William, stone mason, 32,

Sumner, Helen, John, Roger, Vincent, bus operators, 108-09,

Switchgear & Equipment, 16, 96-97, 170,

Sylvester, Victor (1900-78), band leader, 204, 210, 214-15,

Talbot café, 69,
Taverne, King Kong, wrestler, 205,
Taylor, Albert, school caretaker, 149,
Taylor, A R, air raid warden, 229,
Taylor, Cllr Colin, 203,
Taylor, Suzanne, dance school proprietor, 101,
Taylors, haulage contractors, 103,
Tew, A L, farmer, 90,
Thomas, Vernon, lecturer, 153,
Thomas, -, baker, 132,
Thompson, Eddie (1925-86), jazz musician, 207,
Thompson, S W, chemist, 219,
Thornitt, A A & Son, victuallers, 21,
Thornton & Thornton, accountants, 162,
Timms, Walter, builder, 130-31,
Tobin, Caroline & James (b 1875), 115,
Todd, Douglas, schoolmaster & ATC officer, 202,
Tooley's Boat Yard, 54, 132,
Townsend, Irene, bowls player, 173,
Trew, Alice, Ellen, Henry, Priscilla, landowners, 45,
Trinder Bros, cycle & toy dealers, 174, 186, 219,
Truss, W A, fishmonger, 70,
Tubb, Harold, timber yard worker, 82,
Turnbull, Gail, 'Miss Littlewoods', 77,
Turner, Avis, Spencer factory worker, 108,
Turner, Jack, Switchgear & Equipment manager, 97,
Turner, Nan & Neville, amateur actors, 192-94,
Turney, P A, motor mechanic, 87,
Turpin brothers, boxers, 158,
Turvey, Edward, bus driver, 107,
Tustain, Ralph, pigeon fancier, 155,
Tustain, -, of Great Tew, 84,
Tyler, Mrs -, of Milcombe, 76,
Tysoe-Smith, Miss, 46,

Upton, W, Steam Society secretary, 186,
Usher, Ethel, entrepreneur, 22-23, 116, 203-04,

Vacher, Polly, aviator, 202,
Verney, -, carrier, 108,
Vestey, David, 2nd Baron 1882-1954}, 32,
Victoria, Queen (1819-1901), 86, 115,
Viggers, -, milkman, 48,

Wakelin, Biddy, Guide captain, 197,

Walker, Josiah L, landowner, 127-28,
Walker, M F, motor cyclist, 176-77,
Walkley, Ald John, coal merchant, 111-12,
Wall family, rope makers, 30, 115,
Ward-Jackson, Rev, 81,
Wardyard & Co, builders, 130,
Warriner, George, farmer, 74,
Watson, Frank, publican 24, 204,
Watson, George, publican, 21, 24,
Watts & Co, seed merchants, 110,
Waugh, Evelyn (1903-66), writer, 18,
Weaver, Maurice, journalist, 103,
Webb, Frederick, musician, 211,
Webb, Henry, foundry worker, 92,
Webb, John C, Automotive Products worker, 101,
Webb, Randolph, newspaper editor, 191,
Webb, William (Bill), motor mechanic, 87-88,
Webb, Winifred Doris, singer, 191,
Webb, Cllr, farmer, 132,
Wentworth, Clayton, amateur actor, 192,
Wheeler, Miss E, cyclist, 174,
Wheelwright, -, 46,
Whitcher, Arthur, outfitter, 60-61,
White, R O, structural engineer, 57,
White, -, groundsman, 172,
Whitlock, Mrs, cook, 69,
Whittle, Tommy (1926-2913), jazz musician, 207,
Whittle, William, aluminium factory manager, 94,
Wildgoose & Sons, outfitters, 60,
Wilks, Gwyneth, secretary & amateur actor, 192, 194,
Williams, Revd Canon A L E, 137-38,
Williams, C G, motor cyclist, 178,
Wills, Irissa, singer, 213,
Wilson, Robert, fairground showman, 157,
Wilson, Revd William, 124, 127,
Wimpey Bar, 113
Wincott, Arthur, baker & ballroom proprietor, 37, 119, 155, 161-62, 213-15,
Wise, Dick, musician, 213,
Withey, L R, milkman, 136,
Wood, Edward, first Earl of Halifax (1881-1959), 89-90,
Webb, John C, Automotive Products worker, 101,
Wood, Julie, Girl Guide, 196,
Wood, Keith, newspaper editor, 99, 204,
Wood, Vera, historian, 167,
Woodbridge, Eric, Switchgear & Equipment manager, 96,
Woodhull, William, 46,

Woods, H, burlesque artist, 213,
Woodward, Douglas, footballer, 170,
Woolgrove, Cllr A J, farmer, 147,
Woolworth, F W & Co, 15-17, 74-77, 113, 218,
Wrench's Garage, 87,
Wright, Charles, motorcyclist, 180,
Wrigley, -, borough surveyor, 116, 137-38, 140,
Wyatt, Baron Woodrow (1918-97), politician
    and newspaper publisher, 103-04,
Wyatt, William, assistant in canvas shop, 68,

Wyatt, -, carrier, 34,
Wyatt, Misses, 124,
Wyncoll, T & Sons, greengrocers, 37,

Yaters, Carl, printer, 103-04,
Ye Odds & Ends, 66,
Young's Garage, 86-88, 214,
Young, Jack, timber yard worker, 81,
Young, Sidney, garage proprietor, 17, 86-88,
    214,

General Index of subjects, places, &c.

Abingdon, Oxon, 202,

Abyssinia, 226,

Adderbury, Oxon, 12, 46, 97, 128, 169, 196, 212, 218, 227

Alkerton, Oxon, 35

Altrincham, Ches, 132,

Amersham, Bucks, 180,

Apprenticeships, 30, 33, 72, 87, 133, 151-52,

Ardley, Oxon, 113,

Argentina, 17, 80,

Aston Clinton, Bucks, 67,

Astrop, Northants, 198,

Australia, 205,

Austria, 66,

Aynho, Northants, 72.

Banbury:
Allotments, 32

Athletics, 39, 168-69,

Bingo, 190,

Bowls, 18, 21-22, 160, 162, 172-73, 183, 203,

Boxing, 158, 169, 204, 206,

Brickmaking, 49, 115,

Cakes, 15, 17, 25, 37,

Castle, 27, 98,

Banbury, chapels & churches:
Baptist, Bridge Street, 27,

Baptist, South Bar, 214,

Christ Church, South Banbury, 135, 178, 193-95, 221,

Methodist, Church Lane, 127, 140,

Methodist, Grimsbury, 149,

Methodist, Marlborough Road, 18, 40, 69, 127, 147, 184, 191, 197, 219,

Methodist, Neithrop, 127-49,

St Hugh, 12, 31, 137-39,

St John RC, 74,

St Leonard, 83, 135-36, 169,

St Mary, 33, 45, 65, 72, 115, 125, 127, 132, 135, 169, 212, 231,

St Paul, 124-26,

Salvation Army, 157,

Warwick Road Mission, 129,

Banbury:
Cherwell, River, 132, 135,

Christmas celebrations, 55, 74, 95, 123, 127-29, 210,

Church House, 23, 64-65, 155, 191,

Banbury: cinemas:
Grand, 108, 133, 188-90, 222,

Palace, 36-37, 108, 214, 219-20, 222, 224,

Regal, 108, 221

Banbury:
Co-op Assembly Rooms, 18, 164, 166,

Coronation celebrations 1953, 118,

Corn Exchange, 101, 160,

Country carriers, 30, 34, 36, 66, 89, 108, 159,

Cricket, 13-15, 29, 59, 92, 170, 210,

Cross, 15, 17, 29, 32-33, 73, 83-85, 98, 163, 174, 204,

Cycling, 18, 87, 174-75,

Drill Hall, 198,

Early Closing, 39, 44, 60, 230,

Electricity supply, 46,

Farmers' Ball, 203-04,

Fish and chips, 70-71,

Football, 18, 44, 77-79, 86, 88, 92, 95, 103, 147-48, 150, 198, 230,

Horton Infirmary, 40, 57, 73-74, 122-23, 188, 194-95, 210, 214, 221, 232,

Hunt Balls, 25,

Industrial Exhibition 1951, 23-25, 67, 93,

Lady on the White Horse statue, 31,

Market, livestock, 37, 47, 49, 60, 69, 89-90, 113, 163,

Market, retail, 12, 36-38, 60,

Michaelmas Fair, 18, 47, 49, 60, 69, 89-90, 113, 163,

Motor Cycling, 152, 176-81, 186-87,

Municipal Buildings, 92,

Museums, 155,

Banbury, organisations:
Air Training Corps, 201-02,

Arts & Crafts Festival, 184-85,

Auto Club, 180-81,

Banbury Run, 176-79,

Black Diamond Dance Band, 52,

Board of Health, 127,

Boy Scouts, scouting, 17, 57-58, 81, 184, 188, 196,

Caledonian Society, 164-66,

Central Bowls Club, 172-73,

Chamber of Trade, 69,

Cheney's Piscatorial Club, 155,

Cherwell Fishing Association, 95,

Chestnuts Bowls Club, 15, 21-22, 160, 163, 172,

Conservative Bowls Club, 172,

Conservative Party, 225-26,

Co-operative Choir, 40, 43,
Co-operative Society, 39-44, 138, 231,
Cross Players, 18, 191-95,
Dramatic Society, 191,
Easington Sports FC, 158, 170-71
Fishing Association, 168,
Freehold Land Society, 17, 133,
Freemasons, 1, 56, 212, 214-15, 231,
Futurists Band, 155, 209-10,
Girl Guides, 18, 196-97,
Harriers Athletic Club, 137-38, 147-48, 167-69,
    231,
Jazz Club, 207-08,
Labour Party, 225-26, 231,
Liberal Party, 226,
Licensed Victuallers' Association, 122, 155,
Midland Whippet Club, 155-56,
Mothers' Union, 122,
North Oxfordshire Car Club, 88,
Nursing Association, 188,
Oddfellows, 37,
Operatic Society, 53-54,
Red Cross, 228,
Rotary Club, 18, 56, 82, 162-63, 212,
St John Ambulance Brigade, 117, 228,
Sea Cadets, 18, 198-200,
Society for the Mentally Handicapped, 187,
Spencer FC, 14, 78, 158, 169-70, 230,
Star Cycling Club, 168, 174-75,
Steam Society, 186-87,
TocH, 115-16,
Trades & Labour Club, 76, 106,
United Homing Club, 84, 155-56,
Vintage Motorcycle Club, 178-79,
Volunteer Fire Brigade, 82,
West End Tennis Club, 50,
Work People's Hospital Association, 40, 122,
    221,

Banbury, public houses & hotels:
Banbury House, 207,
Barley Mow, 29, 121-23,
Bear, 108,
Bell, 86,
Blacklocks Arms, 97,
Case is Altered, 142,
Catherine Wheel, 57, 80, 115,
Coach & Horses, 121,
Cock & Greyhound, 159,
Constitution Tavern, 142,
Cricketers, 132, 157,
Criterion, 142,
Crown, 155-56, 158, 165, 177-79,
Dog & Gun, 21, 174,

Duke of Wellington, 122,
Eagle Tavern, 140,
Easington Hotel, 142-43, 170,
Flying Horse, 108, 140, 172,
Fox, 142-43,
Gazey's Wine & Spirit Vaults, 23, 203-04,
Globe, 115,
Hare & Hounds, 108, 140,
Inn Within, 203, 205,
King's Arms, 140,
Leathern Bottle, 106,
Mount House, 207,
Old George, 167-68,
Plough, 108,
Prince of Wales, 123, 132-33, 135,
Red Lion, 22, 75, 147, 159-60, 188,
Reindeer, 34, 121, 140,
Seven Stars, 127,
Shakespeare, 140,
Ship, 140,
Star, 140,
Strugglers, 37, 81,
Unicorn, 133, 172,
Vine, 117,
Warwick Arms, 87,
Watson's Wine Vaults, 203,
Whately Hall, 33, 60, 209-11, 221-2,
White Hart, 45,
White Horse, 168, 174,
White Lion, 34, 159, 188, 192,
Windmill, 37,

Banbury:
Remembrance Sunday, 197

Banbury, schools & colleges:
Banbury Municipal/County/Grammar, 31,
    118, 149-50, 201, 219, 229,
Britannia Road/Cherwell Infants 92, 217-18,
British School, Crouch Street, 17-18, 140,
    145-46,
Cooke's Academy, 124,
Dashwood Road, 72, 108, 145-46, 219, 229,
Drayton School, 29,
Easington Girls', 31
Grimsbury County/Hall, 29, 32, 133, 170,
Harriers Primary, 147-48,
North Oxfordshire Technical College &
School of Art, 11, 18, 44, 96, 151-54, 164-65,
Roman Catholic, 115,
St Mary's, 74, 117-18, 218,
Tudor Hall, 30,
Woodgreen, Secondary Technical, 18, 149-50,

Banbury:
Sor Brook, 5, 219,
Sportsmen's Ball, 215,
Steeplechases, 145,
Swimming, 149, 229, 231,

Banbury, streets, houses & locations:
Addison Road, 170-71,
Alma Terrace, 67-69,
Arran Grove, 29
Austin House, 214,
Bath Road, 151-53,
Beargarden Road, 70, 126,
Berrymore Road, 164,
Bidston, 142,
Bloxham Road, 30, 139, 142, 169,
Boxhedge Square, 127-28,
Bretch Hill, 106 110,
Bridge Street, 27, 32, 34, 37, 45-54, 57, 61,
    76-77, 80-81, 87, 108, 115, 155, 157-58, 165,
    177-78, 230-31,
Britannia Road, 62, 98-100, 108, 131,
Broad Street, 22, 39, 40-44, 78, 108, 119, 133,
    164, 166, 174, 188-89, 194, 221,
Broughton Road, 126, 164, 191, 219,
Butcher Row, 22, 67, 121,
Calthorpe Gardens, 182,
Calthorpe Manor House, 24, 182,
Calthorpe Street, 1, 17, 23-24, 45, 72-73, 111,
    115, 151, 223,
Castle Quay Centre, 27, 33, 37, 53, 59, 113,
Castle streets, 17, 27-32, 107, 115-18, 217-18,
Causeway, The, 49, 133,
Centre Street, 41, 135,
Cheney's Yard, 115,
Cherwell Heights, 70-71,
Cherwell streets, 17, 27, 30, 32, 47, 50, 99, 110,
    115, 135, 223, 226,
Church Lane, 34, 57-59, 152, 198,
Church Passage, 28, 168,
Compton Street, 27, 118,
Coningsby, 188-89,
Cope Road, 29,
Cornhill, 21, 117, 141,
Cow Fair, 49, 157, 182, 223,
Crouch Hill, 55, 70, 219,
Crouch Street, 17, 140, 145-46, 224,
Dashwood Road, 182,
Dashwood Terrace, 120,
Daventry Road, 132, 180,
Duke Street, 49, 117,
Easington, 17, 31, 130, 137-43, 147-48, 170-71,
    219-20, 224, 229,
Easington Road, 138,

East Close, 55,
East Street, 132, 232,
Factory Street, 27 54,
Fish Street, see George Street,
Gatteridge Street, 80-81, 217,
George Street, 22, 32, 40, 42, 45, 80, 194,
Gibbs Road, 72, 132-33,
Globe Room, 17,
Globe Yard, 115-16,
Golden Villa, 127-28, 231,
Gould's Villa, 125,
Grange Road, 138,
Green, The, 124,
Green Lane, 115,
Grimsbury, 17, 78, 86, 89, 94, 96, 123, 130,
    132-36, 140, 145, 186, 196, 223,
Grimsbury Manor, 132,
Hardwick, 93, 224,
Havenfield, 47-48,
High Street, 21, 24, 34, 43-44, 62, 64-66, 74-76,
    83, 240, 268, 174, 188, 204, 223, 231,
Hill View, 130,
Hilton Road, 147,
Horsefair, 22, 32, 65, 72, 86, 108, 176-77, 183,
    221,
Horton View, 137-39, 273 219,
Huscote, 180,
Ivy House, 212-14,
King's Road, 26,
Manor Road, 72, 130, 132,
Margaret Close, 232,
Market Place, 22, 31, 36-37, 49, 60, 67-69, 74,
    105, 108, 130, 132, 140, 157-58, 172,
    220-21,
Marlborough Place/Mews, 85, 182,
Marlborough Road, 40, 66, 83, 151, 160, 184,
    217,
Mascord Road/Close, 232,
Merton Street, 17, 49, 135,
Mewburn Road, 70,
Middleton Road, 33, 86, 157, 186,
Mill Lane, 37, 72,
Monument Street, 17,
Neithrop, 17, 124-29, 223,
Neithrop House, 182-83,
Newland Road, 39, 130, 182, 219,
North Bar, 21, 30, 32, 37, 60, 105, 151, 174,
North Street, 132,
Old Grimsbury Road, 72, 135,
Old Parr Road, 193m 201,
Orchard Way, 130,
Oxford Road, 130, 138, 147, 188-89, 197-98,
    220, 229,
Paradise Square, 182,

Parsons Street, 22, 24, 31, 34, 37, 55-56, 60-61, 118, 121, 140, 163, 172, 182, 191,
Park Farm, 70,
Park Road, 231,
Penrose Close, 202
Penrose House, 210,
People's Park, 18, 182-83, 221, 226,
Pepper Alley, 190,
Queen's Road, 22,
Queensway, 70-71, 106,
Ruscote, 17, 59, 130,
Railway station, 111-12, 121, 227,
Ruskin Road, 138, 219,
St George's Crescent, 137,
Salt Way, 130, 218,
Scalding Lane, see George Street,
Shades, The, 21-22,
South Bar, 34, 128, 155, 214-15, 223,
South Street, 132-33, 164,
Southam Road, 29, 32, 74, 76, 96, 99, 115, 117, 227-28,
Spiceball Park, 27, 197,
Springfield, 139, 142,
Springfield Avenue, 137-38, 140-42,
Swan Close, 151,
Townsend, 147,
Town Hall, 57, 105, 119, 142, 158, 160, 184, 197, 201, 210, 223, 226, 231,
Tramway Road, 103,
Upper Windsor Street, 113,
Warwick Road, 15, 29-30, 86-88, 119-26, 129, 141, 201, 210, 214, 225,
Water Lane, see Warwick Road,
West Bar, 27, 72, 106,
West Street, 130, 132,
White Lion Walk, 73,
Woodgreen, 149-50,
Woodgreen Avenue, 128,
Wykham, 17, 50, 125, 127, 170, 205,

Banbury:
Swimming, 149, 229, 231,
War Memorial, 182-83,
Winter Gardens, 18, 22, 44, 116, 203-06, 210, 214, 216,
Workhouse, 15, 119-20, 210,
World War 1: 121, 129, 169, 182-83,
Wrestling, 204-06,

Banbury, World War 2: 18, 26, 48, 50, 72, 74-75, 87, 96, 109, 117, 158, 191, 194,
Agricultural sprays, introduction of, 50,
Army experiences, 210
Black-out, 229,

Bombing raids, 117, 227,
Civil Defence, 72
Cold Store, 97,
Election 1945, 225-26,
Evacuees, 217-18,
Home Guard, 228,
Mayors, 229-30,
RAF experiences, 158,
Royal Navy experiences, 199-200,
Shops, effects on, 74-75,
VE and VJ Day street parties, 118, 223-24, 228, 231-32,
Wings Week, 221-22
Women workers, 227,

Barford, Oxon, 90,
Basingstoke, Hants, 13,
Bearwood, Staffs, 105,
Bicester, Oxon, 110-12,
Birmingham, 11, 22, 37, 78, 113, 157, 176-78, 198, 206, 225,
Birmingham Mail, 78,
Birmingham Planet, 102,
Birmingham Sports Argus, 78-79,
Blackpool, Lancs, 76-77,
Bloxham, Oxon, 24, 30, 34, 140, 158, 169, 184, 186, 193-94,
Bodicote, Oxon, 46, 92, 131, 184, 198,
Bolton, Lancs, 177,
Boys' Brigade, 81,
Brackley, Northants, 59, 76, 97,
Brailes, Warks, 177,
Brecon, 119,
Brentwood, Essex, 34,
Brighton, Sussex, 177,
Broughton, Oxon, 30, 32,
Buckingham, 152,
Burford, Oxon, 32,

Cambridge, 12,
Canada, 32, 205,
Canons Ashby, Northants, 30,
Carlisle, Cumb, 178,
Chacombe, Northants, 30,
Chadlington, Oxon, 186,
Channel Islands, 184, 227,
Charlbury, Oxon, 62,
Charlton, Northants, 105,
Charmouth, Dorset, 197,
Cheltenham, Gloucs, 12, 26, 33, 111,
Chesham, Bucks, 225,
Chesterfield, Derbys, 60, 85,
China, 60, 103,
Chipping Norton, Oxon, 38, 103, 105, 194,

Chipping Warden, Northants, 72, 105,
Claydon, Oxon, 106,
Clifton, Oxon, 154,
Coventry, 26, 30, 60, 70, 78, 103, 170 178,
    198-99, 206.
Cropredy, Oxon, 68, 119,
Crosby, Lancs, 76,
Croughton, Northants, 110,
Crystal Palace, 91, 186,
Cyprus, 71,

Dagenham, Essex, 86,
Deddington, Oxon, 30, 35, 81, 105, 155, 186,
    201,
Drayton, Oxon, 47, 12,
Duns Tew, Oxon, 34,

Edge Hill, Warks, 176,
Edinburgh, 201,
Epwell, Oxon, 30,
Ettington, Warks, 51,
Evenley, Northants, 105,
Exeter, Devon, 11,
Eydon, Northants, 34, 38

Farnborough, Warks, 30, 105, 176,
Farnham, Surrey, 177,
Fenny Compton, Warks, 34, 88, 110, 155, 201,
Festival of Britain 1951, 23-25,
Forest of Dean, 71,
France, 93, 110,

Gaydon, Warks, 60, 177,
Germany, 62, 158, 227, 229,
Great Bourton, Oxon, 227,
Great Rollright, Oxon, 226,
Great Tew, Oxon, 84,
Grenadier Guards, 213-15,

Hanwell, Oxon, 108, 229,
Harbury, Warks, 177,
Harrow, Middsx, 176,
Helston, Cornwall, 196,
Hemel Hempstead, Herts, 219,
Henley-on-Thames, Oxon, 153, 180,
Heythrop Park, Oxon, 64,
High Wycombe, Bucks, 171, 214,
Hinckley, Leics, 60, 117,
Hitchin, Herts, 199,
Hook Norton, Oxon, 46, 186, 196,
Hopcroft's Holt, Oxon, 81, 180,
Horley, Oxon, 30, 108, 119, 196,
Hornton, Oxon, 33, 108, 170, 191,

India, 32, 226,
Ireland, Irish people, 78, 206,
Isle of Wight, 60,
Istanbul, Turkey, 177,

Jarrow, Co Durham, 119,

Kenilworth, Warks, 110, 177,
Kineton, Warks, 171, 177,
King's Sutton, Northants, 46, 198,
Knowle, Warks, 177,

Lake District, 196,
Leamington Spa, Warks, 62, 101, 105, 180,
Leicester, 13, 34, 36, 60,
Liberal Party, 104,
Little Rissington, Gloucs, 202,
London, 26, 57, 94, 96, 106, 111-13, 115, 124,
    147, 163, 177, 189, 191, 196, 199, 207, 217-18,
    226-27, 229,
Long Itchington, Warks, 62,
Loughton, Essex, 32,

Malden, Surrey, 186,
Mallory Park, Leics, 179,
Malvern Hills, 202,
Manchester, 76,
Marlborough Farm Camp, 170,
Marston St Lawrence, Northants, 108,
Middle Barton, Oxon, 117,
Middleton Cheney, Northants, 34, 92,
Milcombe, Oxon, 76, 101, 105,
Milton, Hants, 171,
Mollington, Oxon, 170,
Moreton-in-Marsh, Gloucs, 83,
Motorway M40, 16, 29, 113,

Newcastle-upon-Tyne, 79,
Newport, Isle of Wight, 60,
Newport, Mon, 111,
New York, 192,
Northampton, 13, 57-59, 221,
Northend, Warks, 170,
North Newington, Oxon, 30, 72, 158,
Nottingham, 11, 13, 157, 212,
Nuneaton, Warks, 199,

Oban, Argyll, 34,
Offcurch, Warks, 177,
Oxford, 22, 7, 93, 111, 124, 147, 158-59, 180,
    184, 193, 225, 230,
Oxford Canal, 50, 92, 103, 113, 198,
Oxfordshire & Buckinghamshire Light
    Infantry, 27-27, 116,

Paris, France, 188,
Pelaw, Co Durham, 39,
Plymouth, Devon, 149,
Poole, Dorset, 43,
Porthmadog, Gwynedd, 34,
Prescote Manor, Oxon, 89,
Princes Risborough, Bucks, 111,

Reading, Berks, 11,
Romsey, Hants, 94,
Ross-on-Wye, Herefs, 142,
Rousham, Oxon, 84, 78, 108, 152,
Rugby, Warks,
Ruislip, Middsx, 205,
Russia, 226,
Ryde, Isle of Wight, 60,

Sandhurst, Berks, 160,
Scotland, Scottish people, 77, 89, 164-66, 171, 208,
Shalstone, Bucks, 105,
Sharnford, Leics, 117,
Sheffield, Yorks, 30,
Shipton-on-Cherwell, Oxon, 50,
Shotteswell, Warks, 68,
Shutford, Oxon, 177,
Sibford Gower, Oxon, 60, 177,
Silverstone, Northants, 80,
Slough, Bucks, 180,
Snowdonia, 202,
Souldern, Oxon, 140
Southampton, 11, 13-14, 212,
Southport, Lancs, 186,
Speedway, 14,
Spithead, 188
Stafford, 76,
Stourport, Worcs, 46,
Stow-on-the-Wold, Gloucs, 83,
Stratford-upon-Avon, Warks, 21, 66, 121,
Stroud, Gloucs, 60,
Sturdy's Castle, Oxon, 174,
Sulgrave, Northants, 80,
Sunbury-on-Thames, Surrey, 212,
Sunderland, Co Durham, 111,

Sunrising Hill, Warks, 177-78,
Swalcliffe, Oxon, 57,
Swerford, Oxon, 105,
Swindon, Wilts, 83,

Tackley, Oxon, 81,
Teddy Boys, 203,
Thame, Oxon, 170, 229,
Tredegar, Mon, 119,
Traction engines, 186-87,
Tysoe, Warks, 177,
Twyford, Oxon, 46,

United States of America, 76, 80, 98, 110, 200, 219-20,
Upper Heyford, Oxon, 110, 115, 202,
Upton House, Warks, 57, 184,
Uxbridge, Middsx, 13,
Uzbekistan, 103-04,

Waddesdon, Bucks, 51,
Wales, Welsh people, 34, 165,
Walsall, Staffs, 78,
Wardington, Oxon, 105,
Warkworth, Northants, 135,
Warmington, Warks, 122,
Warwick, 80, 110, 121,
Water Orton, Warks, 110,
Wednesbury, Staffs, 60-61,
Weedon, Northants, 34, 55,
Wellesbourne, Warks, 64,
West Bromwich, Staffs, 78, 94, 104,
Wigginton, Oxon, 160,
Williamscot, Oxon, 67-68, 105,
Windsor, Berks, 115, 188, 213,
Witney, Oxon, 218, 226,
Wolverhampton, Staffs, 78, 170, 186,
Woodford Halse, Northants, 96, 111, 201,
Woodstock, Oxon, 82,
Worcester, 13, 180,
Wroxton, Oxon, 30, 116, 166, 168-69,

Yugoslavia, 32,
Zululand, 188,